Curriculum ~TION

English and the
National Curriculum

For 'the parents',
and my teachers

Curriculum Continuity in English and the National Curriculum:
Working Together at Transition

Daniel C. Tabor

with contributions from
Jo Cumberland-Harper, John Follett
and Jackie Turner

Foreword by
Norman Thomas CBE,
Emeritus Professor of Education,
University of Warwick

 The Falmer Press

(A Member of the Taylor & Francis Group)
London • New York • Philadelphia

UK The Falmer Press, 4 John St., London WC1N 2ET
USA The Falmer Press, Taylor & Francis Inc., 1900 Frost Road, Suite 101, Bristol, PA 19007

First published 1991

A catalogue record for this book is available from the British Library

Library of Congress Cataloguing in Publication Data are available on request

Jacket design by Benedict Evans

Typeset in 10/11.5 pt. Bembo
by Graphicraft Typesetters Ltd., Hong Kong

Printed in Great Britain by Burgess Science Press, Basingstoke on paper which has a specified pH value on final paper manufacture of not less than 7.5 and is therefore 'acid free'.

Contents

Contents

List of Figures and Tables

Figures

Tables

List of Abbreviations

AT   Attainment Target
DES   Department of Education and Science
IT   Information Technology
KS   Key Stage
NCC   National Curriculum Council
PDC   Professional Development Centre
PoS   Programmes of Study
RE   Religious Education
SEAC School Examinations and Assessment Council
SCDC Schools' Curriculum Development Committee

**A New Description for School Year Groups
(Text of NCC Circular No. 2: February 1989)**

1 There has in England been no agreed description of the progress of pupils through all stages of schooling such as that in use in Scotland, in many European countries and in North America. Schools have used their own descriptions, usually based on a break at age 11, which is no longer universal. There is need for a simple and easily understood system.

2 The introduction of the National Curriculum from September 1989 underlines the need and provides the opportunity for a uniform description. The Secretary of State for Education and Science has agreed to the proposal of the National Curriculum Council that a system should be introduced. It will be used by DES, HMI and, we expect, local authorities and schools. NCC will use it in all circulars and guidance. It will not however be statutory.

3 The new description is as follows:

Key Stage*	New description	Abbreviation	Age of majority of pupils at the end of the academic year
	Reception†	R	5
1	Year 1	Y1	6
	Year 2	Y2	7
2	Year 3	Y3	8
	Year 4	Y4	9
	Year 5	Y5	10
	Year 6	Y6	11
3	Year 7	Y7	12
	Year 8	Y8	13
	Year 9	Y9	14
4	Year 10	Y10	15
	Year 11	Y11	16
—	Year 12	Y12	17
	Year 13	Y13	18

* The key stages of compulsory education are described in section 3 of the Education Reform Act. Assessment under the National Curriculum takes place at or near the end of each key stage.
† Key Stage 1 for the National Curriculum also includes those pupils in reception classes (R) who have reached compulsory school age. The new description does not cover nursery provision. Special arrangements for applying the National Curriculum to five year olds in school year 1989/90 are contained in NCC circular number 1.

4 The new description will emphasise continuity from the beginning of compulsory schooling at 5 to the age of 18. It will encourage pupils and their parents to regard as normal the completion of thirteen years of full-time education.
5 Schools may wish to number age groups in accordance with the new description but will be under no obligation to do so.
(Reproduced with permission of the National Curriculum Council.)

The new description of school year groups will be used throughout the book, in accordance with current practice.

SEAC Notation for the National Curriculum

Where appropriate, the current SEAC notation for identifying Attainment Targets, levels and strands in the National Curriculum will be used. For example, if a writing activity has 'hit' one of the strands for editing and redrafting, this will be referred to as En 3/4e. 'En' clearly indicates the subject, 3 identifies Attainment Target 3 (Writing), and 4e refers to Level 4, strand e '. . . discuss the organization of their own writing; revise and redraft the writing as appropriate, independently, in the light of that discussion.'

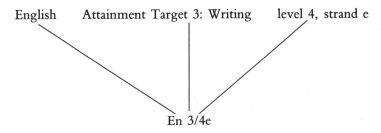

English   Attainment Target 3: Writing   level 4, strand e

En 3/4e

Though this notation will be used most of the time, more explicit reference to Attainment Targets will be used instead, if this makes the meaning clearer e.g.: AT 3: Writing, strand 4e. (The Attainment Targets and levels for English in the National Curriculum will be found in Appendix 2.) The main concern will be that use of the SEAC notation should not obscure the points that we are trying to make.

Acknowledgments

I am grateful to many people for their help and encouragement: to Mr. Doherty (Headmaster, Daventry William Parker School) and the Governors and the Headteachers of our contributory schools, for their support and encouragement; to Jo Cumberland-Harper, for her unwavering support, and for writing part of Chapter 1; to Jackie Turner (Head of English) for writing most of Chapter 12; and to the English Faculty of Daventry William Parker School, and other colleagues in our contributory schools who have put so much into these projects. I am grateful to our pupils, who have participated in these projects with such commitment and enthusiasm. Thanks are also due to the PTA of Daventry William Parker School, for financial assistance. I am most grateful to Professor Norman Thomas for writing the Foreword to this book; and to Tim Boswell M.P., for his interest and support.

I am grateful to the committee of Daventry PDC for financial support through our group's INSET programme, and to Frances Start (Head of Centre 1987–88) and John Follett (Head of Centre since 1988) for evaluating our projects. I am grateful to Northamptonshire LEA for my flexi-secondment; and to Bert Gill of 'Arts in the Curriculum' for funding the writers' workshops.

I am grateful to SCDC for a grant from the Teachers' Fund in 1987; to Mr. P. Candlish, HMI, for encouraging me to write my first article; and to Jim Andrews, for helpful advice. I am grateful to HMSO for permission to reproduce pages 3–19 from *English in the National Curriculum (No. 2)* (DES 1990a) in Appendix 2, and to quote extensively from these pages and from pages 21–42 in the rest of the book. I am grateful to the National Curriculum Council for permission to reproduce the text of NCC Circular No. 2: February 1989. I am also grateful to Valerie Hogg for typing most of the manuscript; and to Marie, for humorous encouragement.

Foreword

The Board of Education Report for 1908/1909 included the following:

> Education is one thing; any dislocation in it is at the best but a necessary evil. It ought to be continuous from the time when a child first passes beyond the home and goes to school up to the time when he ceases to be under educational tutelage, has been taught how to learn and can henceforth go on to learn for himself.

Aspects of that quotation jar eighty years later, not least its masculinity. However, its general sentiment is as much a matter of concern in the 1990s as it was then. We, and more importantly the children, cannot afford discontinuity which interferes with their learning. The National Curriculum is now in place, or in plan which ought to aid continuity and progression. It will not, by itself, secure them for individuals, especially as they pass from one school to another. Despite its complexity, the National Curriculum is, rightly, too crude for this purpose.

In this book, the author and his colleagues reveal complexities that arise when promoting development in children transferring to secondary schools. Change is not always a disclocation. It can be a spur. If the best is to be made of new opportunities, the children should know that the school they move to will require them to use knowledge and skills already acquired, will be a welcoming place, and will not bewilder by its size and shape.

There are practical difficulties in the way of linking primary and secondary schools. They come from differences between the two kinds of schools — differences of size, staff responsibilities, the maturity of the pupils — and from admissions arrangements that can make it difficult to establish close and consistent relations between a secondary school and a primary school. I believe that they also arise because teachers in a school, whether primary or secondary, are substantially occupied with their day to day responsibilities. It takes a wider than average vision to pay attention to what children do before or — somewhat easier — after they are one's own responsibility. This book shows that the wider vision pays off for children and teachers.

This book describes an important set of practices by which pupils in primary and secondary schools, and their teachers, came together in ways that stimulated learning for all. It is not simply that the secondary school teachers have worked to ensure that their next group of pupils will settle more quickly, and that their strengths and shortcomings will be better known. The language and social abilities of the secondary school pupils have gained from working with younger children, from having to explain, to encourage, and to promote ideas that younger and older students can display together. The primary school children have gained from glimpsing what is to be their school future, but have also been stimulated immediately in their social and language development, oral and written.

If progress and continuity are to be achieved, teachers in primary and secondary schools need to know and trust each other, or at least be able to translate each other's words so that messages about pupils convey usable meanings rather than confusion best disregarded. Mutual comprehension has clearly been vital in the exercises described here. When children and teachers are actually to work alongside each other in the coming term, as they are shown to do here, any misunderstanding is soon revealed and must, for practical purposes, be resolved.

Two encouraging messages from this book are of growing confidence in both primary and secondary school pupils, and of growing mutual respect between primary and secondary school teachers. For those alone, the book deserves attention.

Norman Thomas
August 1990

Chapter 1

Working Together at Transition

The little bit (two inches wide) of ivory on which I work with so fine a brush as produces little effect after much labour. (Jane Austen, Letter, 16 December 1816.)

Continuity. 1543. [a.F. *continuité*, ad. L. *continuitatem*.] 1. The state of being continuous; uninterrupted connection or succession; coherence, unbrokenness. 2. Uninterrupted duration (*rare*) 1646. 3. quasi-*concr*. A continuous or connected whole 1601. (SOED)

Introduction

This book describes a programme of curriculum continuity projects in English, between Daventry William Parker School, a mixed 11–16 comprehensive school in rural Northamptonshire, and its contributory schools. The programme started with a pilot project in 1986, and this was extended with support from the SCDC in the following year. Since 1988 the programme has been part of the English Curriculum at Daventry William Parker School, and virtually all our contributory schools have been involved.

At Daventry William Parker School, English is taught in mixed-ability tutor groups in Year 7. In Years 8–11 pupils are put into sets according to ability; the sets are usually ranked 1–5 or 1–6. Each member of the English faculty works with a colleague at a contributory school, planning a joint project to run over one to three terms. The projects involve primary school pupils in Years 5 and 6, and a class of secondary school pupils from Years 7–9. The children work *with* each other and *for* each other, the sense of audience being an important aspect of most projects. The joint sessions have usually taken place at Daventry William Parker School, but the majority of projects have involved at least one session in the contributory school. Most projects have had a specific outcome, in terms of producing a book of poems, an anthology of stories, a presentation etc. Practising poets and writers have also been involved in joint workshops.

This book examines the projects in detail, looking at the interactions that occurred across the primary-secondary divide, largely through the written and spoken words of the pupils and teachers involved. We shall show how these projects contributed towards the development of curriculum continuity in English, and promoted good liaison between our schools.[1] Independent evaluation of the projects has been provided by the Head of Daventry PDC. We shall also show how the projects developed pupils' language skills, and hit a wide range of levels in the Attainment Targets for English in the National Curriculum (DES 1990a). The projects also covered many elements in the Programmes of Study for Key Stages 2 and 3. Follow-up interviews with primary school pupils before and after transition revealed how the projects helped pupils to settle in more easily at the secondary school, at the beginning of Year 7. Where appropriate, the approach used in this case study is related to the wider issues of continuity and liaison, and selective reference will be made to research in these areas. We shall suggest that the approach developed at Daventry William Parker School could be used as a model for cross-phase projects in other curriculum areas.

The discussions about the Attainment Targets in the National Curriculum, and their relation to the activities described in the projects, have been set in smaller type. This is to help the reader who wishes to gain an overview of the projects, and our approach to curriculum continuity in English. Thus the material dealing with the National Curriculum may be omitted at a first reading.

The Schools

Daventry William Parker School traces its descent from the original Daventry Grammar School, founded by a local worthy, William Parker, almost 400 years ago. In 1967 the grammar school and the secondary modern school in Daventry were amalgamated to form Daventry School, an 11–18 school with approximately 850 pupils.

Daventry is a small market town, twelve miles west of Northampton, which has grown to a population of over 14,000 as a result of new estates which house overspill families, mainly from Birmingham. It supports a range of light industry. Until 1989, the town had three 11–18 comprehensive schools: Daventry School, Southbrook School, and the Grange Comprehensive School. As a result of the reorganization of education within the town in 1988–89, the Grange Comprehensive School was turned into a 16–19 Tertiary College, and the other two schools were transformed into enlarged 11–16 schools. Daventry School was reborn in September 1989 as Daventry William Parker School, with over 1000 pupils.

The school enjoys a reputation within Northamptonshire for excellent pastoral and liaison links with its contributory schools. In the past these comprised two schools within Daventry itself, and six or seven small county primary schools, to the north of the town. As a result of reorganization, the Grange Junior School also became one of the town contributory schools (formerly its pupils went to the Grange Comprehensive School). The Grange

Junior School is the largest junior school in Northamptonshire, with approximately ninety pupils in Year 6. The majority come to Daventry William Parker School, though a proportion choose to go to Danetre School (formerly Southbrook School). A detailed description of the contributory schools will be found in Appendix 1.

The next section deals with concepts and issues, in particular the notions of curriculum continuity (with a note about the teaching of English), transfer and transition, and liaison. The final section of the chapter, by Jo Cumberland-Harper, describes pastoral liaison at Daventry William Parker School, and provides the context for our curriculum continuity programme. Over 1100 children have participated in these projects so far. Most of them are still at Daventry William Parker School, and in Chapters 2 through 12 their names have been changed.

Concepts and Issues

Daniel C. Tabor

Curriculum Continuity

Since the Hadow Report (1926) a great deal has been written about the need to ensure continuity of the curriculum, and the related issues of transition, transfer and liaison. Creasey, Findlay and Walsh (1983) suggested that '"Continuity" is about content and to some extent methodology in subject, whereas "liaison" is about the processes and procedures that can facilitate that continuity' (p. 9). It is thus important to distinguish between the different elements that are usually grouped together when curriculum continuity is discussed. For example, in 'Continuity, Liaison and Progression: The Northamptonshire Approach' a clear distinction was made between transition or transfer arrangements, and continuity of the curriculum (Spencer, 1988, p. 36). In practice, the process of transferring pupils from one phase to another was considered to involve three areas:

1 General transfer or induction arrangements.
2 Curriculum continuity, including teaching styles and organization.
3 Exchange of written information and record keeping.

Derricott (1985, p. 16) provided a somewhat different perspective, when he said that curriculum continuity should involve agreement between schools about

— aims and objectives
— the selection and organization of content
— skills
— methods of assessment
— understanding and/or agreement about approaches to reading.

However, the importance of curriculum continuity has been highlighted by the findings of the ORACLE project. The project found that a significant proportion of pupils in Year 7 regress, in terms of attainments in Maths and English, compared to their levels of achievement in Year 6 (i.e.: their last year at primary school). In general, girls tended to do considerably better than boys in their first year at secondary school (Galton and Willcocks, 1983).

The English lessons observed at secondary schools in the project were rather monotonous, with a lot of solitary writing; indeed writing was seen as the main medium of learning. The researchers were also struck by the dominant influence of teaching style on pupils' performance, and the ways pupils quickly adjusted to a variety of teaching styles at secondary school (Galton and Wilcocks, 1983, Chapter 7; see also Dodds and Lawrence, 1984, pp. 61–2; Collin, 1984, p. 62).

In summarizing the findings of the ORACLE project, Croll observed

.. Of all the primary comparisons that we made, only 3 per cent of the children went backwards. In the secondary school, on the other hand, 30 per cent of children did worse on the tests at the end of their first year in the Secondary School than they had done at the end of their last year in the Primary School ... and whatever the reasons for this ... the experience of progress has been replaced by (for many pupils) the experience of actually going backwards (1984, p. 74).

These findings should heighten the concerns of secondary school teachers about the content of the curriculum, and the way it is delivered in Year 7. To ignore much of what pupils have achieved in Year 6 (in whatever curriculum area), or to 'go back to basics' in Year 7, undervalues the experiences pupils bring with them from primary school, and can result in regression.

Concern for curriculum continuity is also reflected in recent DES/HMI documents. For example, the HMI *Curriculum Matters* series (DES 1984) focused on the 5–16 age range. *Better Schools* (DES, 1985a) emphasized the need for whole curriculum planning across phases. *Science 5–16* (DES, 1985b) listed continuity as one of its ten principles. The SCDC Teachers' Fund requested proposals for 1987 relating to three themes, one of which was 'curriculum continuity, within and between all phases of schooling' (1986).

While curriculum continuity, like motherhood, is something everyone is in favour of, it remains a difficult concept to define. As Derricott (1985) observed '... When we examine practices we still find continuity to be a slippery concept, difficult to define and identify' (p. 155). Discussion about curriculum continuity should involve some consideration of the nature of the curriculum. The concept of 'the curriculum' can be regarded as consisting of content (syllabuses etc.); process (how children learn; approaches to teaching and assessment); context (where children learn; school and classroom management); and aims and objectives (the purposes of learning at school) (SCDC 1988, Unit 1, p. 4).

Continuity of the curriculum, with the implicit idea of progression, is important within schools, as well as between schools. However, some would argue that there are 'linear subjects' (perhaps Maths) where continuity is particularly important, and possibly easier to identify than in a subject such as English. At a general level, we can say that the notion of 'curriculum continuity' implies an agreed curriculum plan between the contributory schools, and the secondary school to which children are transferred (Derricott 1985, p. 16).

Though there is a consensus that continuity in the curriculum is desirable, one could argue that 'discontinuity' (meaning a break or radical change in children's learning experiences) can also be beneficial. The Plowden Committee (1967) accepted that children, like adults, are stimulated by novelty and change, but that it must be carefully prepared for, if the pupils are to be stimulated, and not disheartened (cited by Gorwood, 1986, p. 10). Whalen and Fried (1973) suggested that bright pupils in fact benefit from the stimulus of a new environment after transfer. Similarly, Derricott argued that 'planned discontinuity' could have a beneficial effect on some pupils, if by this we mean that the change from one school to another could act as a stimulus. While not advocating anything as extreme as 'a clean break' or a 'second birth', Derricott suggested that 'the challenge is to provide continuity of experience as a general goal, but to recognise those areas in which discontinuity is likely to be fruitful' (1985, p. 157).

The ORACLE project found that while transfer impaired progress for many pupils (one assumes only temporarily), motivation and enjoyment were high. One group of pupils, who Galton and Wilcocks (1983) termed 'accelerators', made substantial gains in their first year at secondary school. A small number of these pupils felt that they had not been particularly successful at their primary school, and were going to do better at their new school. They were not generally able children. These findings support the view that there are some benefits associated with transition.

The National Curriculum, with its statutory programmes of study, will lead schools to work together more closely. Nonetheless, there are practical difficulties that are likely to impede the collaborative planning of the curriculum across the phases. For example, a move towards continuity in one or more curriculum areas involves a further surrender of school autonomy, something jealously guarded by the primary schools (Beynon 1981, p. 37; Derricott 1985, p. 31; Dodds 1984, pp. 22–23 and p. 111; Stillman and Maychell 1984, p. 29). Difference in teaching styles also appears to be an obstacle. In the primary school, pupils are usually taught by one teacher for the whole year, and project work is widely used as the vehicle for delivering most of the curriculum. By contrast, pupils at secondary school are taught by specialist teachers, often with widely differing teaching styles. These differences are of crucial importance where the joint planning of the curriculum is concerned. The SCDC questionnaire on curriculum continuity activities, and teachers' perceptions of them, identified the main focus of current continuity work: 'Over 50 per cent of mentions identified teaching methods/styles and pupils' learning strategies as the main focus. A significant number also reviewed record-keeping procedures' (SCDC 1988, Unit 1, p. 13).

Lack of communication between phases is often a problem. This was noted by the Bullock Report, though research suggests that the situation has steadily improved since 1975 (Dodds 1984, p. 24). The National Curriculum has highlighted the need for better communication between schools, and given added impetus to cross-phase visits by teachers.

Planning the curriculum together is only possible when good working relationships exist between teachers; otherwise curriculum continuity is unlikely to develop. For example, Stillman and Maychell (1984) in their case study on the Isle of Wight, focused on liaison and continuity between middle and high schools. Liaison procedures between schools were usually satisfactory, particularly where ways of introducing pupils to a new environment were concerned. Provision for curriculum continuity, usually in terms of meetings between subject teachers in different schools, was variable and often unsatisfactory. Stillman and Maychell identified 'lack of mutual trust between sectors' (p. 28) as one of the main obstacles to the development of curriculum continuity. There was little communication between teachers about classroom practice in the different phases: 'We found the open and frank discussion of classroom teaching with immediate colleagues to be rare, and in consequence, when attempted, difficult' (p. 118). Yet it is the willingness of teachers to come together in groups to share experiences and perceptions 'which lies at the heart of a successful continuity activity' (SCDC 1986).

While continuity cannot take place without good relationships between teachers, support from the senior management teams of the schools concerned is clearly necessary if initiatives are to be successful. The active involvement of the LEA is also necessary, so that curriculum policy can be agreed, and appropriate resourcing supplied. Various models have been suggested for facilitating curriculum continuity (e.g. Castle and Lawrence 1987), though these are no substitute for the commitment of practising teachers.

Many secondary schools have set up continuity and liaison groups with their contributory schools (primary, junior and middle), in an attempt to plan the curriculum together, or to find areas where agreement can be reached. Cross-phase visits, joint planning of the syllabus, or a common policy on assessment and record keeping (e.g. Laycock 1987), are all important in developing curriculum continuity, either in specific subject areas, or on a 'whole school' basis.[2] The implementation of the National Curriculum has made agreement on assessment and record keeping between the phases particularly important.

Most initiatives have involved teachers meeting together to discuss policy, and trying to reach agreement in shared concerns in different subject areas. However the present study approaches curriculum continuity in English from a different perspective. We shall show how pairs of teachers working together across the primary-secondary divide developed a joint approach, as part of an ongoing curriculum continuity programme in English. The projects described in Chapters 2 through 12 often grew out of the topic work that the primary colleagues had already planned for their classes. The English teachers at Daventry William Parker School were able to adapt these topics to the language and/or literature work of their particular classes.

The joint sessions, when primary and secondary pupils worked together, constituted the 'core' of the projects. Preparatory and follow-up activities for each class took place between these sessions, and could involve additional 'extension' work, if the teacher considered that this was appropriate for his/her group. Cross-phase visits by teachers, and working with each other's classes, occurred when possible.

The joint planning and ownership of these projects helped to bridge a curriculum gap between primary and secondary phases in language work. The projects have provided continuity of curricular experience for primary school pupils in Year 6, who were about to move to Daventry William Parker School. At a practical level, we have crossed the 'Humpback Bridge' which for Steed and Sudworth (1985) symbolized the obstacles to the development of liaison and continuity between primary and secondary schools.

Within Northamptonshire the Chenderit School Humanities Local Study project is another example of cross-phase collaborative planning. The project in 1987–88 ran over eight Wednesdays, involving ten contributory primary schools, with approximately ninety primary pupils and one hundred and thirty pupils in Year 7. The project covered 'Farming, Buildings and People in the Local Area', and had been prepared by secondary staff in consultation with primary teachers (SCDC 1988, Unit 2, p. N90). There are several differences between this scheme, and the projects described below. Our curriculum continuity projects in English are 'owned' by the primary-secondary pairs of teachers who plan them; the pupils are allocated with partners at the other school, who provide the initial sense of audience; and the working relationships between pupils develop over one, two or (in some cases) three terms.

A Note about 'English'

Primary and secondary school teachers may have different ideas of what 'English' and 'language work' entail. Allen (1987) has suggested that

> ... Primary teachers think of 'language development' to cover the whole broad area and 'English' is often used to describe some particular work such as comprehension exercises. In the secondary school 'English' specialists, while asserting the importance of their work, all readily admit that children learn language outside the subject. Even more, some uses of 'language' omit 'literature' ... The confusion of terms represents differences of perception, differences of emphasis ... (pp. 6–7).

The difference in emphasis is largely a result of the way the whole curriculum is delivered by one teacher in the primary school, with the difference in teaching style (compared to a secondary school) that this entails. The primary teacher also has greater flexibility in the use of time.

The Sheffield Writing at the Transition Project showed that, in the two

7

pyramids of secondary-primary schools studied, on average over 60 per cent of the writing in primary schools was 'English' whilst in secondary schools 32 per cent of the writing was done in English lessons. All the English work in the secondary schools gave evidence of engagement by pupils in their writing, and this contrasted with the writing in English in the primary schools where it was much less likely to show evidence of involvement. These differences were entirely accounted for by the setting of exercises in the primary schools for more than 40 per cent of the tasks in English. By contrast, there were *no* exercises done in English in the secondary schools during the week of the collection of the material. Furthermore, in the primary schools only a minority of teachers related any literature to writing, whereas this was the norm in the secondary schools (Horner 1987). While one should be cautious about generalizing from these findings (and they do not apply to the creative, child-centred teaching of English in many of the primary schools in Daventry), nevertheless they should make us aware of the possible differences in pupils' experiences of English at transition.

Whatever one's view of curriculum continuity, and the effect of transition on children's development, the role of English/language work in this process is surely crucial.

> Whether there is continuity in other areas of the curriculum, there is a case for the emotional/imaginative aspects of transfer to be dealt with by teachers of English language. By using suitable texts, video or photo presentations, as well as poetry writing and discussion, the informal passage can be made easier for the pupils, as well as being a point of contact for the staff (Crinson 1988, p. 90).

The projects described in Chapters 2 through 12 illustrate how 'discontinuity' can be a stimulus for the creativity of both teachers of English and their pupils.

Transfer and Transition

The terms 'transition' and 'transfer' are sometimes used interchangeably. For example Sumner and Bradley (1977) suggested that 'transition' should apply to moves between recognized stages of education, whilst 'transfer' can be used for any change of school. Stillman (1984) took a different view, arguing that 'transfer' described just the physical displacement of the child from one place to another. 'Transition' implied changes in the lives of pupils, in the teaching they received, and the expectations made of them. Derricott (1985) considered that 'the *process* involved in moving from stage to stage is *transition*' (p. 13). Whichever term is used (we shall be using Derricott's definition here), the pupils' transition from one school to another involves considerable anxiety. There is a strong need to maintain some continuity of social experience, such as friendship groups, in the new school.

The anxieties that pupils at primary school feel about transition have been well documented. Much of the research carried out in the 1970s showed that

> ... prior to transfer over two-thirds of the ·pupils express some measure of anxiety about the change, but that these may be sub-divided into children who are apprehensive, and wish to remain with their own teacher, and those who look forward but with some trepidation to the challenges provided by the new school (Galton 1983, p. 8).

Research has shown that by the end of the first six months, only 10 per cent of children have not adapted to life in the secondary school (Nisbet and Entwistle 1969; Youngman and Lunzer 1977).

A sample of the research conducted since the mid-1970s into pupils' anxieties about transition, reveals certain common elements. For example, Neal's study in Birmingham showed that the most common anxieties associated with transfer were about the size of school, and the complexities of organization, school work, and relationships with older pupils. Many pupils felt lonely when separated from primary school friends (Neal 1975). The more general *Continuity in Education* project carried out in Birmingham showed that it was relationships with teachers that really mattered. One year after transition, when asked what they missed about their primary school, 33 per cent said they still missed their teachers, but approved of the 'adult treatment' they received at secondary school, with its different teachers (cited by Gorwood 1986, p. 56).

A small-scale study carried out by a group of middle-school teachers in Norfolk, compared pupils' attitudes before and after transition. The most common anxieties which pupils had in the final year of middle school about going to the high school were about bullying, the size of school and getting lost in it, new teachers, new subjects, homework, punishments, and separation from friends. After transition most of the anxieties were allayed before the pupils had been in the new school for very long, but the pupils became more anxious about curriculum matters. Homework tests, new subjects and new styles of teaching were all mentioned as problems after transfer (Norfolk 1983). These findings were also similar to the results of research into infant-junior transition (e.g. Jones 1985).

Measor and Woods (1984) studied the school careers of pupils from an 8–12 middle school who transferred to a 12 to 18 comprehensive, over a period of eighteen months. By using participant observation, they were able to gain an understanding of how pupils experienced transition. Many children (and their parents) regarded the move to secondary school as a 'rite of passage': a modern version of tribal initiation rites (see Van Gennep 1909). It was the informal (pupil) hierarchy which imposed this view, with an elaborate mythology and corresponding activities (for example, putting a new pupil's head down the toilet) which signalled the tough semi-adult world the pupils were joining.

Measor and Woods also described developments in the child's identity or self-concept over the 10–13 age range studied. They noted that the pupils tended to position themselves on one side or the other of two divides: conformist/deviant, and gender. With reference to the conformist/deviant divide, a small minority were highly conformist or highly deviant, while the majority clustered on the central line, slightly to one side or the other. Secondly, pupils began to align themselves much more strongly with gender groupings, and to develop stereotyped responses to subjects; for example, girls tended to show boredom in more traditional male areas such as sciences and Design and Technology. Most of these attitudes crystallized within a year of transfer. Measor and Woods felt that induction schemes usually helped the process of transfer, but more could be done to intermesh teaching and organization at the divide between primary or middle schools, and the secondary school. The 'discontinuity' experienced by pupils at transition was in fact beneficial, signifying the change 'from one stage of life to another' (p. 170).

Anne Murdoch also used the model provided by Van Gennep's 'rites of passage', to describe how leaving the primary school, and starting at the secondary school, were accompanied by social rituals associated with this change of status. Transition was identified by pupils with the process of growing up. However, the extent of pupils' anxieties suggested that more emphasis should be placed on 'preparing pupils for the move, and encouraging realistic expectations of the new school' (Murdoch 1986). Brown and Armstrong (1986) found that the most prominent fears among pupils in Year 6 about transition were about getting lost in the school, classwork, homework, strict teachers, and a general feeling of anxiety. On the positive side, sport and new and different subjects, were the activities the children were most looking forward to. Research shows that most pupils made the social adjustment to the secondary school successfully by the end of their first year. However, the fact that 10 per cent were still disenchanted 'suggests a potential waste of talent that could possibly be prevented by closer monitoring of pupils at time of transfer' (Gorwood 1986, p. 61).

The interviews conducted as part of the present study with pupils in Year 6 revealed that some of them experienced the anxieties described above. Follow-up interviews and surveys were conducted with the same pupils after transition, in the autumn term of Year 7. The pupils felt that their participation in a project with secondary school children had made is easier for them to settle in at the beginning of the new term at Daventry William Parker School.

Liaison

The process of transition is accompanied by liaison procedures. The different categories of procedures are

1 The exchange of documentation about pupils;
2 The organization of activities for pupils and teachers;

3   Staff consultations about related pastoral matters (Derricott 1985, p. 15).

A cynical note about the value of liaison links was struck by Marland (1977) who wrote

> One of the romantic vaguenesses peddled frequently in educational exhortation is that we should create a closer liaison between educational institutions. In fact it is one of the hardest things to achieve and can consume considerable time to little effect (p. 213).

Nonetheless, liaison links at a pastoral level are highly important in making transition smoother, and enabling pupils to settle in more easily at their new school. Exchanges of pupils' work, cross-phase visits by teachers and pupils, induction days, inter-school sports and social activities, and other good practices are widely used to promote liaison.[3] Findlay felt that there was a need for primary and secondary teachers to build on pastoral liaison links, to achieve a shared understanding in common curriculum areas. She lamented the fact that teachers do not usually have the opportunities to develop working relationships with each other across the phases (Findlay 1983, p. 24). The present study describes one way in which such working relationships can be established.

The curriculum continuity work in English at Daventry William Parker School would not have been possible without the pastoral links that have been developed with our contributory schools over many years. I am grateful to Jo Cumberland-Harper for describing these liaison procedures.

Pastoral Liaison at Daventry William Parker School

Jo Cumberland-Harper (Head of Lower School 1980–90)

Pastoral liaison should enable the transferring of children from primary to secondary school to be as smooth and as worry-free as possible. For some children this could be a traumatic experience for a number of reasons: the journey to the new school; unfamiliar environment; unfamiliar routines; tuition by a variety of staff, both male and female, in different classrooms; and the establishment of new personal relationships.

Most primary school children have a short distance to travel to their school but on transfer many find that they have to travel longer distances to school by car or public bus. Bus times must be learned and the use and care of bus passes learned. It is the responsibility of the secondary school to make sure that behaviour of all pupils is good so this journey is not so formidable as the children may fear, but without pastoral care, smoking and other anti-social behaviour by a minority would prevail and jeopardize the safety and comfort of others.

The new school can appear to the new pupils as a strange conglomerate of rooms, passages, exits and entrances and staircases so different from their compact and friendly primary schools. Therefore, a knowledge of the secondary school before transfer removes the fear of this unknown vastness and, instead, there is a feeling of adventure and eager anticipation of what is ahead of them in their first autumn term. Intake Day, liaison of the curriculum, Open Days and PTA activities help the pupils to become familiar with their new school.

The routines of the new school will differ in times and length of lessons and assemblies, breaks, and lunchtimes. New disciplines must be learned such as regular homework, uniforms to be worn and school guidelines to be followed. Tuition by such a variety of staff both male and female in different classes can be daunting, although most children are ready for different classes; when questioned later about this variety, most of them answer that they prefer a range of teachers and the moving to different teaching areas and are glad not to be closetted in one room with one teacher.

There is an unfortunate universal tendency for rumours to circulate in primary schools concerning horrendous initiation procedures devised by the older children for the discomfort of the new arrivals, such as 'bog-washing' and other forms of bullying. It is necessary to alleviate these fears as soon as possible. In the primary schools the top juniors have been regarded as the senior members of the school, responsible and reliable and caring towards the younger children, and on transfer the situation is reversed. The new pupils are helped to adjust to this without loss of confidence by being valued and made useful within their tutor groups, within their year group and as part of the whole school taking responsibility on such committees as the Environmental Issues Committee, Debating and Literary Societies, School Council and so on.

All the foregoing applies equally to the transition from any school to another. In Daventry William Parker School the pastoral liaison is an ongoing function throughout the year and a good, close relationship with eight junior schools has been developed. Visits to the primary schools to talk to the next school year's intake begin in the spring term. The pastoral staff and I are already known to the children and staff of the primary schools and our visits are carried out in an atmosphere of friendliness and trust. Two or three ex-pupils of each primary school always accompany me, they enjoy returning to their old school ready to inform and advise on matters concerning buses, routines of Daventry William Parker School, different lessons, different teachers, lunchtime clubs and their sporting achievements. Homework diaries are produced and examined, the uniform is appraised, school bags are scrutinized and useful tips given, such as always carry a plastic bag in the school bag for dirty things like football/hockey boots and trainers. On Intake Day these children will act as escorts to the children of their old primary school, a much sought-after duty and always performed very well indeed. After a while the children are left alone together without adults.

In the question and answer session the primary children realize that there is not a lot of difference in the rules of their school and those of the secondary school. There are the same reasons, for instance, why they should not rush about the school corridors, why they need absent notes, why they should not bully and so on. There is the main rule to care and respect for others, and all things follow from that.

A discussion about the pupils to be transferred takes place with the class teacher and sometimes the headteacher. I receive Richmond Test results along with other vital information from the primary school staff which helps me to make transition easier for each individual child. The children are issued with a uniform list to take home and also a pastoral form for their parents/ guardians to fill in and return to me either via the primary school or straight to Daventry William Parker School. The pastoral form is sometimes my first contact with parents and it asks for address and telephone numbers of workplace of parents and of the family doctor, also an emergency telephone number. So that I can take proper care of their child, I ask for details of any problem or worry they or their child might have and also an example of parents'/guardians' signatures. This pastoral form is warmly received by parents, further knowledge of the child is acquired and valuable parent involvement has begun. Some parents prefer to ring me about certain matters concerning their children and only wish the tutor, Head of Year and myself to be party to their information.

At the beginning of the summer term, with this information from primary schools, I am able to compile my lists:

— Tutor groups
— Special care
—Children of high academic potential
— Children needing education support
— Promising athletes
— Promising musicians

Tutor groups contain, as near as possible, the same proportion of boys and girls, children from town and country areas, friendship groupings, high academic potential, above average academic potential, average academic potential, below average academic potential, children in need of educational support, children with physical problems, children with emotional problems, promising athletes, promising musicians and children with leadership qualities. The first draft of tutor group lists are then sent to the primary schools to be scrutinized and, if necessary, altered.

The Special Case List contains information about children with particular problems which all members of staff should know about if they are to understand the children they teach. This list includes, for instance, children recently bereaved, one-parent families through divorce or separation, children with a physical handicap, children with emotional problems, children with dietary problems and children with attendance problems, and so on. After the Induction Evening when parents have the opportunity to talk to tutors and other pastoral staff, the Special Care List may need adding to, and the final draft is circulated to all members of staff on the first day of the autumn term. All members also have information on the children of high academic potential and those probably needing educational support, thus they know the children who need stretching and those who need extra help at the beginning of the term. The PE Department receives a list of promising athletes, the Music Department receives a list of promising musicians in the summer term so that provision can be made for peripatetic music staff.

The Induction Evening usually occurs in the penultimate week of the summer term. It is held mainly for parents but, of course, children are welcome too. As they enter the door of the Main Hall, parents are given a card on which is written their child's Tutor Group and tutor's name. The tutor will wear a label with his name and Tutor Group, and the object is to enable the tutors to meet all the parents of the children in his group. The tutor will have his tutor list together with all the information concerning them. This knowledge pleases parents; they realize we do care about their children and we want them to be able to continue learning without setbacks caused by poor transition. At the beginning of the Induction Evening, the Headmaster addresses the parents, he stresses the need for their support and makes it clear that the pastoral staff welcome parent involvement and are never too busy to make appointments to discuss their children. The pastoral staff flank the Headmaster on the platform and, although this may appear formal, parents like to have a good view of the teachers who are to be concerned with their children. They also need to be able to recognize their child's teachers so that in the time set aside for refreshments and informal chat contact can be made easily. This informal part of the evening is appreciated by parents; they ask many questions and get to know the staff. During the evening there is also a uniform display and sometimes a drama/dance or maybe a French or German drama performance.

Before Intake Day children are sent their individual programmes for the day which include times and place of assembly, timetable of lessons and leisure and names of escorts for the group. The day begins with an assembly the children sit in their tutor groups in their particular place in the Main Hall. This is a very important beginning as it gives them a feeling of belonging and security. The Intake Day also ends with a short assembly and they then know exactly where to come and where to sit on the first day of the autumn term. Pupils in Year 7, and some in Year 8, act as escorts, they take them to the different teaching areas stay with them and help them. In leisure time they show them where the toilets and playground areas are, and also where pastoral staff are to be found. Their timetables will include: Science, Modern Language, Design and Technology, Drama/PE, Computer Studies/Maths, English/Humanities and a Tutor Period. The primary school children derive a great deal of pleasure, interest and confidence from their Intake Day.

The new intake receive an ABC Booklet of the first Year at Daventry William Parker School. This enables them better to understand the workings of the school particularly as they apply to pupils in Year 7 in their earliest days at secondary school. Syllabuses of all subjects are explained, lunchtime clubs are listed, the bookshop is described, Parents' Evenings explained and so on. After my letter of welcome and encouragement there is a section of help and advice written by pupils at present in Year 7, which is intended to quell anxieties and to entertain. Recent contributions include:

First things first, you don't need to be frightened because everyone is kind and helpful.

Your tutor or Head of Year are always to be found if you need them.

You need not be unhappy but if you are you are not a wimp, just go for help.

Bullying is absolutely not allowed.

If you are naughty you always get a warning first but if you do not take any notice you will soon wish you had.

Dinners are quite tasty, lots of teachers eat them.

You can have fun in lessons without mucking about.

I like Maths now. Work is set at your standard and it is up to you to keep it high.

The best thing that happened to me at Daventry William Parker School was meeting my Tutor and to find that he is my English teacher as well.

You don't have to be brilliant but you must put effort in your work.

At the end of my first day I was really tired but I couldn't wait for the next day.

Beware of detention! Do your homework.

My dad said that I have come out of my shell since I came to this school.

I never thought I'd be good at rugby. Now I am in the school team.

Remember, everyone has a lesson she doesn't like.

It's good to have a school uniform because you don't have to bother about the latest fashion or what you are going to wear each day.

You'll love Frontier Camp. The instructors make you listen and give you confidence when you need it. I got to know my friends better and myself because I never thought I would be brave enough to abseil and canoe.

I'm looking forward to showing you round on Intake Day.

In the last week all records are received from the primary schools and filed in Tutor Groups in the Lower School office for the perusal of tutors and any other staff who teach the children.

The first day of the autumn term is a smooth-running affair. The children assemble in the Main Hall with ease, they know their tutors who are there to greet them and after a short welcome they go off for a Tutor Period with their tutor. This is a quiet time for receiving timetables, maybe maps if they have lost the ones they had on Intake Day, school prayer and general discussion. They know where the toilets are; they know where the pastoral staff are should they need help because this was all part of the escorts' duties on Intake Day. At the end of their first day the children are tired but secure.

After three weeks or so a 'Cause for Concern' form is sent out to every member of staff involved with Year 7, as sometimes problems concerning children have been overlooked. It is at this time the junior school staff come to Daventry William Parker School to lunch with their ex-pupils and in rooms set aside for them, talk to them about lessons, teachers and how they have settled in to their new school. This is a time for frankness; there may be anxieties about the school bus or some lesson or some teacher. The junior school staff then discuss any problems that may have been thrown up with Head of Lower School. Quite often one worry will be about movement around the school as there are many more children in the secondary school compared to primary schools. This usually sorts itself out when the younger children cease to rush to the next lesson or playground area. Another worry may be having to wait a long time for food to be served in the canteen, this again solves itself when the pupils do not hurry to the canteen at once. Sometimes there are problems with lessons, either too hard or too easy. Since the English liaison work there have been no concerns about English.

The Junior Heads meet formally with the Headmaster and Head of Lower School every term. In these meetings many subjects of mutual interest are discussed:

— new intake opening of autumn term
— school transport
— liaison initiatives in English
— National Curriculum
— training days
— PTA activities

We enjoy a very good relationship with the Junior Heads and staff of our contributory schools; their knowledge of the children and their families, their advice and contributions are invaluable when effecting a trouble-free transfer from primary school to Daventry William Parker School.

Notes

1 The Maths and Science Departments at Daventry William Parker School have also established continuity links with our contributory schools. In 1987 the Maths Department organized a problem-solving day for over a hundred primary school pupils and selected pupils in Year 7. The Head of Science has visited all our contributory schools, and organized a training session for the staff of our adjacent junior school.
2 For examples of good practice in developing curriculum continuity, see Derricott 1985, Chapter 4; Dixon 1985, pp. 29–31 on Language; Findlay 1987a, on English; Gorwood 1986, Chapter 8, a review of several continuity and liaison initiatives; SCDC 1988.

3 For examples of good liaison practices see Creasey *et al.* 1983, Chapter 4; Cutler 1984; Dodds and Lawrence 1984, p. 21 and Chapter 3; Doherty 1984; Findlay 1983; Gorwood 1986, Chapter 8; SCDC 1988, Curriculum Continuity Information Pack: Unit 1.

Chapter 2

Children's Writing and the Sense of Audience

Introduction

Francis Bacon wrote: 'Reading maketh a full man; conference a ready man; and writing an exact man'. This Renaissance view of the complete man sums up many of the aims found in today's teaching of English. It certainly applied to our pilot curriculum continuity project in English and Drama, which was started in the autumn term 1986 at Daventry School.[1]

Our project involved the pupils in the top English set in Year 8 (aged 12 to 13), and the class of pupils in Years 5 and 6 (aged 9 to 11) at Falconer's Hill Junior School, the adjacent contributory school. The aims of the scheme were to develop a range of language skills and to foster creativity, through project work involving both groups of children. We will show that, focused by a sense of audience the two groups of pupils were stimulated to write stories for each other. In the process, the junior school children also benefited from curriculum continuity in both English and Drama. We shall also show that the range of activities which the pupils engaged in would have hit several levels in each of the three main Attainment Targets, as defined by the National Curriculum for English.

The Autumn Term

In the autumn term, the pupils from Daventry School studied a selection of readers on all subjects from the junior school, which they analyzed in detail. The Daventry School pupils were required to study the content, presentation, use of language and suitability of the book, and to devise an activity based on a part of the book for use in the classroom.

The reviews were usually perceptive and analytical. A number of pupils studied story books that were published over twenty or thirty years ago, and they commented on the old-fashioned nature of the content or the gender bias of the stories. All the pupils had to produce a worksheet for use by a child at the junior school, based on a part of the reader they had analyzed.

The worksheets included cloze tests (where pupils fill in missing words in a passage), crosswords, word searches, questions and answers, word games, and were often attractively illustrated.

On our first visit to Falconer's Hill, the pupils from Daventry School were paired up at random with pupils from the junior school. The older pupils had to interview the junior school children about their families, background and interests, and to give them the worksheets. The pupils worked in small groups, in four or five rooms around the school.

All the pupils enjoyed the activities, and this was reflected in their reports. For example, Sarah wrote that her pupil, Phillip,

> ... liked doing my worksheet because he said it was brilliant fun.

Rebecca was also enthusiastic about the work of her pupil, Diana. After describing Diana's family background and interests, she noted that

> ... Diana coped with the cloze test I had set extremely well ... The crossword puzzle I had set caused no problems either [and] she got all the answers right again ... Diana said she had found the work very easy.

Communication between the groups of children was very good, and we were struck from the start by the interest and rapport that developed between the two groups of pupils.

For the follow-up activity, the Daventry School pupils wrote stories for 'their' particular pupil, knowing his or her particular interests and abilities. The stories were written in two stages. The first draft was corrected by the teacher, and improvements suggested. The second draft was then turned into a booklet, with a special cover, illustrations, and one or more worksheets. Focused by a sense of audience, the Daventry School pupils produced some excellent stories, taking a lot of care with the presentation of their work. Many of the stories featured the children for whom they were written.

During our final visit in the autumn term, the Daventry School pupils presented the booklets to the children at Falconer's Hill, read the stories to them, and assessed their performance on the worksheet. The younger pupils were very excited to receive their stories, and the visit was highly successful.

Robert, for example, had written a story for Darren. This story featured Darren as a bounty hunter, who was trying to find a man called Nick Hamilton in the Amazon jungle. Robert wrote:

> He told me that he had enjoyed the story very much. I think it was a good idea to use your pupils as a star in the story. I was pleased but I had made my materials a little bit too hard.

In the reports the Daventry School pupils described how the younger children reacted to the stories, and the suitability of their worksheets. Samantha was typical of many when she said:

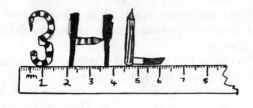

Figure 2.1 '3HL HAVE DONE IT AGAIN', by a pupil at Daventry School

I enjoyed this visit and I hope we go back there some day.

It is clear that by this stage the pupils' work would have fulfilled a range of levels in the three main Attainment Targets. The interviews and discussions between the children would have hit several strands in Attainment Target 1: Speaking and Listening. For example, strand 2a: '... participate as speakers and listeners in a group engaged in a given task'; strand 3a: '... relate real or imaginary events in a connected narrative which conveys meaning to a group of pupils ...' etc.; and strand 4b: '... ask and respond to questions in a range of situations with increased confidence'. The editing and redrafting which the Daventry School pupils undertook within their own class would have hit strand 4c: 'take part as a speaker and listener in a group discussion or activity, expressing a personal view and commenting constructively on what is being discussed or experienced...'.

For the Falconer's Hill pupils, reading extracts aloud from junior school books, and completing the accompanying worksheets, would have met part of En 2/3a: '... read aloud from familiar stories and poems fluently and with appropriate expression'.

The Daventry School pupils' analyses of the readers which they discussed in class, would have partly hit En 2/4b: '... demonstrate, in talking about a range of fiction and poetry which they have read, an ability to explore preferences'.

Writing stories for their junior school partners would have enabled the Daventry School pupils to hit most of the strands in AT 3: Writing, level 4. For example, strand 4b: '... write stories which have an opening, a setting, characters, or sense of events ...' etc.; and strand 4e: '... discuss the organization of their own writing; revise and redraft the writing as appropriate, independently, in the light of that discussion'. The fact that each story was written for a specific audience would also have hit strand 5a: '... write in a variety of forms for a range of purpose and audiences, in ways which attempt to engage the interest of the reader'.

The Spring Term 1987

In the spring term we decided to reverse the roles that the pupils had played, so that the pupils from the junior school would have to help write stories for the pupils from Daventry School, with help from the latter.

At about this time, twelve of the pupils at Falconer's Hill who had been involved in the project, were interviewed in groups of three or four. The pupils were asked what they felt about the two visits from the Daventry School pupils; their feelings about going to the senior school next year; and how they viewed the prospect of writing stories for the older children.

The pupils were chosen at random, and were representative of the range of talent within the class. They all said that they had enjoyed meeting and working with the older pupils from Daventry School, particularly as many of the stories featured them as the main characters.

The children did not find the stories particularly difficult to read; in most cases they thought they were easy, and liked doing the accompanying worksheets. The stories written by the pupils from Daventry School were kept in the children's classroom at Falconer's Hill Junior School, and they read each other's stories with interest.

Most of the pupils were worried about going to the Secondary School; the most commonly voiced fears were that the work would be too hard, that they would get lost or picked on. One boy was worried because he couldn't tie a neck-tie. Most of the pupils going from Falconer's Hill School to Daventry School (one of the three secondary schools in the area) had siblings or other relatives there. Working with Daventry School pupils on two occasions in the autumn term had enabled the younger children to ask about life at the Secondary School and to form contacts with pupils already there.

The children were also asked what they found difficult in writing stories, and how they felt about writing for the pupils at Daventry School. They all said they liked writing; pupils such as Stephen, Janet and Nicola were articulate and enjoyed expressing themselves verbally and in writing. Other pupils appeared to have more limited language skills, and to find writing difficult. Different problems in writing were mentioned; the beginnings and endings, and the overall structure of stories. Jane, for example, said that once she got it started, 'it's all right', and Stephen found it difficult to stop once he had started writing.

Stories written in class were often started by the teacher, though several pupils prefered to choose their own topics, e.g. adventure or magic. Choosing the right words could be a problem, as Jill said:

> You know what you mean, but find it difficult to find the right words.

Both Jill and Stephen said they used dictionaries. John was worried that his spelling might not be good enough and that he might look stupid. Punctuation and paragraphing were not mentioned.

Many of the children interviewed were, understandably, anxious about the likely responses of the older children to their work. A number were worried that they might make mistakes or appear stupid. However, their enthusiasm came through clearly, as the following extract shows:

Nicola: I'm worried in case I don't do a good enough story or something, because they're older.

Teacher: Are you all worried about that?

Darren
John ⎤ Yes
Nicola ⎦

Teacher: I think the older pupils will want to help you. How do you feel about writing stories generally?

Nicola: I like writing stories, it's one of my hobbies.

Teacher: What do you like most about it?

Nicola: I don't know really, I just enjoy it. When I've thought of the beginning sometimes I forget to think of the end bit and I have to think of the story all the way through. I always write long stories so I have to make sure I don't write them too long 'cause I won't get to finish them.

Teacher: Yes! How does Darren feel?

Darren: I like writing stories and I like drawing to go with the stories.

Teacher: Do you like writing any particular type of story?

Darren: Adventures!

Teacher: Anything you find difficult about writing stories?

Darren: No, not unless you get to a part when you can't carry on and you have to finish the story.

The interviews revealed problems pupils had with vocabulary, spelling and sentence structure, though the idea of writing for a specific audience did not appear important at this stage. However, all the pupils interviewed at

Falconer's Hill were looking forward to working again with pupils from Daventry School.

To prepare the pupils from Daventry School for the first visit to the junior school, they studied three examples of writing produced by the younger children. We analyzed some of the difficulties that the less able pupils had in expressing themselves, in forming proper sentences, in using tenses correctly, etc. We discussed the need for the older pupils to have an understanding and encouraging attitude.

The pupils were put into new pairs during the spring term. We paired pupils whom we thought would get on well together, or would complement each other in terms of ability and/or personality. During the first visit to the junior school, the Daventry School pupils interviewed their new partners about their interests, discussed possible topics for stories, and gave short reading or writing tests. These were designed to test the language skills of the junior school pupils, and some of the older pupils were very inventive in their approach.

Many pupils asked the younger children to read from a book they liked, and to write something connected with one of the characters. Other pupils were more concerned to find stimulating materials directly related to their partner's particular interests. A week later, the pupils from Daventry School brought materials with them to help the younger children start their stories at Falconer's Hill School. There was complete freedom as to the choice of stimuli — so long as they were suitable for the particular child. For example, Clive's pupil, Ricky, was very willing but found it difficult to start his story about a visit to Wembley. Clive reported:

> To help him I gave him a short magazine article, word list, a title and advice when needed. He started quite enthusiastically but got rather bored so I helped him out.
>
> I feel he will enjoy this project if he tries hard enough and has plenty of support. He is capable of a great deal if the support is there
> . . .
> I cannot wait to see my child's work as I think he will do his best even though he is not as capable as most. The only thing is I wish I were there to help him . . .

The other pupils shared a similar degree of concern, in providing word-lists, pictures, and above all, support and encouragement for their young partners. The discussion in pairs of themes, vocabulary and stimulus materials, helped the junior school pupils to develop their ideas, and to start writing. The Daventry School pupils had to show maturity and flexibility in adapting to the abilities and needs of their partners.

The first drafts of the stories were completed by the Falconer's Hill children at school and delivered to the Daventry School pupils for marking and correction prior to the third visit. A short assessment had to be written for each of the younger children.

A few days later the pupils from Falconer's Hill came over to Daventry

School, and in pairs the pupils went over the first drafts of the stories. The Daventry School pupils were encouraging, but tended to concentrate on points such as spelling and punctuation. The Falconer's Hill pupils had come expecting help in improving the content of the stories and there was some mismatch of expectations. Some of the younger pupils were disappointed and turned to the teachers for help.

However, some pupils helped the younger children to improve the content of their stories as well. For example, Nicola suggested that the beginning of Susan's story should be longer, and contain more detailed descriptions. Susan thought she could put more adventures into the story if it included a time machine, and Nicola discussed several possible endings with her.

A week later the Daventry School pupils returned to Falconer's Hill School to see the final version of the stories, and to attempt the worksheets and exercises which the younger pupils had prepared for them.

The Daventry School pupils were impressed by the care which the junior school children had taken over the presentation of the second draft, with colourful covers, numerous illustrations, worksheets, etc.

Typical was Ruth's assessment of Jim's final draft. She thought it was 'really good', as he had taken her advice about improving the presentation, correcting spelling and the use of illustrations ... 'I thought it was an excellent effort overall'.

Nicola praised the presentation of Susan's final version, and described how she had incorporated the improvements which Nicola had suggested from the previous visit. Clive was pleased with Ricky's efforts, and felt the wordsearch he had prepared was very good. Clive wrote:

> At the end we had a photo session with all the members of our class and our pupils. I think this was a fitting finale to a great series of fantastic visits. I hope we can have another visit to Falconer's Hill.

We can see from these extracts how closely both groups of children were involved in the task of producing stories, and that writing the story for someone else (not the teacher) was an important part of this process. Through working in pairs, the younger pupils were given a degree of individual help that they would rarely receive in the classroom.

The enthusiasm of the younger pupils was also reflected in the reports they wrote about the project. They all appreciated the help they received in writing their stories, and were clearly motivated by a sense of audience. The following extracts are typical:

> Chris wrote:

> We wrote some stories, they helped us with spelling mistakes and punctuation. I hope we can do more work with the seniors. I liked writing a story for somebody. I would like to write one again.

Malcolm wrote:

I found it was a great help only writing the story for one person. I would like to do drama next term.

Felicity found:

... it very useful working with one partner only, because they can help you and listen to you without being bothered by anyone else.

The interviewing and discussion of ideas for stories would have hit En 1/4b: '... ask and respond to questions in a range of situations with increased confidence'; and En 1/4c '... take part as a speaker and listener in a group discussion or activity, expressing a personal view and commenting constructively on what is being discussed or experienced'. In addition to the reading (of books, pupils' stories) which took place, the juniors wrote and redrafted their stories, thereby hitting En 3/3c: '... write more complex stories with detail beyond simple events and with a defined ending'; and En 3/3d: '... begin to revise and redraft in discussion with the teacher, other adults, or other children in the class ...' etc.

Summer Term 1987

One outcome of the project was that many of the pupils from Falconer's Hill Junior School became more interested in writing. Two girls at the school decided to write a play which their class would act for pupils from Daventry School, and this led to joint drama work during the summer term.

The play, divided into four main episodes, described the adventures of a group of children at a Children's Home in London, looked after by a formidable Principal, Mrs. Martin. She organized two trips for them, to a zoo and to a Pirates' Island. The play ended with the children arriving on the Island, though without describing what happened there.

The two girls who wrote the play, Louise and Jane, wrote the play together, in long-hand and using a work processor over a two week period, though Louise provided most of the ideas. Both girls felt that working with the pupils from Daventry School during the spring term had helped them to develop their ideas:

Teacher: How was the writing of the play affected by what you did last term with Daventry School pupils?

Louise: Well, if we hadn't done the work with them, I don't think we would have had the good ideas, because they put it into our heads, you see.

Teacher: You mean for the play, or the ideas of adding bits?

Louise Adding some bits.

Teacher: Had you done that before, writing a story and then doing a second version?

Louise: No, I hadn't.
Jane: Nor me.
Teacher: So do you think the idea of going over a piece of writing,
          adding bits and doing a second draft . . . is something you
          learned from those children?
Louise: Yes.
Jane: Yes.

The play was produced by the children, with very little help from their form teacher. Initially only a few children in the class wanted to act, but Louise was able to persuade the others, helping some of them learn their lines. Over half the class was involved in the performance; a total of sixteen children. The children brought in their own props and costumes, and worked closely together, adding extra jokes and ideas in rehearsal.

The play was acted in the school hall; the Daventry School pupils sat in the centre and the play was acted in the round. It lasted about twenty minutes, with a narrator providing the continuity between episodes. The children acted with confidence and appeared very natural, and the play ended with the children arriving on Pirates' Island.

At the end of the performance, all the children sat in a circle, and gave their first responses to the play. The Daventry School pupils were clearly highly impressed. The older children then paired up with the junior school partners from the spring term, and were put into groups of six or eight. Each group had to discuss the play, and start developing ideas for a sequel.

All the groups praised the acting and production. Mandy was typical of many Daventry School pupils when she wrote:

> Overall, this play was well thought out, brilliantly presented, and a
> really well-written production. It was a lot different from what I
> expected. I thought it was going to be some sort of fairy tale, but it
> was a very grown-up, mature play.

Two days later the pupils from Falconer's Hill Junior School came over to Daventry School, and in the same groups, improvised a sequel to the play. This activity, involving about sixty children, took place in the Dance and Drama Studio and adjacent Activity Hall.

The pupils continued to develop the ideas that they had discussed during the previous session. Some of the younger pupils were nervous or shy about acting with the older children, but by the end of the session (lasting an hour), all the groups had worked well at their improvisations.

Five days later the pupils met again at Daventry School to finish their work, and to show it to the other groups. By the end of this session most of the groups had been able to develop their ideas successfully, and to present an improvisation that was enjoyable to watch. This work would have fulfilled En 1/4d: '. . . participate in a presentation'.

These drama sessions were filmed, and at the end of the final session the Daventry School pupils discussed their work with the teacher. All had enjoyed doing drama with the pupils from Falconer's Hill, though some felt that a number of the younger children were nervous about acting with the seniors.

In their reports, the Daventry School pupils decribed the benefits they felt they had gained from three terms' work with the children from Falconer's Hill. A couple of extracts illustrate their enthusiastic assessments of the project:

Nicola wrote:

I have enjoyed this work and all the other work we have done with the Falconer's Hill children over this year, and I am sure the pupils have enjoyed it too. I would like very much to do some more work along these lines next year.

Robert wrote:

I think our class had had a flashback to Junior School life. We were able to see if we had changed in any way as well. We also got a taste of teaching life which was good ... I enjoyed all the sessions. They were great fun.

Programmes of Study

The project would have clearly covered numerous elements in the Programmes of Study for ATs 1–3 at Key Stages 2 and 3. For example, in AT 1 both junior and secondary school pupils had opportunities to attempt many of the activities and skills in section 6 (either partly or wholly) such as:

recount events and narrate stories;

assess and interpret arguments and opinions with increasing precision and discrimination;

ask increasingly precise or detailed questions;

respond to increasingly complex instructions and questions;

listen and respond to an increasing range of fiction, non-fiction, poetry and plays, including those which have been seen;

discuss issues in small and large groups, taking account of the views of others, and negotiating a consensus (DES 1990, p. 24).

The juniors also had the opportunity to:

'work with or devise an increasing range of drama scripts, taking on a variety of dramatic roles' (DES 1990a, p. 24), as well as being involved in 'role-play, simulations and group drama' (section 8; DES 1990a, p. 25). The range of opportunities provided by the project enabled all the pupils 'to work in groups of various size, both single sex and mixed where possible, with and without direct teacher supervision' (section 7; DES 1990a, p. 25). The production of the juniors' play would have covered 'planning and taking part in a group presentation, which at this level (i.e. level 6) might include performance of a playscript for a school production' (section 17; DES 1990a, p. 26).

In AT 2 at Key Stage 2, the juniors had (some) opportunities 'to participate in all reading activities'; and to 'read aloud and to talk about the books they have been reading', giving their opinions where appropriate (section 10; DES 1990a, pp. 30–31). The secondary pupils studied the junior school readers, and discussed them with their younger partners. Thus they had the opportunity (in part) to 'discuss the themes, settings and characters of the texts they read in order to make a personal response to them' (section 20; DES 1990a, p. 32).

The editing and redrafting of stories which took place covered a range of opportunities described in AT 3 at Key Stages 2 and 3. For example, at KS 2 pupils should have opportunities to write for others (section 16). The project would have enabled then to 'undertake chronological writing' (e.g. work diaries); 'have opportunities to create, polish and produce individually or together, by hand or on a word processor, extended written texts, appropriately laid out and illustrated (etc.); 'be encouraged to be adventurous with vocabulary choices'; 'think about ways of making their meaning clear to their intended reader in redrafting their writing'; and 'consider features of layout' (etc.) (section 18; DES 1990a, pp. 37–38).

For the secondary school pupils at KS 3, the project would have enabled them to demonstrate 'an increasing proficiency in rereading and revising or redrafting the text' (section 22; DES 1990a, p. 38). The project also offered them opportunities to 'handle the following elements of a story structure with increasing effectiveness: an opening, setting, characters, events and a resolution; and 'organize and express their meaning appropriately for different specified audiences' (etc.) (section 25; DES 1990a, p. 39). These examples indicate the range of provisions within the Programmes of Study that the project would have satisfied.

The Benefits of the Project

At the end of the pilot project we assessed the benefits as follows:

Curriculum Continuity

There was considerable benefit to the pupils from the junior school through continuity of curricular experience in English and Drama. Furthermore, pupils from both schools developed all their language skills through discussion, analysis, reading, writing, editing, listening, acting, etc. A great deal was demanded of the older pupils, because they had to act in the role of the teachers, though without a teacher's training. They responded very well to this challenge, and in the process developed their critical faculties, and deepened their understanding of how language is used in different contexts.

Increased Interest in Writing

As we have seen, the junior school pupils became much more interested in writing stories as a result of the project. We have shown that the younger pupils were helped with their writing by the older pupils, and the efforts of both groups were focused and stimulated by a sense of audience. The play produced by the younger children was also evidence of their motivation, and their desire to act for a specific audience. Thus the pupils were not only working *with* each other, but also *for* each other. Writing for a purpose was clearly a powerful stimulus. As Allen (1987) has put it:

> Since all writing should take place in context, with a purpose and an intended audience, the classroom needs to be a place where the circumstances sustain a community of 'real writers' (p. 25).

A successful cross-phase project is more than the sum of its Attainment Targets. However, I have tried to demonstrate the range of levels in the three main Attainment Targets that the project would have hit.

Liaison

Liaison between the two schools was considerably enhanced by the project. The younger children became more familiar with Daventry School through visits they paid to the school, and working with the older pupils. Those children that were coming to Daventry School in September said they felt happier about the move because of their involvement in the project. An edited version of the video was shown at our induction evening for parents of new first year pupils.

Social Skills

The reports written by the junior school pupils show that they gained greatly in self-confidence through the friendly relationships established with the older pupils. The two groups of pupils were unlikely to have met, or formed relationships, it it had not been for this project.

There are some similarities between this project, and initiatives which have taken place as part of the National Writing Project in Dorset. For example, pupils in Year 8 at an 11–18 comprehensive school wrote individually to pupils aged 5 and upwards at their contributory infant, junior and primary schools, inviting them to a visit. They performed short entertainments for each other, and at the end of the visit the older pupils presented their guests with storybooks which they had written individually for them. These were based on a study of books for young children, and information about the readers' interests supplied by their teachers. In another project, boys of 12 and 13 at a grammar school worked in groups to write complex adventure books for pupils in the top year of one of their contributory primary schools (Wallen 1987).

Our project was somewhat different, in that close relationships developed pairs and groups of pupils from the two schools over three terms, and they helped each other with their writing and improvisations. The sense of audience was therefore important for both age-groups.

On the basis of the project, we were awarded a grant of £640 by the Schools' Curriculum Development Committee to extend the scheme to some of our other contributory schools in the academic year 1987/88. The projects which took place then are described in Chapters 3 through 5.[2] The scheme developed in scope, so that by 1988/89 all the members of the English Faculty at Daventry School and the majority of our contributory schools, were involved; five of these projects are described in Chapters 6 through 10.

Notes

1 I am indebted to Neil Richards, of Falconer's Hill Junior School, for his collaboration and help in devising this project. A shorter version of this chapter was published in *Education 3–3*, **16**, 2 (June 1988). A brief account of this project: 'Building Bridges', by Tabor, D.C. and Richards, N. (1987) was published in *Junior Education*, **11**, 12, pp. 30–31.
2 For an overview of the projects which took place in 1987/88, see Tabor, D.C. (1988) 'Building More Bridges', in *SCDC Curriculum Continuity Information Pack*, Unit 1, p. 34.

Chapter 3

Poetry Across the Divide

Introduction

Wordsworth's famous aphorism: 'Poetry is the spontaneous overflow of powerful feelings; it takes its origin from emotion recollected in tranquillity' describes the creative impulse which we, as teachers, try to stimulate and guide in the classroom. Workshops with practising poets and writers are widely used in schools to develop pupils' writing, and to deepen their appreciation of literature. In 1987/88 we combined this approach with curriculum continuity work in English, as one of a series of projects with our contributory schools.

My top English set in Year 9 (pupils aged 13–14) worked with the top class of juniors in Years 5 and 6 (aged 9–11) at Falconer's Hill Junior School, which is adjacent to us. The Daventry School pupils had participated in the pilot project in the previous year.[1]

Each class had poetry workshops with Leicester poet Chris Challis. As part of the project, the children worked in junior–senior pairs, writing poems for each other about school, and in response to various stimuli. Workshops were also held with both groups of children working together. The goal of the project was to produce a book of poems which could be sold to raise money for 'Children in Need'. This chapter will look in detail at the way the children responded to a practising poet, how they worked together, and the different language skills that were developed as a result. I shall suggest that the approach used here provides a model that could be used for other projects in curricular continuity. In addition, the project fulfilled several levels in each of the three main Attainment Targets for English, and these will be highlighted where appropriate.

Poetry Workshops

When I first mentioned the poetry workshops to my class, they were intrigued by the colourful life Chris Challis had led, as described in his c.v. The first workshop was very successful; Chris Challis looked like a poet, with long hair, a flowing beard … and a three-piece suit! In the first hour he talked about his life, and read his poems, which he discussed with the class. In the second hour he produced six enlarged photographs which he had taken, and these were the stimuli for the pupils to write their poems, a few of which where read out at the end of the session. The pupils worked with intense concentration, and greatly enjoyed the workshop.

Gail commented:

We had an excellent lesson with Chris Challis. I listened intently to what he had to say and enjoyed all the poems he read to us. I wrote 'The Tramp' which I am quite pleased with. I was surprised Chris could sit down like us and write a brilliant poem. The pictures of what we were writing about helped me actually find ideas because I could see what I was writing about.

Mandy wrote:

It was great! I have never really met a poet before and I am really glad I did. Chris Challis was a very interesting and happy person … I have learned that poetry can be fun even if you are not an expert.

The oral work generated by this session would have hit several levels and strands of AT 1: Speaking and Listening, for example En 1/4c: '… take part as speakers and listeners in a group discussion or activity, expressing a personal view and commenting constructively on what is being discussed or experienced'; and En 1/5b: '… contribute to and respond constructively in discussion, including the development of ideas …' etc. AT 3: Writing does not specifically stipulate the writing of poems. However, this activity would have hit several strands, for example En 3/4c: '… organize non-chronological writing for different purposes in orderly ways'; part of En 3/5a: '… write in a variety of forms for a range of purposes and audiences, in ways which attempt to engage the interest of the reader'; and En 3/4e and En 3/5d, which cover editing and redrafting.

Take Your Partners

We discussed the workshop in the next lesson, and prepared for our first joint lesson with the juniors. The following week I took the class over to Falconer's Hill Junior School for their first session with the juniors, and paired the pupils up at random. My pupils had to interview their partners and fill in a personal questionnaire about him/her. Then they had to read a couple of poems from 'Junior Voices' with their partner, and give him/her a short test (using a worksheet) based on one of the poems. These activities enabled the children to get to know each other, and afterwards my pupils had to write a poem about school for their partners. The children worked very well together in small groups round the junior school. Good relationships were quickly established between the pairs, with the older pupils adapting to their roles as teachers with ease. Mandy wrote:

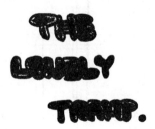

I lie in comfort in my four-poster bed,
A fine silk pillow supports my head,
Luxury surrounds me as I doze,
Not moving from under my bedclothes.

My room is something to be desired,
The velvet drapes and welcome fire,
The plush, leather armchair stands on its ow
As I live a life of wealth, in my own home.

I wake up - into reality,
And there's no bedroom near to see.
The park keeper nudges me in the back,
I struggle up and grab my cap.

In shabby attire I go on my way,
I say goodbye to the 'good old days.'
I pull my cap down over my ears.
It's moth-eaten now and has seen better
                                    years.

I trudge along out of the park,
Down secluded alleys I wait for the dark ......

Figure 3.1 *'The Lonely Tramp', by a pupil at Daventry School*

Figure 3.2 'The First Day of Term!', by a pupil at Daventry School

... I had a girl called Susan, and she is really nice. I asked her to read out the poem 'Oliphaunt'. Susan read it out with a lot of feeling ... using her voice to vary the tone ... Then I asked Susan if she would like to choose a poem, and she replied, 'When I'm choosing a poem, I like to read them through, is that OK?' I thought that was very sensible, and let her read through the book. Susan chose one called 'Meeting Mary', and she read it brilliantly ... I told her I was hoping to write a poem about school for her and asked her whether she would like the poem to be funny, serious, narrative, rhyming etc. and she replied, 'Cheerful!' I really enjoyed this visit, and I think Susan did too!

Sarah wrote:

I really enjoyed working with John. I worked very hard during the lesson to try and make it interesting for John and me. He thought that poetry was boring, so I hope I might be able to change his mind.

The junior school pupils were also very enthusiastic about their first session with the senior pupils. Julie was typical of many when she wrote:

> This is an exciting experience. Alice [my partner] is really nice, and she comes from the village of Braunston. First of all we read a poem called 'The Hairy Toe'. After we read it I did a wordsearch Alice had made, it was about the poem. Then I answered some questions. Who do you think owns the hairy toe? Or what do you think the thing or person who owns the hairy toe looks like? Then we read 'Tramp Tree' and I did a crossword for that. Then we both tried to answer riddles at the front of the book, but we only got one right ...

Some of the juniors were initially apprehensive about working with an older pupil, but these anxieties were quickly dispelled. For example, Bill wrote:

> I enjoyed Michael coming to interview me from the seniors. He said to me 'Don't look so worried' ... I felt embarrassed. Michael had already picked some poems, they were 'Two Dumb Boys' and 'A Dull Day'. They were most interesting ...'

The interviews and discussions which took place would have hit several levels and strands in AT 1: Speaking and Listening. For the younger pupils this would have included En 1/3c: '... listen with an increased span of concentration to other children and adults, asking and responding to questions, and commenting on what has been said.' Conducting the interviews, by the Daventry School pupils, would have fulfilled in part En 1/4b: '... ask and respond to questions in a range of situations with increased confidence.' Reading the poems to each other, and the writing of diary entries, would also have hit several levels in Attainment Targets 2 and 3.

Poetry Review

The Daventry School pupils had to write the first drafts of their poems about school for their partners. A fortnight later the seniors had their second poetry workshop with Chris Challis. In the first hour he read out all the poems which the pupils had written during his first visit and a few of the 'school' poems, all of which he commented upon. Towards the end of the session everyone wrote poems on the theme of a journey, and a few of them were read out.

Mary particularly appreciated Dr. Challis' comments about the pupils' poems. She wrote:

> He read out twenty-six of our poems from the last workshop, telling us the parts he liked, where the poem could be improved, whether the use of words was good, and whether the words flowed in a pattern. I think this was an extremely good idea because he is an

expert after all, and he could tell us how to produce a better standard of poems, and help us to develop our skill at poetry. Also the praise from him would make writing the poem worthwhile ... He was just as interesting and enjoyable as last time.

Robert reflected the opinion of many pupils when he commented:

My behaviour was good, and so was everyone's in the class. The atmosphere was very relaxed ... I have learned that poetry is more complicated than you think.

The pupils' discussions about their poems would have hit En 1/4c: '... take part as a speaker and listener in a group discussion or activity, commenting constructively on what is being discussed or experienced.' The editing and redrafting of the poems would have hit En 3/4e and En 3/5d; the final versions would have hit part of En 3/6c: '... demonstrate the ability to use literary stylistic features' (etc.).

The idea of the journey was interpreted in several ways; most pupils wrote about journeys they'd made in England or abroad, or would like to make. Steven responded to the idea by choosing a theme from classical mythology. His poem, which went through several drafts before reaching its final form, was about Icarus and Daedalus:

Daedalus' Wings

Out of Crete flew a father and son,
Daedalus the mad scientist, it is said.
Flying joyfully in the sea air
Borne by wings of wax and owls' feathers
Happiness spread across his face
For the ecstacy of flying was such a delight.

His son, Icarus,
Soared and dived in the sky,
But delight turned to sorrow,
As Icarus flew too high,
The wings melted in the heat of the day,
And his wings bore him no more.
Falling out of the sky he called aloud
'Athene, help thy servant.'

The gracious goddess came,
But Icarus still crashed into the glittering sea,
As a proud courageous man,
Not a weeping child.
Daedalus searched hour upon hour,
No sight of Icarus could he see,
So at last, a man burdened with sorrow,
He flew over to Greece.

Improving Your Work

The following week the Daventry School pupils paid their second visit to Falconer's Hill, working in the same pairs as before. The pupils looked at some more poems from 'Junior Voices', and talked about what made a 'good' poem. The Daventry School pupils then read the first drafts of their poems about school, and asked for comments from the juniors about how their poems could be improved. The juniors then interviewed their partners (reversing the roles from last time) and with help from the senior pupils started to write their poems about school.

Mandy gave a detailed account of her visit. After a discussion about what made a good poem, she was interviewed by her junior school partner, Susan:

> ... Now it was my turn, for about the next half an hour Susan asked me lots of questions. They were really good; she asked me about my favourite pop group, where I lived, animals, pets, my favourite book ... there were loads!
>
> Eventually I read my poem to Susan. I was a bit embarrassed, but I was pleased to say that Susan said she enjoyed it. Maybe she was just saying it to make me feel good, but she said she was telling the truth.
>
> Susan said she liked the way I went through my life at school, and she said it made her think of her feelings and memories of playschool. She thinks it tells people a lot about my feelings. Susan doesn't think it is too long; overall I think she enjoyed it ...
>
> Then came the time for Susan to start to think about her poem, which she would write for me. She didn't really seem very eager to start ... In the end Susan said she wanted to write a poem where all the children bring their animals ... she explained it really well, but it was too detailed to be a poem.

Communications between these two pupils was obviously very easy, even though Susan found written work difficult. Other Daventry School pupils, while having good relationships with their partners, had to work harder to get a response. For example, David read his poem 'The Register' to Tricia, and then tried to elicit her comments, so that he could write an improved version.

The Register

We crowd into the classroom,
As the morning bell rings.
Miss gets out the register,
As through our names she sings.

> Richard Abbott, Tony Bell,
> Cuthbert Hall, Timothy Lings,
> Jonathan Neat, Simon Pennie,
> Jason Putworth, John Rennings.

Every morning It's the same old gabble,
Through the register she goes,
Down the alphabetical list,
Through our names she flows.

> Jean Bains, Janice Fish,
> Lisa Goodard, Jenny Lowes,
> Ann Porter, Janet Thomas,
> Karen Willis, Sarah Rose.

Why does she want to know these things,
Whether we are here or not?
Now she wants to know what I'm doing for lunch,
What a nosey teacher I've got!

David: Is there anything you liked about it? You said you like rhyming poems last time, so I've tried to make it rhyme, and you said you liked funny poems, so I've tried to make it funny. Is there anything you particularly like about this poem? [Pause] ... at the beginning I've put 'We come into the classroom'. Do you all crowd into the classroom, or do you amble in late?

Tricia: We tend to take our time.

David: But as soon as you're in the classroom, you all have to sit down. You get a book out while Miss reads the register?

Tricia: Yes.

David: And you liked that about it. Is there anything else you liked about it? [Pause] ... Sometimes the teacher does gabble on, doesn't she?

Tricia: Yes.

David: Going on with the names ... you think it'll never end. Trouble is, it's all the same, it's not as if every day it's different ... What else do you find interesting in this poem?

Tricia: I like some of the names you've got in it ... I like 'Cuthbert Hall'.

David: Any particular reason?

Tricia: It's unusual.

David: Do you know anyone called Cuthbert Hall?

Tricia: No ... it's unusual.

David: Anything else you like?

Tricia: I like 'Sarah Rose'.

David: Well, when I was writing this poem, I had to have something which rhymed with 'Lowes'!

Tricia wrote afterwards:

We read David's poem, it was good ... I like the verses where the teacher sings through the names and being nosey, and asking them what they like and are doing for lunch.

A great deal was being expected of both pupils. The open–ended questions from David required a sophisticated level of response from Tricia. The critical skills involved in this type of discussion can only be developed gradually. A number of the other Daventry School pupils also discovered that the juniors found the activity of criticizing a poem difficult.

Yet when it came to creative work, pupils worked well together. For example, Robert's partner knew exactly what he wanted to do:

> ... Martin asked me some questions about myself and my family. My partner had typed out a questionnaire, which I thought was good. After this he started to write out his poem. He didn't need any help, as he had thought about the poem before the lesson.

The enjoyment and motivation of the juniors was reflected in their diary entries. For example, Claire was a new girl at Falconer's Hill, and she had been paired up with Penny, a new girl at Daventry School. The two girls hit it off straight away, and found they had a lot in common. They discussed Penny's poem 'The New Girl', about her experiences. Afterwards Claire wrote:

> Penny is new, and I am new. We enjoyed being together and I hope to see her again. I loved her poem. She has a nice voice and she is interesting to talk to. When we were together we talked about being new and what we thought of it ... Now I am her friend and wish to see her again.

The cross–phase discussions about the secondary school pupil's poems would have hit En 1/3c and En 1/4c.

Primary School Poetry

The Daventry School pupils had all prepared word–lists or brought other stimuli to help their partners start their poems about school during the same session. The older pupils helped the juniors sort out their ideas for a poem, as this transcript illustrates:

Sarah:	What sort of things do you want your poem to be about? I know it's about school, but do you want it to be about the first day at junior school?
John:	The first day at junior school.
Sarah:	That's better, because you know people there ... Can you remember your first day at junior school?
John:	Yes, I can remember going down there ...
Sarah:	Did you want to come?
John:	Yeah.
Sarah:	Can you remember your first thoughts coming into school?

John: It seemed big ...
Sarah: How did the other children strike you?
John: Some of them seemed friendly ...
Sarah: I've done a word list on somethings on school, and
         there's a list of of some things in school. Those are descrip-
         tions of children, and those are teachers, and that's what
         you think of when you first come into school. OK? So you
         can choose some words and I'll help you write them down
         ... How are you going to start off?
John: School was very big ...
Sarah: Are you going to start it getting up and having breakfast
         and thinking 'I've got to go to school', or are you going to
         start it going into school?
John: I'll say 'School's very big and ...'
Sarah: Are you going to have it rhyming?
John: Dunno ... it depends how it turns out!
Sarah: Are you going to say something about the teachers? What
         did you think of them?
John: They were very good, they helped me a lot.
Sarah: So you could put 'The teachers are very helpful' ... or
         'very nice' ... or friendly'.
John: [Writing] 'The teachers are very ... helpful.'

This extract indicates the sort of interaction that was taking place. Sarah was articulate, and if anything, almost over-eager in her desire to help John. The transcript may suggest that she was largely dictating the structure of the poem, though in reality John was able to be assertive and express his own views.

Several levels in AT 1 and AT 3 were met in the process. For example, Sarah's attempts to help John would have hit En 1/5b: '... contribute to and respond constructively in discussion, including the development of ideas' etc. John's responses would have met (at least in part) En 1/3a and En 1/3c.

What is perhaps more interesting is the way John and Sarah were doing what every poet attempts in some form or another. They were grappling with the raw material of John's early experiences of school, and trying to find suitable words to convey that experience. Ted Hughes (1967) has described succinctly the difficulty of bridging the gap between the word, and the experience.

It is when we set out to find words for some seemingly quite simple experience that we begin to realize what a huge gap there is between our understanding of what happens around us and inside us, and the words we have at our command to say something about it (p. 119).

The process is bound to raise pupils' awareness of language, and the different ways in which language can be used.

A Messy Morning

The paint was splattered everywhere,
It even went onto the clay.
The roller was on the paper.
The paper was getting dirty.
The felt tips had all run out.
The paint brushes had all gone hard.
The newspaper was very clean,
But the pots and pallets were dirty.
My drawing was all smudged with finger prints.
The background went all wrong.
The colours had all mixed,
The shading had been rubbed out.
The shadows had all gone.
Everything had gone wrong,
But it was worth staying in at break.

Figure 3.3 'A Messy Morning', by a pupil at Falconer's Hill Junior School

Oral Work

During the next lesson my class was divided into friendship groups, and the pupils were given four questions about the project as a starting point for discussion. Most pupils responded well, discussing their experiences with insight and maturity, as the following extract shows.

Gail: [Reading] How did you get on with your pupil at Falconer's Hill, and if you had any problems, what were they?

David: My pupil was very good. I had two pupils, a boy and a girl, though on the second visit the boy wasn't there. She worked very hard and enjoyed the poetry, and she's very critical so I can always change my poems to what she likes.

Sarah: Mine's the opposite to that because he's not critical at all and just says my poem's rubbish.

Robert: I read my poem to Martin and said 'How could I improve it?' He just didn't know, and when he was writing his poem he didn't write it about school, but about the sky.

Mandy: Susan couldn't start writing her poem, she kept asking questions all the time.

Sarah: John kept saying 'This is going to be a brilliant poem' and 'My poem is so brilliant', and he kept saying my poem was rubbish. He kept boasting how brilliant his poem was.

Robert: I don't think they'd done much poetry before.

Gail: No, it didn't seem like it.

Mandy: Mine just likes nursery rhyme type of poems.

David: I think what we've done is a very good introduction for them to poetry. I think they've enjoyed it.

This discussion shows the sort of understanding the pupils had gained into the problems with language and poetry that their partners had. This activity would have met En 1/5b: '. . . contribute to and respond constructively in discussion, including the development of ideas; advocate and justify a point of view'; and En 1/6a: '. . . contribute, to group discussions, considered opinions or clear statements of personal feeling which are clearly responsive to the contributions of others.'

Primary Workshop

Chris Challis conducted his first workshop with the junior school class, and he quickly established a rapport with the younger children. They enjoyed his poems, and responded enthusiastically to the photographs, which he discussed with them. The children wrote their own poems, and some were read out in class.

Helen gave this account of the workshop:

Today Chris Challis came to talk to us about poems. I thought he would be all posh because most poem writers are, but he was just ordinary. When he came in he read two poems. One was about a hat, and another was about a fancy dress party. Then he showed us six pictures: one was a tramp, a rock band, two skeletons, a prison, and some policemen.

Chris said, 'You write a poem about the one that interests you most, then you can choose a picture for me to write about.'

We all chose skeletons, then we all wrote our poems. I read mine out, and Anne read hers out and I liked it. I went up to get Chris's autograph, and then he left.

It seemed a good idea for the teachers to spend a lesson with each other's classes, talking about the project. Paula, my colleague from Falconer's Hill, spent a lesson talking to the third years about her pupils, and the language problems they had. She brought several examples of their writing, which were duplicated, so as to illustrate the different ability levels. Then she talked to pupils individually about difficulties they were having with their partners, and gave them advice. The pupils found this visit interesting and helpful.

I made a return visit to Falconer's Hill and spent a lesson with the top class. For part of the lesson I split the pupils up into groups of four to six and gave them a few questions about the project for discussion. The pupils had not done this sort of work before, so we first of all discussed the difference between a 'discussion' and a 'question and answer' session. Each group then chose a chairperson, who took notes and reported back to the class what the children in his/her group felt about the poetry workshops, and working with the pupils at Daventry School. It was clear that all the pupils had enjoyed the project, and felt they had learned something. We were constrained by the lack of supply teachers (who could have taken our normal lessons), from spending more time with each other's classes. This group work would have fulfilled En 1/3c: '. . . listen with an increased span of concentration to other children and adults, asking and responding to questions, and commenting on what has been said.'

We had planned the last poetry workshop with Chris Challis and both groups of children together for the end of term. Unfortunately his car broke down, so the session was spent with the children talking to each other about their poems, improving their work and making display copies of the final versions. The pupils continued to work very well together.

Claire, from Falconer's Hill, was very pleased to see her friend Penny again at Daventry School. Claire wrote:

On Thursday 10th December my class went to see the Secondary School pupils to improve our poems. When I got there I did not expect what I saw. There were coats all over the front corridor, and we could not get in, so my teacher moved the coats and we went in. The school was big, and if I had got lost I would have got lost. Penny and I went to the library to work. We worked on my poem and then it was playtime at 10:15. When we came in we finished my poem and then I copied it onto yellow paper and backed it onto blue. Then I showed it to Mr. Tabor, and he loved it. I enjoyed going, and I hope to go again.

This is Claire's poem:

School is a Book

A school is a book of
interesting words.

Pages of things to
look at and learn.

A school is a book of
different folk,

Of teachers, pupils,
Heads and cleaners.

A school is a book of
colourful pictures.

Each picture uniques
and full of ideas.

A school is a book of
puzzles to learn.

Like Maths and English
and Poems.

The good working atmosphere was also reflected in the diary entries of the Daventry School pupils. Gail was typical of many when she wrote:

> To my surpise Andrew settled to his work quickly. I followed the teacher's instruction and set to work. Andrew hadn't written a poem as I asked, so I helped him to put pen to paper. Andrew carried on writing until break! (Amazing).
>
> After break Andrew selected some red paper and began writing out his final draft of the poem. He kept making errors, but after the third attempt, he produced quite a nice piece of work ... I enjoyed today's session immensely.

Sarah had a productive lesson with John, though he continued to demonstrate that he had a mind of his own:

> First he showed me his poem which was very good. The only thing I didn't like was that he put 'I burn up hot'. I didn't understand this so he told me that it meant getting angry. I asked him if he wouldn't mind changing it to 'I get angry' because some people might not understand it. At this he created a fuss, saying he didn't want to change anything because his poem was brilliant. I managed to calm him down and eventually I got him change it.
>
> John particularly enjoyed decorating his poem, which he did very well ... and I have enjoyed working with him, although he is a bit boastful.

The care the pupils took in producing display copies of their poems would have hit En 4/3d: '... in revising and redrafting their writing, begin to check the accuracy of their spelling.' The older pupils (and perhaps some of the younger ones) would have hit AT 4/5: Presentation, strand 6b: '... check final drafts of writing for misspelling and other errors of presentation'; strand 6d: '... show some ability to use any available presentational devices that are appropriate to the task, so that finished work is presented clearly and attractively'; and strand 7d: '... show an increased ability to present finished work appropriately, clearly and attractively.'

Final Workshop

We were able to arrange the final workshop for all the pupils, and this took place at Daventry School in the middle of the spring term. Chris Challis spent part of the time reading and discussing his poems, and then he produced half a dozen enlarged photographs which he had taken, and which he discussed with the class. Like the earlier workshops, but working in pairs and small groups, pupils chose a photo as the starting point for their poems.

In senior-junior pairs the pupils discussed their poems as they were writing them. They worked intently on their poems, some starting to produce display copies. Chris Challis and the two teachers circulated among the different groups, giving help and advice. For the last twenty minutes of the session all the pupils came together in the school library, and several read out their poems, which were commented upon by Chris Challis. The Falconer's Hill pupils were less self-conscious than the seniors, and read their poems confidently. This activity would have fulfilled En 1/4d: '... participate in a presentation.' The success of the workshop was reflected in the pupils' work diaries, as a couple of entries show. Bill, from Falconer's Hill, wrote:

> I was feeling great this morning because we were going over to Mr. Tabor's third year class for a poetry lesson with Chris Challis. I was looking forward to meeting with my partner and meeting with other seniors ... We went over, we were muttering and laughing. We got to the double doors ... it smelt like a hospital! I felt great, I knew my way around. We got to the library door, the seniors were there. I was afraid now! I was the first to meet my partner, Michael, who was at the back of the room. I felt an idiot, but I forgot that.
>
> Chris Challis pulled up in an Escort with a dent. I thought, 'What a heap.' Then I noticed that he had a private registration. Chris walks in with a cool jumper on with 'C.C.' Then he gets out some photographs of a Cathedral, Notre Dame where Quasimodo used to clang the bells; a swan in a pond; and a funeral. The one that Michael and I chose was of a spider's web on a window pane. The bell rang for break and we rushed outside and nearly got pushed over. I heard the bell again. I thought, not another collision!
>
> When we got back Michael and I got on with our poetry. Michael finished first, he said, 'Have a read.' I thought his poem was great. Then he gave me some ideas. The teacher said, 'You have thirty minutes to finished.' I was on my last verse at that time. Chris Challis came round to help us. The teacher said, 'Time to pack away!' Chris asked, 'Who wants to read their poem?' Many pupils read their poems. I hope to meet the seniors again.

Bill's partner at Daventry School was Michael, who wrote:

> This was the last poetry workshop to be held with Chris Challis and pupils from Daventry School and Falconer's Hill, but it was one of the best. The juniors came over about 9 a.m. and we found our partners and got down to work. The first double period was taken up by Chris Challis reading us some of his poems, and then he showed some photos and we had to write a poem on one of them. I managed to get mine done with a bit of time left to help my partner, Bill. He got stuck after the first two verses, but I helped him out, and it was finished in no time.
>
> A good ending to an extremely interesting series of poetry workshops with Dr. Challis.

In the summer term we produced a book of the poems, illustrated with the children's decorations, and with extracts from their work diaries. Chris Challis came over for a short session with all the pupils together, to read and discuss their poems. The book went on sale in the two schools and local bookshop, and we raised £50 for 'Children in Need'. A couple of articles about the project appeared in the local press. We received an appreciative letter from our MP, and from the Secretary of State for Education, who praised the book as 'a fine collection'.

Programmes of Study

We shall select a few of the more prominent elements from the Programmes of Study which the project would have covered. For example, in AT 1 the project would have given all the pupils opportunities to 'recite and read aloud in a variety of contexts, with increasing fluency and awareness of audience'; 'discuss issues in small and large groups, taking account of the views of others, and negotiating a consensus'; and 'reflect on their own effectiveness in the use of the spoken word' (section 6; DES 1990a, pp. 24–25). Talking about poems covered part of one element in section 8 (DES 1990a, p. 25). Pupils' discussions about their own poems would also have enabled them to consider 'language appropriate to situation, topic and purpose' (section 18; DES 1990a, p. 26 — usually associated with level 7).

In AT 2: Reading at KS 2, the pupils had opportunities to read poems aloud (section 10; DES 1990a, p. 30). Both age groups gained in awareness of how literary (i.e. poetic) language 'works' and conveys meaning (section 19; DES 1990a, p. 32). Discussing the imagery in their poems, and other technical effects, made the pupils more aware of the uses of alliteration, rhymes, figures of speech etc. (section 24; DES 1990a, p. 33).

In AT 3: Writing at KS 2, the project gave the junior school pupils opportunities 'to write poetry (individually, in small groups, or as a class) and to experiment with different layouts, rhymes, rhythms, verse structures, and with all kinds of sound effects and verbal play' (section 18; DES 1990a, p. 37). At KS 3 the older pupils also had opportunities (in part) to 'build on their experience of reading and hearing a wide range of poetry, and write, both individually and in groups, using poetic features such as rhythm, rhyme and alliteration in verse forms such as jingles, limericks, ballads, haiku etc.' (section 25, DES 1990a, p. 39). At both KS 2 and KS 3 pupils were editing and redrafting their poems (DES 1990a, pp. 37–39).

The Benefits of the Project

Interest in Poetry

It will be apparent from the diary entries and transcripts quoted above how much the pupils enjoyed the poetry workshops, and working with a partner from another school. Many of the older pupils said that working with a professional poet had made them realize how interesting poetry could be.

Liaison and Continuity

Liaison between the two schools was improved by the close working relationship which developed between pupils and teachers. The juniors in Year 6 were going to Daventry School in September 1988, so the project gave them a good opportunity to learn more about the senior school. At the same time, a sense of continuity was created through the joint project. As a result the younger pupils gained an understanding of the sort of work which Daventry School pupils did in English. The social skills of both classes were also improved by working together in pairs and groups, in each other's schools, and with different adults. Independent evaluation was provided by the Head of Daventry PDC, whose comments helped us to improve our planning in 1988/89.

Language Skills

The range of activities which this project involved developed all the pupils' language skills. I was particularly pleased with the quality of oral work produced by both junior and senior pupils, the editing and redrafting that took place, and the attentive way pupils listened when poems were read by Chris Challis or their peers.

The Falconer's Hill pupils gave an assembly about the project to the rest of their school. Their Deputy Head later said that he was amazed how successfully some of the children had communicated their feelings about the project. 'For those children,' he said, 'the poetry project was obviously the highlight of the year.'

I have also demonstrated in a selective manner how the project fulfilled a range of levels and strands in each of the Attainment Targets. The pupils' discussions about poetry also developed their knowledge about language, which will be discussed in detail in Chapter 6.

Motivation

Working in pairs, and with Chris Challis, gave the pupils a strong sense of audience. Pupils were thus writing for each other, and also for possible publication in a book. It could be argued that we have not proved that the *quality* of the children's work was improved through working in pairs or groups. However we cannot know what the outcome of the workshops would have been *without* the age mix. Certainly all the pupils worked hard, and tried to produce their best work for each other.

Easing the Process of Transition

In the following autumn term a survey was conducted among the top juniors who had participated in the project, and were in their first year (i.e. Year 7)

47

at Daventry School. The survey form asked the pupils what they remembered about the project, what they had or had not enjoyed about it, how the project had helped them with English, and with settling in at Daventry School. All the pupils wrote that they had enjoyed the project, especially working with a practising poet, and most felt that it had helped them to write poems.

All the pupils wrote that the project made them feel happier about coming to Daventry School. Typical replies were '... It made me feel more confident' ... 'I knew some people there and I had been to the school' ... 'It helped me not to worry about coming to Daventry School' ... 'It helped me with making friends' ... 'I felt better about coming to Daventry School because I had already visited and worked here.'

Cross-Phase Poetry Project in March

It is instructive to compare this project with the cross-phase poetry project organized in March, Cambridgeshire in 1986 by Findlay and Potter. Richard Burns, a local Cambridge poet, worked for fourteen half-days in an 11–18 secondary school and one of its two large contributory primary schools. In all, 370 pupils in the 9 to 13 age range and ten teachers were involved in the workshops. A joint poetry anthology was produced, and a Poetry Evening was held in the secondary school, during which about fifty pupils from both schools read their poems to their parents.

Much of the writing produced by the primary pupils was more developed and more polished than some of that produced by the secondary pupils. In part this was accounted for by differences in the organization of learning between primary and secondary schools, and the differences in conditions for writing between phases:

> Firstly, the primary school could offer a more flexible approach to writing and rewriting whereas many secondary pupils would, because of the demands of the rigid timetable, have to work at home on their ideas without the support of a teacher. Most secondary pupils will have about two and hours of 'English' per week on a conventional timetable, whereas most primary pupils have up to five hours of 'Language' work. 'Language' work is a part of everyday's work in the primary school whereas there could be a three-day gap between the workshop and the secondary pupil's opportunities to follow-up workshop ideas (Findlay 1987b, p. 43).

Thus the primary school pupils were able to follow-up the workshops immediately, and to spend as long as was needed to improve the first drafts of their poems. Given the quality of poetry produced, the biggest problem for the primary school teachers was deciding which poems to select for the anthology (Potter 1987, p. 44).

The poetry project described in this chapter was different in several respects. The workshops were held with the pupils in their separate teaching groups, *and* with all the pupils together. The primary–secondary divide was used to accentuate the sense of audience, and each pupil was allocated a partner at the other school. The pupils worked together during workshops and between workshops, developing close relationships as a result. The quality of poetry produced by both secondary and junior pupils was high, helped by the fact that the secondary pupils were in the top set. Both projects clearly stimulated the children's enthusiasm for poetry, and contributed towards continuity and liaison between the schools involved.

Two other cross-phase projects took place in 1987/88 between Daventry School, and two contributory schools, involving pupils of low ability who wrote stories for each other. These projects will be described in the next two chapters.

Note

1   We are grateful to Chris Challis for his unique contribution to our Poetry Project. Thanks are due to SCDC and the 'Arts in the Curriculum Project' (Northants. LEA) for funding, and to the Headteachers of our two schools for their support. I am particularly grateful to Paula Raynham of Falconer's Hill Junior School, with whom this project was planned. I am also grateful to 'Steven', 'David' and 'Claire' for permission to reprint their poems.

    For another account of this project see Tabor, D.C. and Raynham, P. (1989) 'Poetry in the Making', in *Junior Education*, **13**, 3, pp. 36–37.

    A shorter version of this chapter was originally published as 'Poetry Across the Divide' by Tabor, D.C. (1990) in *Education 3–13*, **18**, 1, pp. 33–44.

Chapter 4

'Their Tables and Chairs are Really Small'

Introduction

... The Mock Turtle went on.

'We had the best of educations — in fact, we went to school every day —'

'*I've* been to a day-school, too,' said Alice, 'you needn't be so proud as all that.'

'With extras?' asked the Mock Turtle a little anxiously.

'Yes,' said Alice, 'we learned French and music.'

'And washing?' asked the Mock Turtle.

'Certainly not!' said Alice indignantly.

'Ah! then your wasn't a really good school,' said the Mock Turtle in a tone of great relief. 'Now at *ours* they had at the end of the bill, "French, music *and washing* — extra."'

'You couldn't have wanted it much,' said Alice, 'living at the bottom of the sea.'

'I couldn't afford to learn it,' said the Mock Turtle with a sigh. 'I only took the regular course.'

'What was that?' enquired Alice.

'Reeling and Writhing, of course, to begin with,' the Mock Turtle replied, 'and then the different branches of Arithmetic — Ambition, Distraction, Uglification, and Derision.'

(Lewis Carroll: *Alice in Wonderland*)

Any teacher, trying to grasp the implications of the Education Reform Act, will immediately understand what this conversation is about. The Mock Turtle and Alice are discussing the core curriculum. The names of the subjects enumerated by the Mock Turtle might even describe some of the emotional states which many teachers experience when faced with the National Curriculum. Admittedly, the Mock Turtle does not quantify the relative proportions of subjects in the 'regular course'. However, the

Gryphon's subsequent explanation that lessons are so called because 'they lessen from day to day' hints at fears that most teachers share, namely that the impending deluge of SATs and other administrative work will undermine the ability to teach anything effectively. It is also significant that French, music and washing have to paid for by parents, as extras. Whether the privatization of the water industry will have such far-reaching consequences in today's schools remains to be seen.

Teachers of English are particularly sensitive to the likely effects of Attainment Targets, profiles and testing procedures on classroom practice. In spite of widely held reservations about these proposed changes, several of the recommendations of the Cox Report (1989) are of particular relevance to the curriculum continuity project described in this chapter.

Take for example, the emphasis on oracy, as a means of learning, and of evaluating pupils' progress (para. 8.2). The Cox Report also recommends that for children with learning difficulties 'oral work should be given greater emphasis initially ...' (para. 13.9). This chapter will demonstrate the importance of oral work, not only for primary school pupils, but also for less able pupils at secondary school, in the framework of curriculum continuity project work. It is heartening to note that AT 1: Speaking and Listening, now has equal weighting with Reading and Writing in the National Curriculum up to Level 10 (NCC Consultation Report 1989, p. 23; this recommendation has been accepted by SEAC).

The plight of children with learning difficulties is central to this chapter. I shall argue that the curriculum continuity project described below provided a context within which all the language skills were developed, and that less able children benefited considerably from these activities. By looking at the work of a few children I shall also show how argument and discussion stimulated the development of narrative.

Our pilot project in 1986/87 had shown that cross-phase writing of stories was highly successful, especially when the groups were mature and intelligent. The challenge in 1987/88 was to see whether similar projects could be successful with less able groups. In 1987/88 I taught a bottom set in Year 8, and a fifth set in Year 10 (working for GCSE). I wanted both groups to be involved in curriculum continuity activities with our contributory schools, and with my primary colleagues decided to follow the pattern of our storybook project of the previous year.

This chapter describes the project that involved pupils in my bottom set class in Year 8 (aged 12 to 13), and a class of pupils in Years 4 and 5 (aged 8 to 10 years) at Falconer's Hill Junior School, the adjacent junior school. Both groups of children wrote stories for each other. The junior pupils were not particularly academic and their teacher, Eileen Barbett, felt that we would have difficulties in getting these pupils to produce any sustained work. All the Daventry School pupils worked in special project folders, in which notes and drafts of stories were kept, along with work diaries and self-assessment sheets. The juniors were not able, on the whole, to keep diaries of our joint sessions.[1]

Getting Started

My class was very interested in the project, and excited at the prospect of working with the juniors. Following the pattern of the previous year, the pupils started by analyzing a junior school reader, and devising a worksheet for their junior school partner. I had prepared an analysis sheet on the reader for them, which involved supplying factual information e.g. title, author, number of pages etc. and ticking boxes about the content of the book. Most pupils did not know what the date of publication was, nor where to look for it — they had to be shown. The pupils were able to add their own opinions about the books. For example, Derek (who had come into the class from Educational Support) had to analyze a Wide Range Reader pubished in 1951. His overall comment was, 'Well it is a bit old-fashioned, and the drawings are a bit babyish'. Anita's reader was the story 'Mindar of Brannin' by M.L. Salter, written for 8-year-olds. She felt it was '. . . an old-fashioned book about History, Religion, fiction and about a King'. She commented, 'I think the book is okay for older pupils, but it is a bit far-fetched for an eight year old!' Ralph had a Wide Range Reader about Indians. He thought' that the illustrations were quite good, 'Because the pictures look like the descriptions', and his overall comment about the book was, 'I think it's very good for the Junior School pupils.' This activity would have hit (at least in part) En 2/5a: '. . . demonstrate, in talking and writing about a range of stories and poems which they have read, an ability to explain preferences.'

These examples illustrate (typically) the pupils' willingness to give an opinion, though without much detailed analysis. Most of the pupils worked hard to produce their own worksheets based on a part of the reader, though nearly all of them made wordsearches, often brightly coloured. Some of the other pupils, like Derek, added a series of comprehension questions, or a spelling test.

In mid-November we paid our first visit to Falconer's Hill. The pupils had been paired at random. My pupils had to interview their partners, get them to read a short extract from the reader, and attempt the worksheet.

All the pupils enjoyed the session, and my pupils recorded their observations afterwards. Derek's self-assessment sheet showed that he'd enjoyed the session because, 'I enjoy working with other people.' In answer to the question, 'What have I learnt from this project so far?' he wrote, 'I have learnt so far that their tables and chairs are really small.' He felt he could have improved his work '. . . by making harder questions'. Derek made brief notes on his pupil's progress during the session. He wrote '. . . She reads fast. She is no good at wordsearch and when she reads she gets muddled up with other words.'

Irene, a more able pupil, wrote, 'I enjoyed the lesson very much because I thought I did the worksheet very well . . . so far I have learnt from this project how well I can help somebody to work.' Irene was able to evaluate her performance when she wrote '. . . I could have improved my work by making the "spot the difference" and wordsearch a little easier, because I think she found it a little hard.' It is clear that Irene understood what was required of her, and tried to be self-critical. Work diaries, where the pupils were meant to record their thoughts and feelings about the project, usually contained brief summaries of what the pupils had done, while the self-assessment sheets sometimes elicited a more personal response.

The interviews and discussions would have hit En 1/2a: '... participate as speakers and listeners in a group engaged in a given task'; and En 1/4b: '... ask and respond to questions in a range of situations with increased confidence.'

At our next lesson in the classroom, I organized my class into four groups of four to six pupils, and gave them five questions to discuss about their visit to the junior school. Each group chose a chairperson to run the discussion. The discussions were taped, and extracts played back to the class at the end of the lesson. Three of the groups discussed their visit quite well, though in general pupils found it difficult to move much beyond a question and answer session, and engage in a real discussion. This activity was one way of teaching the children what a discussion was. The liveliest group contained Heather, Mike, Nigel, Laura, and Derek. Heather chaired the discussion in a confident manner, and the pupils responded maturely, even though the vocabulary was fairly simple. This is shown by the following extract:

Heather: Did you enjoy your visit to Falconer's Hill last Friday?

Mike: Yes, it was quite enjoyable, and my partner worked well and was cooperative.

Heather: Nigel, can you tell us what your pupil was like?

Nigel: I enjoyed it because Heather, Francis and Mary and myself all enjoyed it, and we all enjoyed the work and I'm sure our partners did.

Heather: Derek, what can you tell us?

Derek: Well, I enjoyed it and our group all worked together.

Heather: Right Laura, can you tell us what your partner was like?

Laura: It was all right, but he kept talking to Martin.

Heather: On to question 2: 'How did you get on with your partner, and did you have any discipline problems?'

Mike: No, not really, she worked quite well, but she did talk a bit to her friends.

Heather: Derek?

Derek: Not really. She got on with the work quite well, except for some of it, which she couldn't do.

Heather: Did you find it difficult to handle her?

Derek: Mmm ...

Heather: Laura?

Laura: Well, he was alright, he kept talking to his friends, but he kept on with his work, I suppose.

Heather: Mine was alright, she got all the things right, and everythings, so she worked quite well. Question 3: 'What did you learn about his/her problems with reading and writing?' Mike?

Mike:	She was quite slow at writing, the reading was very good and ... she got on with her work very well.
Heather:	Nigel?
Nigel:	She was pretty good writing but had to pay more attention to work a bit.
Derek:	She wasn't very good at reading, but was alright at doing her writing, but it's just that she can't read very well.
Laura:	He was quite good at reading, but needed to pay more attention to it.
Heather:	Well, my pupil ... she was good at writing, a pretty fast reader because I told her to read the whole book. I shouldn't have, but I did and she read it all in about ten minutes ... quite well.

This group discussion would have hit En 1/4b (see above), and En 1/4c: '... take part as a speaker and listener in a group discussion or activity, commenting constructively on what is being discussed or experienced.'

The following week I visited the class of second and third years at Falconer's Hill, and discussed the aims of the project with them. I talked to the class about what made a good story, and we looked at a sheet of five 'beginnings' which I had prepared from their readers. They had to give each 'beginning' a mark out of ten, and give their reasons. The pupils responded well, and there were interesting differences of opinions. Then I gave out a sheet of five 'endings', which the pupils also had to mark. Finally they cut out the 'endings' and paired them with the right 'beginnings'. All the pupils claimed that they got 5/5! The class was attentive and interested, and their teacher, Eileen Barbett, said that I had 'made them think'. Her follow-up lesson was on the 'middles' of stories.

The oral work generated by this lesson would have hit En 1/2d: '... talk with the teacher, listen and ask and answer questions'; part of En 1/2e: '... respond appropriately to range of more complex instructions given by a teacher' (etc.); and En 1/3c: '... listen with an increased span of concentration to other children and adults, asking and responding to questions and commenting on what has been said.'

Since our last visit to Falconer's Hill, my class had been writing the first draft of the stories for their partners. They started by making a spider diagram or flow chart for ideas, and I had suggested that the story should feature their partner as the main character. In our project the previous year, with the top English set in Year 8, the sense of audience was important in motivating both groups of pupils. I wanted to see if the same applied to the low ability classes, particularly where redrafting and improving the quality of writing was concerned. This is not always easy to evaluate, but I shall look at the work of a few pupils in detail.

Derek, for example, wrote a story on the word-processor about robbers, with his partner Isabel as the main character. Gloria, one of the more able pupils in the class, wrote a story for her pupil called 'The Chip Factory', which was mainly dialogue. Nadine wrote a story in which her pupil met

Madonna. The stories were on average 200–400 words long, and some pupils had considerable problems with spelling, punctuation and presentation, which I had expected. However at this stage I was primarily concerned with the development of ideas and vocabulary. I sent photocopies of the first drafts to Falconer's Hill, so that the juniors could read them before our visit. Eileen Barbett had prepared a check list with her class of 'what makes a good story', so that they could tick the relevant sections when reading the drafts.

At our joint session my pupils read out the first drafts of their stories (or got their partners to do so), and then asked for suggestions as to how the story could be improved. The pairs also discussed the sorts of illustrations that could accompany the story. The session was a success in terms of good relationships between pupils, though the task was a difficult one for both groups of children, since they had not previously learned how to be critical of each other's writing. The following extract shows the sort of interaction that took place:

Anita: What suggestions would you give me to make the story a bit more exciting for you?

Linda: Well, you should put some more action in it.

Anita: More action?

Linda: Yeah.

Anita: What else?

Linda: Make it a bit longer as well.

Anita: Yes, you said you didn't like the ending bit. What sort of things would you put for the ending if you were writing the story?

Linda: Make it more interesting.

Anita: More interesting ... do you mean so it was a more exciting ending than just being a dream of something like that?

Linda: Yeah.

Anita: Yeah ... if I was to draw pictures [to illustrate the story] what sort of pictures would you want me to draw for you?

Linda: Space pictures.

Anita: With aliens and things?

Linda: Yes.

Anita: Bogey men?

Linda: Yes.

Anita: Now I've got to find out what ... sort of books do you like to read at school?

Linda: With long words in and and exciting with adventures ... and horror stories.

Anita: Have you read any horror stories?

Linda: No, but I've heard some.

Anita: Going back to the the story ... say some things that you don't like about it, because it says here [reading] 'Ask for suggestions to improve the story.' How do you think I ...

> I've asked you this but but if you were being really critical
> about it how could you ... say which bit you didn't like at
> the beginning or the ending.
>
> Linda: Well, I don't know, because it's good, I don't think you
> should improve it.
>
> Anita: Is it good: Do you like it?
>
> Linda: Yes.
>
> Anita: What bits do you like about it?
>
> Linda: Don't know. [They continued to talk about the previous
> session and the preparation for this one].

It is clear from this extract, and from the rest of the conversation, that both pupils were trying hard, particularly Anita. However neither pupil was sure how to proceed beyond a simple exchange of opinions, and this highlighted the need for such skills need to be taught at both phases. In her project folder Anita wrote:

> ... She said it didn't need to be improved, but the ending was a bit
> boring. She said that it needed more action and longer and more
> exciting ending.

Some of the juniors were able to be more critical of the stories that were read to them. For example, Alan (from Daventry School) read the first draft of his story to Sandra (from Falconer's Hill). It was about how Sandra became a singer, and won a competition and became a pop star.

> Sandra: You've used the main character too much I think, and
> you've put where it takes place, but not *when* it takes place.
> You haven't put [any] other character.
>
> Alan: Mmm.
>
> Sandra: You haven't put too many characters, you should put
> more in, and you haven't put anything about what the
> main character looked like ... It's better if don't put *too*
> many characters in, but you should describe the child's
> appearance and personality ... You haven't put much
> adventure in it, you haven't put much comedy or mystery,
> and I think you should put an adventure element in ...
> You haven't put suspense or a good description.

Alan did not expect such a critical response to his first draft, and this was reflected in his work diary:

> ... Today we had to write a story about what she likes and I think it
> is a bit hard and I think she will not like it when I give it to her.

In these discussions the younger pupils were hitting several levels in AT 1. The Daventry School pupils were hitting En 3/3e and En 3/4e, which describe the revision and redrafting of the work in discussion with the teacher, other pupils, or adults.

At the next lesson, back in the classroom, we had a good discussion about the session. Five pupils reported that their partners had not suggested any improvements. I told them to write a short sequel to their stories, while the rest of the class improved their first drafts.

I had also read through the stories, and added my suggestions as to how the stories might be improved (e.g. where more descriptions or conversations would be appropriate), as well as correcting spelling, punctuation and paragraphing. Several pupils tried to utilize the comments of the juniors, as well as my suggestions, when redrafting their stories. I will look in detail at a couple of examples, which show how the project motivated pupils to improve their writing.

Mandy's Story

Mandy's first version of her story was about Alan (her partner) who had netball practice and a dog training session.

Alan's Surprise

One day I saw Alan in the cafe eating his favourite food Beef Burgers, Chips and Peas. He jumped on his last Burger, he had just remembered he had to go to netball practice.

Then after the training he hurried up to the courts, he was only three minutes late but that did not matter.

Once the netball practice had finished he had to go to the Palladium where the dogs were kept. He had his own dog there, its name was Fonzie. He was like an Alsatian. It was his practice at 3.00 p.m. but he had to set Fonzie up.

Mandy discussed the story with Alan, but unfortunately she did not record his comments in her work diary. However in conversation with me, she agreed that the story needed to be made more exciting, and that it should include some dialogue. The second version was an adventure story about how Alan uses his dog to catch a mugger, and he gets a reward.

The Good-Luck Guide Dog

One day I saw Alan in the cafe eating his favourite food: beef-burgers, chips and peas. He jumped up because he had just remembered he had to go to netball practice. Then after that dog training, he hurried to the courts, he was only three minutes late, but that didn't matter.

Once the netball practice had finished he had to go to the Palladium to see his dogs Benji and Skip. He had to train them, he wanted to be in the Dog Training School in the Army when he grew up.

On the way home he met his best friend Emily. He asked, 'Where are you going?'

She said, 'I am going to netball. Why, where are you going?'

Alan replied, 'If you like, I'll walk you to the netball courts.'

'OK then.'

Emily said to Alan, 'I shall only be a moment.'

On the way Alan's dog spotted two men trying to thieve an old woman's handbag. The dog was tugging the lead to be let loose. The dog was let off and the robbers were still trying to get the handbag off her.

Benji got hold of one of the men's legs and bit it. While Benji was doing this, Alan rang the police. They were there within the minute. They got hold of the robbers and put them into handcuffs. Alan got a reward, but he said, 'Well, Benji deserves it because he caught them.'

Benji agreed, the dog was proud of himself. Later that day Alan got his reward and had his photograph in the paper. He got £300, and he was very proud of himself.

It is clear that the second version represents an improvement, and Mandy had understood the 'why' and 'how' of redrafting a story.

Derek's Story

In contrast to Mandy, Derek was more sensitive to the reactions of his pupil, Isabel. Writing the story on the word processor (which he had learned to do the previous year in Educational Support) made redrafting much easier. I shall look in some detail at the stages through which Derek's work progressed, and reproduce the versions as he wrote them. He started the story with a spider diagram, for the main ideas, and then typed the first draft.

The Robery

One day Isabel was working in her Pet shop. early In the morning when there was a nock at the door. When she open the door she was pushed and she banged her hed on the wall. When she wock-up, the robbers had gone. She took a step forward and she fell down a trap door. She was in a cave and there was and there was four doors and she tride all the doors, and the last one she tride it open. She went through the door and there was a long cave. she started to walk down the cave there was a lond of traps she was nealy stabbed by some spears which come out of the wall. Then she saw sun light she ran towards the sun light when she ricked the end she saw steel bars. She tried to see if she good open them. she tried and she tried and in the end she gave up. Not long after she had gave up the steel bars went up and she ran through them befofe thay closed. Then she found her self in a bullring. At that moment someone though a red sheet at her and at that prosise moment the bull started to ren at her. Then she started ren round the out side of the ring. Then she saw a little thing that look luke a shed and she ran in it for safty. She was in there for about a hour when she herd someone backing on top of the shed. She said who is it and she hard a posh voice say you can come out now the bull and the people have gone. When she got out she found he was telling the trouth and she look at me (the prince) and said who are you. I said 'I am Derek and my father is a king. "I would like to see your father. 'I am afrad you can't see him because he is bisy I am afrad you will have to go home'. Bye". Bye'. Then she started to go home and she keeped turning roud and waving. When she got back to her shop she saw that there was nothing left in her shop so she had to start a gane.

Derek clearly had lots of ideas, though they needed to be more structured. I do not want to consider the obvious mistakes in spelling, punctuation and paragraphing at this stage, though some of the spelling mistakes may have been nothing more than typing errors. I was pleased with the flow of ideas, which could be developed and refined.

After discussing the story with Isabel he agreed with her suggestions that the story should include a description of the heroine, and that there should be more characters. Derek wrote two extra paragraphs and incorporated these in his second draft, which was typed on the word-processor. I discussed the second draft with him, helped him to correct the punctuation and layout of his sotry.

In the third and final version of his story, Derek also rounded off the ending, and by this stage he could see how he had worked through and improved his ideas.

The Robber

Isabel is fearly tall and she had blond hair. She likes rich people and her parents are dead. She lives in a flat. Isabel had a compan in the flat with her which is a goldy coloured cat. She also owns her own pet shop.

One day Isabel was working in her Pet shop. early In the morning when there was a knock at the door. When she open the door she was pushed and she banged her head on the wall. When she wock-up, the robbers had gone. She took a step forward and she fell down a trap door.

She was in a cave and there was and there was four doors and she tried all the doors, and the last one she tried, it opened. She went through the door and there was a long cave.

She started to walk down the cave there was a load of traps, she was nearly stabbed by some spears which come out of the wall. Then she saw steel bars. She tried to see if she good open them. she tried and she tried and in the end she gave up.

Not long after she had gave up the steel bars went up and she ran through them before thay closed. Then she found her self in a bull ring.

At that moment someone threw a red sheet at her and at that precise moment the bull started to run at her. Then she started to run around the out side of the ring. Then she saw a little thing that looked like a shed and she ran in it for safty.

She was in there for about a hour when she heard someone backing on top of the shed. She said, 'who is it?' and she heard a posh voice say, 'You can come out now the bull and people have gone.' When she got out she found that he was telling the trouth and she looked at me (the prince) and said 'who are you.' I said 'I am Derek and my father is a king.' I would like to se your father. 'I am afraid you can't see him because he is busy I am afraid you will have to go home.'

'Bye'.

'Bye'.

Then she started to go home and she kept turning round and waving. Shen she got back to her shop she saw that there was nothing left in her shop so she had to start again.

When she had got all the things back in the shop. The robber had come back, but this time the police were in the shop waiting for him. When the robber came in the police tried to catch him but they missed and they banged heads. The robber nicked an alsatoin and he tried to step over the policemen, but the policemen got up and tripped the robber over then the policemen arrested him.

These versions of the story are exactly as Derek typed them. There are still many errors in spelling, use of tenses and punctuation. It could also be argued the improvements are modest; that the story is limited and raises questions about the characters and story-line. However it is clear that Derek was motivated by the project, and made considerable efforts to improve his story. Discussion and argument, and the sense of a specific audience, helped him to develop his narrative.

The editing and redrafting on a word-processor would have hit En 3/5d: '. . . assemble ideas on paper, or on a VDU, individually or in discussion with others, and show evidence of ability to produce a draft from them and then to revise and redraft as necessary.'

The final drafts of the other stories were typed up by pupils on the 14–16 Project, and photocopied. The class planned their booklets, with illustrations and worksheets, using coloured paper and art materials. They greatly enjoyed making these books, and most of them took great care with the layout and illustrations. This would have fulfilled AT 4/5: Presentation, strand 6d: '... show some ability to use any available presentational devices that are appropriate to the task, so that finished work is presented clearly and attractively.'

In mid-February we paid a return visit to Falconer's Hill, and my class presented the booklets to their partners. My pupils were very excited, and most of the juniors were appreciative. After the juniors had done the work-sheets, my pupils helped them start writing their stories, using spider diagrams and flow charts as ways of sorting out their ideas. In terms of relationships and liaison it was a successful session. Afterwards Anita wrote:

> I gave Linda my booklet, she liked it ... but we didn't get all the tasks finished ... I've learned that unless you're confident and mature you won't get very far with your pupil and you must be very kind to them.

Derek wrote:

> She read my story very quick, she enjoyed it. She started her story. I thought that she was very good and I liked the lesson.

Role Reversal

In May we revisited Falconer's Hill and my class read the first drafts of their pupils' stories. I had prepared a check list to help them evaluate the stories, and we discussed how the intention was to find ways of improving the quality of the story, and not simply correcting obvious spelling mistakes. The sheet asked questions about the beginning and ending of the story, the characters, conversations and descriptions etc. By this stage very good work-ing relationships existed between the pupils, and we were pleased by the busy working atmosphere. The following extracts illustrate the sorts of discussions that took place. Derek, from Daventry School, had talked to Isabel, from Falconer's Hill, about her story:

Teacher: Derek, what have you told Isabel to do?
Derek: She needs to describe the characters at the beginning of the story. Then at the end it gets a bit boring, and she needs to make it more interesting.
Teacher: In what way?
Derek: Well at the end they just kill the dragon by tracking the dragon and it dies of starvation. We want to change that a bit more.
Teacher: Do you agree with that?
Isabel: Yes.
Teacher: How are you going to change the story?
Isabel: I'm not sure.

Afterwards Derek wrote:

I thought the lesson was great and I worked well. It was fairly hard but I coped with it. I enjoyed the lesson a lot and it was fun.

Though the discussions were at a simple level, some of the juniors were able to assert themselves, even if they were unable to justify or explain their choices. This is shown in the conversation between Gloria, from Daventry School, and Leroy, from Falconer's Hill:

Gloria: It was 'I saw a ghost, and two Chinese men tried to kill the ghost and it killed them.' It should have had more ghosts.
Teacher: Do you agree?
Leroy: No, one ghost is enough.
Teacher: Where could your pupil put more descriptions?
Gloria: Where the two Chinese men tried to kill the ghost.
Teacher: How could you help him do that? [Pause]. You could give him more describing words — in his folder. [To Leroy]. Would you find that helpful?
Leroy: Yes.

The teacher's guidance was necessary here, it was doubtful whether Gloria could have thought of ways of helping Leroy, beyond stating her opinion of the story. This simple level of response was reflected in the comments the Daventry School pupils wrote about their partners' stories. For example, Irene's comment on Beverley's story:

It was a little short and it also did not have no conversation or description, but apart from that it was OK.

In her work diary Irene was a little less cryptic:

Today I am quite pleased with my work. I read the story, it was very short but good and then I helped her to make her story longer and improve it. We started to write the improved story out and we got some ideas, but then we was told to pack away but that was the best lesson I have ever had with Falconer's Hill.

Quite apart from the oral work that resulted from the session, the junior pupils were helped to improve their stories, and this would have hit En 3/3e: '... begin to revise and redraft in discussion with the teacher, other adults, or other children in the class ...' (etc.).

The juniors eventually completed their stories, and Eileen Barbett typed all of their stories. Her pupils enjoyed producing the booklets, but they needed a great deal of help and supervision. Our final session was held in mid-July, just before the end of term, when the juniors presented the booklets to my pupils, who were very appreciative. The completion of the project was a great achievement.

In evaluating the project we both felt that it had been too teacher-intensive, particularly for Eileen. If we had repeated the project with the same groups, we would have devised activities which were less teacher-intensive, and which provided more structured language skills work. None the less, the benefits in terms of the development of oral skills and increasing pupils' motivation for writing were considerable. Of relevance here is an observation by Gardiner (1988), in the context of the Kingman Report, about the need to give pupils learning experiences which are meaningful, and enable them to enjoy using language:

> Many people dodge or opt out of using language in unfamiliar and, to them, threatening contexts. It is more often the sound rule-systems that they do not properly understand, and so find alien. They opt out so often that they find it increasingly difficult to opt in. And they find that, in their secondary school years, they can opt out of language in lesson after lesson in many subjects, if they keep quiet about it. If language ceases to delight them, it becomes increasingly difficult for them to discern, linguistically speaking, what is going on, and if their attempts to join in are judged according to criteria they do not understand, then the very purposes which they attribute to being in school may be much changed (p. 18).

This project clearly gave the majority of children involved, who were not usually successful at school in academic terms, opportunities for 'opting-in' for a range of language activities.

The elements in the Programmes of Study covered by this project were very similar to those described in Chapter 2, though without the drama/presentation element in AT 1; and not at such a sophisticated level throughout in either KS 2 or KS 3.

This chapter started with Alice, the Mock Turtle and the Gryphon, and our shared concerns about the National Curriculum. At times we may all feel like 'fainting in coils' when contemplating the task ahead. Those who leave the profession in despair might, like the Mock Turtle, admit with a feeling of sorrow, 'Once I was a real Turtle.' On the other hand, the importance attached by Kingman and Cox to the development of language skills, and the need to develop cross-curricular links (e.g. Cox Report, Chapter 14) may present new possibilities. This chapter has described one approach to motivating less able pupils, and to developing their language skills in the three main profile components, while also improving continuity and liaison with a contributory school.

Note

1 I am grateful to Eileen Barbett for her help and collaboration in planning this project, and for commenting on an earlier draft on this chapter.

Chapter 5

The Storybook Project

Introduction

This project involved my fifth set in Year 10 (aged 14–15) and the top class of juniors in Years 5 and 6 (aged 9–10) from Kilsby Primary School, one of our country contributory schools. Though the project was similar in scope to the one described in the previous chapter, there were also certain significant differences. The Daventry School pupils were four or five years older than the juniors, and there was a considerable range of abilities within the class. Their project work was going to be submitted as a unit in their GCSE English folders. Some of the juniors were very bright — several of my pupils felt the juniors were more intelligent than them. I was particularly pleased by the quality of interaction that took place between the two age groups, and the oral work that was generated. It is these aspects of the project that I shall focus on here.[1]

The juniors had written short stories, in leaflet form, and they had been videoed reading them. I was able to use this to introduce the idea of the project to my class. Most of them were interested in the idea of going to Kilsby. They analyzed a reader and prepared a worksheet based on it. Our first session at the primary school, in the autumn term, went well. For example, Peter wrote:

> I enjoyed the lesson because it was good to get out of school and it was good to work with another pupil. The visit was worthwhile ... so far in this project I have learnt at what standard the fourth year [junior] pupils are and that they are more intelligent than I had expected them to be. I also learnt that next time we meet I will set them harder work.

Brenda wrote:

> I knew exactly what I had to do ... I thought it was very interesting and a lot of fun.

We discussed the session in the next English lesson and my class started work on the first draft of their stories for the juniors. A number of pupils made them rather gruesome, but all included their partner in the story, often as the main character. The involvement of the pupils is shown by these extracts from our discussion in class.

Gerald: I worked with a boy called Simon Purcell. Judging from the way he writes he's very good ... he did the work quite quickly ... I didn't set him enough, but the word-search caused him a lot of trouble, mainly because of my handwriting.

        The story I'm writing him ... it struck me he was very interested in football ... he crawls out of bed one morning and answers the phone ... There's a bloke says he's Brian Clough ... says Simon's just become Foot-baller of the Year ... but the story *he* wrote was about a bank robbery. What it turns out is that he goes off in the car with Bryan, who turns out to be one of the bank robbers in disguise, who's kidnapped him to get revenge ... and it carries on from there.

Teacher: What about you, David?

David: I worked with Michelle. She went through the questions so fast I had to add extra questions at the end ... she's brighter than me.

A week later the juniors came to Daventry School, and listened to or read the first drafts of the stories that had been written for them. They made suggestions for improvements; in pairs the pupils discussed possible illustrations for the story and the layout of the final version. Some of the juniors were very critical in their reponses to the first drafts, as this discussion between Michelle (Kilsby Primary School) and David (Daventry School) demonstrates:

Michelle: I think it was too complicated. You need to explain things more simply. There needs to be more speaking; it was just about what he was doing, and no speaking.

Teacher: What do you think about that, David?

David: Well I agree, because I did make it too complicated. I sort of did it too long ...

Teacher: Michelle, how do you think it could be improved?

Michelle: Well, he needs to write more in my words and style. He uses very grown up words which I don't understand, and he's not explained things enough about computers, and I don't know much about computers.

Teacher: Doesn't that make the the story interesting?

Michelle: Well no, because I don't understand it. What he's writing, it makes the story boring.

Teacher:	What do you think about that, David?
David:	Yes.
Teacher:	What are you going to do about it, then?
David:	I'm going to do another draft, and then type it up.
Teacher:	How are you going to change the content?
David:	I'm going to describe the ... I'm going to change the difficult words and make them easier to understand and put more dialogue in it.
Teacher:	Michelle, what about illustrations? Could you make any suggestions?
Michelle:	He ought to put an explosion, so that it all goes over the story, as he's written about the explosion.

I admired Michelle's articulate response, while at the same time sympathizing with David's position in the hot seat. Michelle's ability to argue her point of view would have hit En 1/5b: '... contribute to and respond constructively in discussion, including the development of ideas; advocate and justify a point of view.' Kevin (Daventry School) was more responsive, and perhaps less threatened by the opinions of his junior school partner, Sandra, about his story.

Sandra:	At times it's hard to follow who's speaking.
Kevin:	Is it? How do you think I could get over that? Do you think it would be better if I had the names of the people before the speaking bit?
Sandra:	Yes.
Kevin:	Where do you think I should use the pictures? I don't know where to use them ... I know you should have illustrations. Do you think I should put them after that monster bit?
Sandra:	Yes.
Kevin:	It would be good, because then you could get a picture of what he looks like.

Kevin summarized his partner's comments afterwards:

The presentation was untidy, needed illustrations. At times it's hard to follow who's speaking. My pupil's comments are of a good quality.

Kevin incorporated these suggestions in his final version, though the overall structure of the story remained unchanged. On the other hand, Peter rewrote his first draft after discussing it with Pauline. His story started as a tale of nightmarish horror, in which Pauline ended up by shooting her best friend. His final version was a more conventional adventure story, where the two girls were kidnapped by a gang of jewel thieves. They escaped, and reported the thieves to the police, who captured them. He felt this version was more suitable for a young girl. However the rewriting was mainly a result of his own second thoughts, rather than due to specific criticisms from his partner. He wrote:

> From this project so far, I have learnt that fourth year [junior] pupils are more intelligent than I thought. If there was another project, I would set harder work for my pupil . . . My pupils did not comment much on my second draft except to make it neater.

Brenda's pupil, Alex, liked her story. She wrote:

> I read the story to him, he said it was good and needed no improvements. He said I should illustrate it but didn't give me any ideas how to.

Most of the juniors had commented on the presentation or spelling of the first drafts; many had found it difficult to suggest improvements in the content. I also discussed the first drafts with my pupils on an individual basis. However some of them did not redraft their stories at all, but merely made a neat copy, correcting spelling, punctuation etc. They had not done much reviewing and editing of work in their first three years at Daventry School, though most of their GCSE assignments went through two stages. However, a lot of oral work had been generated by the cross-phase discussions of the older pupils' stories. Those Daventry School pupils who were able to incorporate their partner's criticisms, and improve their stories as a result, would have hit En 3/6d, which describes editing and redrafting.

Reviewing Progress

After the first visit of the Kilsby pupils, I organized the class into discussion groups, as I had done with my Year 8 bottom set, so that they could talk about the project. I was thus able to monitor their feelings about the project, as well as assessing their oral skills. Mature and thoughtful discussions took place, as the following extract shows:

Gerald: Chris, how did you get on with your pupil?
Chris: Fine, he's alright, a bit shy at first, apart from that, fine.
Gerald: Any real problems?
Chris: No.
Gerald: What about you, Henry?
Henry: I go on quite well. She was a bit shy at first, getting used to knowing me, we didn't have any problems with the work. We sailed through most of it and we didn't disagree

on anything. She helped me with some of my work, and I helped her with some of hers.

Gerald: I got on quite well with Simon, in spite of the fact that we didn't agree on many things. If you look at the form I filled in about him, he was nuts about football, you see, but when you got to this last lesson we got on OK. He liked the story and got on with the library work and so on. What about you, Oscar?

Oscar: I had Michael, and he was very mature and he knew a lot about the work and had no trouble with any of it. He liked the story ... though he didn't like the blood ... it was too gory.

Chris: What did your pupils say about the story — the presentation and the illustrations?

Oscar: He thought the story was good, but he thought it could have been a bit better towards the end ... it got boring.

Gerald: Yes, mine finished in the last paragraph. I summed it all up a bit too quickly. What about you, Henry?

Henry: She enjoyed the story, and had some ideas about the story ... she thought I ended it just right ... she enjoyed it.

Gerald: So your second draft isn't going to be much different?

Henry: No, I'll put some illustrations round the outside, and that's about it.

Gerald: What about you, Oscar? What did your pupil think about your story?

Oscar: Well, I think he did like it, but he thought it was a bit too far-fetched, about being an assassin at his age and killing someone.

Gerald: Yes, yes. Not having read it myself, but from what you've told me, it is a bit too far-fetched. What improvements did your pupil suggest?

Chris: He didn't really suggest any improvements.

Gerald: Any alterations?

Chris: Make it better at the end.

Gerald: Simon looked at the story ... the final paragraph which started with the car pulling away, and then ended with them living happily ever after, that was a bit rapid. He said spread it out, basically ... Overall comments about the project so far, Henry?

Henry: Well, I enjoyed the project and meeting Diane, it's enjoyable meeting other people and setting them work. I enjoyed that. It made a change from us getting set work.

Gerald: What about you, Chris?

Chris: It was good, meeting other people ... seeing how they worked at junior school. You could set them work ...

Oscar: I didn't think we had enough time to finish the work ... apart from that I thought it was great.

This extract, which is typical of the discussions which took place, shows how the pupils were able to reflect on their experiences, and to talk about the primary school pupils. I was pleased with the oral work that the project had generated, and I was able to mark it as part of the pupils' GCSE oral assessment.

This discussion would have hit En 1/6b: '... contribute considered opinions or clear statements of personal feeling to group discussions and show an understanding of the contribution of others'; and En 1/7c: '... take an active part in group discussion, contributing constructively to the development of the argument.'

Gerald also demonstrated that he had learned to chair a discussion. This is something which the majority of 15-year-olds are unable to do satisfactorily, according to surveys carried out by the Assessment of Performance Unit (APU) (Tarleton, 1988, p. 54).

These pupils had more understanding of the problems of the primary school children than my group in Year 8, perhaps because they were two years older. Of the seventeeen pupils in my class who produced booklets, six made some attempt to alter and improve their stories. For example, Luke expanded his story about Sherlock Holmes, providing more details so that it would be more exciting. Gerald rewrote his final paragraph, making it slightly longer. Matt altered his sci-fi story, so that the conflict between the synthetic robotized androids and the spaceship's crew was more dramatic. However he did not include any dialogue in the final version, in spite of my suggestions. John, who had missed the previous joint session, accepted my suggestion that his story 'The Football Riots' would be improved with additional dialogue, which he included in the final version. What impressed me was that most of my pupils typed up the stories in their own time, and took a lot of trouble with illustrations, and the production of the finished booklets.

They would have hit (in part) En 3/6a: '... write in a variety of forms for a range of purposes, presenting subject matter differently to suit the needs of specified known audiences and demonstrating the ability to sustain the interest of the reader', and AT 4/5: Presentation, strand 6d: '... show some ability to use any available presentational devices that are appropriate to the task, so that finished work is presented clearly and attractively.'

We paid our final visit to Kilsby just before the end of the autumn term, when my pupils presented the booklets to their partners. We also had a Christmas quiz, between two teams of four pupils from each class. It was very enjoyable, even though the juniors won! Brenda wrote:

I thought it was great, the quiz was good fun even though we lost ... I have learnt a lot about Alex, his ability, his dislikes and likes. I have now realized how juniors work.

Peter wrote:

I found the quiz very enjoyable and I wish I was in our team, as I could have answered most of the questions.

Concluding the Project

The Kilsby pupils wrote sequels to the stories which they'd been given, or developed the ideas in them, or wrote different stories altogether. The booklets were imaginative, varied and attractively produced, and each of my pupils wrote a brief analysis of his/her booklet. The whole project was entered as a unit of work in their GCSE English folders.

In the summer term, a small group of pupils from Kilsby worked with a small group from my class in the computer room, producing a joint newspapers, using the Newspa computer program. They worked in junior-senior pairs; the juniors were familiar with the program, and explained how it worked to the older pupils. Very good oral work resulted from the session. Several pages of a joint newspaper about Kilsby Primary School and Daventry School were produced.

Several levels in AT 3 would have been hit, such as strand 7a: '... write in a wider variety of forms, with commitment and a clear sense of purpose and awareness of audience' (etc.), and 7d: '... demonstrate an increased awareness that a first draft may be changed, amended and reordered in a variety of ways.'

The Programmes of Study covered by this project were similar to those described in Chapter 2, though some of the activities would have included elements in KS 4. For example, the group work on a joint newspaper, using the Newspa programme, would have furnished (in part) 'many of the materials and topics for discussion for which planned outcomes, e.g. *in written work or presentations*, might emerge' (section 18; DES 1990a, p. 26). For the older pupils, writing for the juniors gave them opportunities to 'write in aesthetic and imaginative ways'; 'extend and refine their competence in drafting, redrafting, rereading and revising' (etc.); and 'craft their writing so that they achieve a readable, pleasing style' (section 31; DES 1990a, p. 41).

Benefits at Transition

At the beginning of the next academic year (autumn term, 1988) a survey was conducted among those ex-juniors who had been involved in the project, and had come to Daventry School. The survey revealed that the majority of pupils had enjoyed writing stories for their older partners, as well as the quiz at the end of the project. A number of pupils felt that their English work had also improved as a result, e.g. '... It helped because my partner was critical and corrected my work. '... I think it helped me with story writing' ... 'the project helped with the use of words in stories.' The project had clearly given some of the children greater confidence about doing English at Daventry School, as a number of responses show: 'It helped because I knew what standard is expected of you at Daventry School' ... 'Pleased to know that English would not be as hard as I thought' ... 'My partner told me what English was like' ... 'I knew more about the sort of thing expected of me.'

All the pupils felt that the project had helped them with the process of transition and settling in at the new school. For example '... it helped me settle in easier, because I got to know a bit about the system' ... 'The project helped me to get ready for the [secondary] school' ... 'I'd learnt quite a bit about it from my partner, and I was more confident about it' ... 'I'd already met some teachers and children and knew my way round the school quite well' ... 'It made me excited about all the lessons at Daventry School.' Overall, both groups of pupils had benefited considerably from the project.

Colin Padgett has described a project which took place in 1986, when his CSE group in Year 10 (similar to my GCSE group) wrote and presented a set of stories for infants, aged 5 years old, at a contributory primary school in Halstead. The older pupils showed the infants the stories as they were being written, and the infants painted illustrations for the completed stories. At the final presentation session, the stories were read out loud to the infants. The infants had 'written' a story as a class, with a text copied out by the teacher, and illustrations by themselves, which they presented to the secondary school pupils.

The older pupils gained the experience of writing for a 'real' audience. Pupils of all abilities and widely differing ages were able to make useful contributions at all stages of the activity. Padgett's pupils learned something about negotiation and control, and the infants gained new stories to complement those they already knew and loved. Various benefits of liaison accrued, such as familiarity with the 'big school', and awareness of its activities (Padgett 1987).

The age-gap between secondary and primary pupils was much narrower in the project described in this chapter. Given the relative sophistication of the Kilsby pupils, a different type of relationship developed between secondary and primary pupils during the course of the project, from that possible with infants. The transcripts of the discussions that took place, and the work diary entries, show how language work was stimulated by the interactions across the primary-secondary divide.

Further Developments

Towards the end of academic year 1987–88 I was awarded a month's flexi-secondment to study language work in all of our contributory schools, concentrating particularly on Years 5 and 6. In December 1987, the Secretary of State for Education, Mr. Baker, had given Northampton County Council permission to go ahead with the reorganization of the secondary schools in Daventry, to take effect from September 1989. As a result, Daventry School and Southbrook School would be changed into enlarged 11–16 schools, and the third comprehensive, the Grange, would be transformed into a Tertiary College. The majority of the intake for the Grange School had come from the Grange Junior School, and most of this intake would be transferred to the reorganized Daventry School.

It made sense to spend a week of the flexi-secondment at the Grange Junior School, and to divide the remaining three weeks between the rest of our contributory schools. The draft of my report was circulated to colleagues at our contributory schools for comments, and they received copies of the final version, as did colleagues in the English Department at Daventry School. The report has been partly superseded by the dictates of the National Curriculum. However, it provides a personal picture of our contributory schools, and the range of English and other language activities which I observed.[2]

Within the English Department it was decided that curriculum continuity would be adopted as departmental policy, and the majority of English teachers chose a contributory school to be linked with in 1988/89. The Deputy Head of one of our contributory schools acted as coordinator for an INSET programme for cross-phase visits, which was funded through our Teachers' Centre. I provided in-service training for my colleagues about the planning of joint projects. Thus by September 1988 we could look forward to a range of such projects with the majority of our contributory schools.

Seven teachers in the English Department paid one of more visits to 'their' contributory school in the autumn term 1988, when most of the planning took place. Seven joint projects were organized, running over one to three terms, though two were not completed due to lack of time. Five of these projects are described in detail in Chapters 6 through 10. In total, over 420 children were involved, of whom over 200 constituted the majority of our new intake in September 1989.

Notes

1 I am grateful to Tim Rose, the Headteacher of Kilsby Primary School, with whom this project was planned.
2 The report of my flexi-secondment is reproduced in Appendix 1.

Chapter 6

The Survival Project

'No man is an Island entire of itself.' (John Donne)

Introduction

This project involved my second set in Year 9 at Daventry School, and the top class of juniors in Years 5 and 6 at Braunston Primary School, one of our country contributory schools. The juniors were taught by Anne Cottingham, the Deputy Head at Braunston. In choosing the theme of 'survival', we wanted to provide a range of activities, suitable for both groups of children, which would develop their language skills, and provide opportunities for cross-curricular tasks.[1]

I paid a half-day liaison visit to the primary school in the autumn term 1988, and we had several meetings after school, to plan the activities together, and to put pupils into suitable pairs and groups. We were also able to involve three pupils from Staverton Primary School, the smallest of our contributory schools.

First Meeting

The first session was held at the end of January 1989, in the library of Daventry School. Several 'ice-breaker' activities were used for this first meeting. For example, each of the Daventry School pupils had analyzed a reader from Braunston Primary School, and prepared a worksheet on an extract from it. During the first half of the hour-long session, the pupils from the three schools interviewed their partners about their families, interests, etc. and the juniors completed the worksheets that had been prepared for them. In the second half of the session the pupils were put into groups of four, and told that they were going on holiday together. They had to decide where they were going, and what they were going to take. The pupils worked well in their pairs and foursomes, and some good oral work resulted

73

from the session. A couple of diary entries will illustrate how the pupils responded. Mary (from Daventry School) wrote:

> Today's lesson was very good. It was fun working with the Braunston Juniors. I though that they were very well behaved and polite. At first Veronica [from Braunston] was very shy, but once we started working she wasn't so shy. I think that it was good working in groups because Veronica got on quite well with Diana's partner, and she felt more relaxed.
>
> Veronica is a very good reader and she reads at a steady pace and pronounced every word very well with no hesitation ... Veronica seems to be a very bright girl ... When I gave her the worksheet to do I didn't even have to explain it to her, she just took it and started it ... she completed the worksheet well and got everything right.

In her work diary, Rebecca (Daventry School) explained that her foursome had considered five different places, before choosing Florida for their holiday. She described the decision-making process as follows:

> ... We came to this decision because we could stay in a hotel near to Disneyland. We could hire a car to go to Disneyland, and to other nearby places ... We could go to the beaches sometimes. We thought if we went in late June–early July, it would be best, because the peak season is in August. It wouldn't be over-busy then, but it would be hot. We could go for lots of fun. Robert and Eleanor [from Braunston] both made interesting contributions to the discussion. Robert is going there this year with his family. I enjoyed working with him, and I found his opinion intriguing. The session was very interesting and enjoyable. I hope the next time we meet will be very soon.

The primary school pupils did not keep work diaries, though each of them wrote a profile or fact-file about his/her partner at Daventry School.

For the younger pupils, the activities of the first session hit several levels in Attainment Targets 1–3. For example, conducting the interviews would have hit En 1/4b: '... ask and respond to questions in a range of situations with increased confidence.' The group planning of the holiday would have hit En 1/3d: '... give, and receive and follow accurately, precise instructions when pursuing task individually or as a member of a group';[2] and En 1/4c: '... take part as speakers and listeners in a group discussion or activity, expressing a personal view and commenting constructively on what is being discussed or experienced.' The Daventry School pupils would have fulfilled these strands as well, and possibly part of En 1/5b: '... contribute to and respond constructively in discussion, including the development of ideas' ... (etc.). The juniors read extracts from readers, either aloud or silently, thereby hitting En 2/3a or 3b. Writing a profile or fact-file of their Daventry School partners would have hit En 3/3d: '... produce a range of types of non-chronological writing'. The Daventry School pupils' work diaries would have fulfilled (in part) En 3/4b: '... produce other kinds of chronologically organised writing' (i.e. apart from stories).

Planning the Holiday

After the joint-session, each pupil had to complete a list of possessions he/she was going to take, as well as working out the cost of the holiday. This involved studying holiday brochures to find the appropriate factual information, such as dates of flights, type of accommodation, special offers, and overall cost. Most pupils in each class needed help in learning to consult a brochure. This was a cross-curricular task, involving media studies, arithmetic, and a degree of economic awareness. The Daventry School pupils also cut out and pasted up their holiday choices, and provided a written commentary on the resort they had chosen. Providing a list of possessions to be taken, and a commentary on the choice of holiday, with a break-down of the cost, would have hit En 3/3d and 4c, which require the organization of non-chronological writing for different purposes.

All the children started fictional 'Holiday Diaries', describing their preparations for the holiday. For example, Susan (Daventry School) wrote in her diary:

> I am looking forward to going on holiday to Disneyland, and getting a good tan. But I am also looking forward to going because I am going with Sandra [from Daventry School] and Robert and Kate [from Braunston]. I think we will all have a great time together. I am sure I will enjoy their company, and I hope they will enjoy mine. I can't wait to see all the fun rides and Disney characters. I know we are going to have a great time. I can't wait.

Rebecca (Daventry School) and her group also decided to go to Florida. In her 'Holiday Diary' she wrote:

> ... Although we aren't going to Florida until 1st September, I am extremely excited. We have looked through hundreds of brochures and the pictures of Disney World and the other places look really brilliant.
> ... The holiday costs a fortune, but I think it's well worth the money, because it's going to be the best holiday I've ever been on. The company of Helen [Daventry School], Eleanor and Alice [Braunston] will help to make it the best.

The work diaries and holiday diaries showed that good relationships had been established between the pupils, that they had enjoyed the first session, and were looking forward to continuing the project.

We're Going on our Summer Holidays!

A week later the Braunston pupils returned to Daventry School and the pupils met up again in the Library. At the beginning of the session they were

Our holiday in the Barrier Reef

My group and I all decided that we would go to Australia

I particularly wanted to go, I have dreamed of going for quite a few years, One reason is that 'The neighbours' come from down under and i would like to think i was in Jason Donovans' home country!

Also there is a lot of touring and sight-seeing to do, all over Australia I really like animals and wildlife and so would enjoy seeing the familiar ozzie kangeroo and the koala bear! Australia is ~~a ~~ good standard of living. My group and ~~are hoping to go to the~~ Barrier Reef, that means staying in different hotels along the way.

The Barrier Reef is 1250 miles long, from sydney to Cairns along the coast. 600 islands (tropical) are along the stretch in the sea. We would stay for 14 days and 13 nights, the prices include :-

Accomodation with private facilities → Air conditioned motor-coach transportation → sight-seeing → Hostess exorted → cruising whitsunday passage → lake Barrine → outer Barrier Reef and Daintree wilderness - most meals.

Highlights - A visit to 6 of the the islands, a glass bottomed boat ride, trainride through a pineapple plantation, unique underwater journey in sub sea coral viewer and a sea-food feast.

We are flying by Quantas and a choice of stopping at in singapore or Bangkok (break the journey). We thought we

Figure 6.1 'Our holiday in the Barrier Reef', by a pupil at Daventry School

told that they had set off (by air) for their holiday, but that the plane had been caught in an electric storm, and had crashed. They were the only survivors. In their groups of four, the pupils had to decide where they had crashed, and to draw a map of the area, as well as designing a shelter. The idea (derived from *The Island* booklet, published by The English Centre, ILEA 1985) was unfortunately already present in everyone's mind, as the Lockerbie air disaster had occurred quite recently. However, all the pupils responded well to the task and animated discussions took place about the crash. All the groups, quite independently, decided that they had crashed on an island. The pupils discussed the geography of the island, the type of shelter that would be built, and the possessions the survivors would be able to salvage from the plane. The following extract was typical; Susan and Sandra were from Daventry School; their junior school partners were Robert and Kate. The extract starts with the pupils discussing how they would build a shelter:

Susan:	Branches which we can use ...
Sandra:	Yes, we can use them to go over the top of the blankets, and to ... well ... reinforce it [the shelter].
Susan:	So the first night's camp we'll stay there [pointing to map] and there should be some food or something lying about.
Sandra:	So we can get that.
Kate:	And there's shelter on the other side of the island so we can carry on and make another shelter, like, in the forest.
Susan:	Yes.
Sandra:	We're going to go through the forest, and then go down over the mountains there [pointing to map].
Robert:	Yes, but you could avoid ...
Kate:	It'll be quite dark, though ... It'll be crowded in the trees, we'll have to find a torch.
Robert:	The trees will block out the sunlight.
Susan:	We'll have to take some stuff with us on the journey.
Sandra:	There might be some back packs or something ... in the passenger ... the stuff where the suitcases are ...
Susan:	Probably, Sandra.
Sandra:	... We could empty it out of their possessions. That's nice, isn't it?
Kate:	Is that where all the people are? [pointing to their map].
Susan:	Civilization ... could be near to a port.
Robert:	Could be an airport.
Susan:	It's only a tiny little area.
Sandra:	Could be a tiny airplane round here.
Kate:	So we could take a plane from there back to our country.
Susan:	It could be near Spain, or something like that.

It is clear from this extract that all four pupils were involved in the task, and ideas about the island were being generated in the course of discussion, without the older pupils dominating the younger ones. The activity would have hit several levels and strands in AT 1, for example En 1/3a: '... relate real or imaginary events in a connected narrative which conveys meaning to a group of pupils, the teacher or another known adult'; En 1/4c: '... take part as a speaker and listener in a group discussion or activity ...' etc. Planning the map, designing the shelter, and discussing what action the group would take on the island, would also have met (at least in part) En 1/5b: '... contribute to and respond constructively in discussion, including the development of ideas ...' (etc.), possibly En 1/6a (which covers group discussion); and En 3/3d (see above).[3]

Afterwards Sandra (from Daventry School) wrote:

> ... I think the group works really well together, everyone joins in well with the discussions. When making the map, everyone drew different parts, so it was everyone's work, not just one person's. I'm looking forward to our next session, because I'm really enjoying it. The project is different from any other that I have done, and it's good fun to do.

Susan (from Daventry School) observed:

> ... Robert and Kate were a little hesitant at first, so I had to draw the outline, but it worked fine. They both made interesting contributions. They were filled with ideas about where we should crash, and why ... We all worked hard on the map and nearly finished [it]. Altogether I think the session went very well, and we are able to work very well with each other.

Clare (from Daventry School) worked with Ruth (from Braunston Primary School) and they teamed up with Laura (from Daventry School) and Bernadette (from Braunston Primary School). After the session Clare wrote:

> ... We all drew our own maps of the areas in which the plane crash landed. We decided it would be an island with a tropical climate. Originally Ruth had wanted it to be an island and Bernadette wanted a forest, so we had an island with a forest on it. We chose Ruth's map — it was the most interesting shape, then we added our own things to it. Because our own map wasn't ready by the end of the lesson, Bernadette and Ruth took it home to finish. Then they would get it photocopied and sent to us.

Ruth had severe hearing difficulties and it was a credit to both her and Clare that they worked well together throughout the project. This showed that a child with special needs could participate successfully in a cross-phase project of this sort, given a sympathetic partner.

The Crash

The Braunston pupils took the A3 size group maps with them, back to their school, where they were reduced to A4 size. These copies were forwarded to the Daventry School pupils, so they could complete the maps for their folders. The follow-up work included finishing the design of the shelter, and writing the holiday diary for the first day after the crash. Most pupils responded imaginatively to the idea, as a few examples will show. The first three extracts are by pupils at Braunston Primary School.

Bernadette started her account of the crash thus:

'This is your Captain speaking. Fasten your seat belt immediately and prepare for emergency landing.'

After he said that, I put my seat belt on quickly, and I could see people panicking, and fastening their seat belts. I quickly put my head between both of my knees. I felt frightened and wanted to know what would happen to me while the plane was falling. When we came nearer the ground I looked out of the window and I could see the trees, mountains, and a river flowing. Then I wondered if the plane would crash into the mountains or if we would land in the river ...

Felicity described the moments before impact:

... Now the roar of the engine was louder, it was making a clattering buzzing sound. I did what I thought best, I hid my face in my knees and waited. Nothing happened. I felt worried and scared. There was no chance of me living now, this was the end!

Alice described her feeling as the plane came down on the island:

... I wasn't panicking and I was managing somehow to keep calm. The engine was rumbling and roaring, moaning as if it was in great pain.

The Daventry School pupils also wrote interesting accounts of the crash. Hannah described the moments before the crash:

... I glanced out of the window on my left as a spark leaped from the side of the plane. I screamed not knowing what to do. My screams were heard all over the plane, but before anyone said anything, we were plunging down and down, and that's when everything went black.

Emily wrote a realistic account of her departure. The flight was almost boring until she looked out of the window:

... The next time I looked out of the window the ground was rising. I thought my imagination was running wild and getting ahead of me, when people started screaming and then we realized we were in danger.

Panic was everywhere. I was screaming loudly, and everyone was holding onto the seats in front of them but it was not good, the force of the crash was too great. I turned my head to the right when something, a hard object, struck me on the head. What it was I will never know. I was unconscious.

These examples show how both groups of pupils were stimulated by the task, and this was reflected in the quality of their writing. The children continued the stories, describing their feelings and reactions when they realized they had crashed, and how they adapted to life on the island. The Braunston pupils also made models of the shelter, which were displayed in their classroom.

Writing the stories hit a range of Levels in AT 3: Writing. For example, the juniors' holiday diaries or stories would have fulfilled En 3/3c: '... write more complex stories with detail beyond simple events and with a defined ending'; En 3/4b: '... write stories which have an opening, a setting, characters, a sense of events and a resolution which engage the sympathy and interest of the reader' ... (etc.). The writing of the older pupils would have hit En 3/5a, b and c.

Holiday Disaster

Our next joint session took place at the beginning of March, when we had planned group radio broadcasts. Ten newsflashes about the holiday flight had been prepared, as if from different sources, giving conflicting information about what might have happened to the plane, e.g. it had been destroyed by a terrorist's bomb, struck by lightning, etc. The bulletins were give out in rapid succession, and the pupils had to produce a coherent news bulletin to a deadline, lasting one minute. The approach adopted was based on the 'Simtex' computer simulation.

Unfortunately the Braunston pupils did not come, because their coach had been inadvertently booked for the wrong day, though the three pupils from Staverton Primary School attended the session. With the Daventry School pupils, they were divided into groups of three or four, and the lesson continued as planned. Lively discussions took place, as the following extract illustrates. Liz and Andrea (from Daventry School) worked with Andrew (from Staverton Primary School). Once the messages had been given out, they started to plan the broadcast.

Liz: You could have someone as radio control.
Andrew: You could have someone on the spot, reporting.
Liz ⎤
Andrea ⎦ Yeah [nodding].

Liz:	It's like radio control. You could be reporter.
Andrea:	Yeah, so I'd be the first one on the scene.
Liz:	Yeah.
	[Andrea starts writing].
Liz:	So what shall I say ... 'Over to the radio controller'?
Andrea:	You could be named ...
Liz:	If you join him you could.
Andrew:	If they say 'Over to so-and-so', they usually say their name.
Liz:	Yeah, you could be interviewing her ...
Andrea:	Yeah ... what should I do now? [to Liz] What sort of name should I have as radio control? I don't know.
Liz:	[To Andrew] What sort of name could she have as a radio control?
Andrew:	Dunno! [All three laugh].
Andrea:	Something like ....
Andrew:	Why don't we have a real name?
Liz:	I can't think of any? Oh, stick to your own name, Andrea!
Andrea:	OK!
Liz:	'Over to Andrea Brown now' [both Liz and Andrea write].
	'Over to our reporter Andrea Brown now'. [All three write].
Liz:	[To Andrea]. Now you're speaking to radio controller ... 'The plane seemed to go off the screen' or something like that ... so it's you who's speaking.
Andrea:	[Reading]. 'We now have here with me Andrew, the radio controller'.

This extract shows the relaxed and friendly manner in which the three pupils were discussing different aspects of their planned broadcast. Though Liz and Andrea took the lead, Andrew was able to contribute his opinions as well.

The Broadcast (script)

Andrea:	And that was Michael Jackson with 'Leave me Alone'.
Liz:	We've just had this news report come in. Three different terrorist groups claim responsibility for blowing up the plane in mid-air. It is not sure whether there are any survivors, but it is highly unlikely that there are. Now over to our reporter, Andrea Brown.
Andrea:	Thank you, Liz. We have a report which suggests that there was a hijacker on the plane, and forced it to crash-land. I now have Andrew Wiles with me, who is Head of the Radio Controllers. Do you think this is highly likely?

Andrew: I don't think so, because from the radio messages the aviation authority denies that there was any hijacker on board. The plane crashed because of an electrical storm.

Andrea: Thank you, Andrew. We will be bringing more reports to you later on in the programme. This is Andrea Brown reporting from Heathrow.

Liz: We now resume with the programme.

Afterwards, Andrea wrote that the activity was 'fun and enjoyable [because] ... working in a group made it a lot easier because you can put all your ideas together.'

Liz wrote:

Andrew, Andrea and I worked as a group of three ... Andrew worked quite hard throughout the hour, and joined in frequently giving his own ideas. The script we had to write was not allowed to be more than a minute long. Throughout the lesson the story was updated with different information, so we had to alter the script accordingly. At the end of the lesson we had read our scripts out loud while being videoed.

Masterman (1985) has pointed out that in news simulations, particularly with primary and lower secondary pupils, the children do not give enough consideration to why they chose particular stories. However, with some input from the teacher, pupils 'quickly discover that value is not inherent within a story, but relates to its usefulness for particular purposes' (Masterman 1985, p. 131). In the simulation described above, the pressure of a deadline for a national radio broadcast, combined with a rapid succession of contradictory messages, provided the context in which the newsflash had to be produced.

The process of working together on the task was valuable, stimulating much oral work about the fate of the plane and the final form of the radio script. The pupils' oral work in planning and presenting the news programmes would have hit several levels and strands in AT 1; for example En 1/4b: '... ask and respond to questions in a range of situations with increased confidence; En 1/4c: '... take part as a speaker and listener in a group discussion or activity, expressing a personal view and commenting constructively on what is being discussed or experienced'; En 1/5c: '... use language to convey information and ideas effectively in a straightforward situation'; and En 1/5d: '... contribute to the planning of, and participate in, a group presentation'[4] etc. The editing and redrafting of the scripts would have hit En 3/4e, and possibly En 3/5d. Through discussing their ideas, and turning them into a script, the pupils would have hit En 3/5c, which requires pupils to '... show an increasing differentiation between speech and writing.'

Media studies have an important place in the teaching of English. As the Cox Report (1989) states:

Media Education and information technology alike enlarge pupils' critical understanding of how messages are generated, conveyed and interpreted in different media [9.2] ... Media education, like drama, deals with fundamental aspects of language, interpretation and meaning. It is, therefore consonant with the aims of English teaching [9.9].

The activity described above will have contributed to the development of the pupils' understanding in these areas. The session was observed by the Head of Daventry PDC in his role as independent evaluator. Afterwards he wrote this assessment:

> The start of this session was somewhat marred by the failure of one of the primary schools to turn up. This meant that the teacher running the session wasted valuable time on the telephone finding out where the missing school was.
>
> The resulting small number of junior pupils present meant that the paired work which had been planned had to be modified accordingly. Fortunately, the children were used to this style of work and the junior school children were not too concerned about being outnumbered.
>
> The secondary pupils were very good at getting the junior children to respond and contribute to the session and ensuring they were involved. The task set was both interesting and challenging, while at the same time achievable by children of all the abilities/phases present.
>
> The time limit imposed, along with the simulation of a real broadcasting situation by introducing updated newsflashes and the actual requirement to perform a short videod scene as a group, ensured that all minds were focused on the task in hand and the finished product was of a high standard.

The next week Anne Cottingham visited my Year 9 class, and talked to them about her pupils and answered their questions about the younger children. At the end of the lesson, she gave out the Braunston pupils' project folders to their Daventry partners, and collected the older pupils' folders for her class to look at. Thus each child had the opportunity to read his/her partner's folder. The children subsequently wrote letters to each other about their work, which were sent with the returned folders.

Writing for Each Other

The next activity was that each pupil had to write a story for his/her partner at the other school about the adventures that happened to them on the island. Some of the Daventry School pupils used or continued with their holiday diaries, while others started a new story. All the pupils met together in March, about five weeks after the previous session. They read each other's stories in pairs and discussed how their first drafts could be improved. A few extracts will illustrate the sorts of interactions that took place. Kate (Braunston Primary School) had read her story to Sandra (Daventry School). After discussing the punctuation errors in Kate's first draft, Sandra looked more closely at some of the descriptions in the story, particularly where Kate had described the survivors crossing a marsh.

Sandra: I think you should make more of when you're going over the marsh. Where's the marsh bit? The parrot's good ... I think you should make more of your feelings going over the marsh, because you've put 'The marsh was full of brown mud.'

Kate: Put a star?

Sandra: Yeah. You get over the marsh bit very quickly. I think you should make more of how you get hot and tired, because you have to push against the mud.

Kate: And we didn't fancy going because it was bubbly [giggles].

Sandra: Yeah, 'very horrible'. You didn't know what was in there. There might be something horrible.

Kate: Where?

Sandra: Just put ... I'll put ... [writes] 'Describe your feelings'.

Kate: I'll cross out that bit and do it again ... Yeah I'll do that bit because that's when they get out.

Sandra: That's alright. It's just in the middle you seem to go across a bit quickly. You could put you were very tired and you wanted to lie down and you couldn't, and your legs were tired after pushing so far.

Kate: It's quite a big marsh.

Sandra: Yeah ... and your legs are tired from pushing against all the mud ... and it's smelly and horrible.

Kate: I'll do that at school.

Sandra: Right ... across the marsh you could have conversations saying it's horrible to me, and I could say things back to you and things, and I think you should have put some speaking in because it's improved it a lot more. Were you told to do it as a diary, or did you decide to do it as a diary?

Kate: I decided to do it like that.

Sandra read her story to Kate, who said she liked it, and that it was exciting, with good conversations; but she wasn't able to offer many suggestions as to how Sandra's first draft could be improved. However, Sandra felt the session had been successful. Afterwards she wrote:

We discussed the stories and I enjoyed reading and listening to Kate's story. She had some really good ideas. I told her to describe more of her feelings ... I think it [the project] is an excellent way of getting children of two different ages to communicate.

This discussion would have hit En 3/3e: '... begin to revise and redraft in discussion with the teacher, other adults, or other children in the class, paying attention to clarity and meaning' ... (etc.), and En 3/4e: '... discuss the organisation of their own writing; revise and redraft the writing as appropriate, independently, in the light of that discussion'. The Daventry School pupils were writing stories and keeping diaries about the project, thereby meeting En 3/4b: '... write stories which have an opening, a setting, characters, a sense of events and a resolution and which engage the interest and sympathy of the reader; produce other kinds of chronologically organized writing.'

Some of the Daventry School pupils worked with two primary school pupils. For example, Susan (Daventry School) worked with Eleanor (Braunston Primary School) and Robert (Staverton Primary School). Eleanor had brought the first draft of her story, though Robert hadn't written anything. Susan helped him to start his story by discussing possible ideas.

Susan: Have you any ideas about the basic story?

Robert: Um ... well, we would be in a plane ...

Susan: You'd be in a plane at first, and you'd have to say about your feelings, and how you feel ... what everyone else is doing. So do you want to put that down for number one? You can put 'In the plane, feelings and thoughts' [Robert writes] ... and then it would be the crash ... and then you'd be going round the island. Have you thought about how we'd go to the civilization on the other side of the island, that we did? ... We get caught by people. Have you thought about it really?

Robert: Well, I wouldn't try to get supplies and food from the plane and I wouldn't stay on the plane because it's pointless to stay at the plane.

Susan: You'd explore round the island?

Robert: Not exactly ... just ...

Susan: Go see what the island is like?

Robert: Yes, explore the island first, ... see which would be the best available approach to civilization, if there *is* any civilization, so we'd sort of go in pairs to see what paths there are.

Susan: Are you actually going to find civilization, or are you going to get captured by men or ... you're going to find civilization, are you?

Robert: We're going to try and find civilization ... We [are] trying to find evidence of civilization, tracks ...

Susan: So the next point would be the crash, and then the description of the island?

Robert: I think we ... should stay by the plane for one night just to get over the shock of the crash ... or maybe even longer.

Though Susan provided a lot of ideas, Robert selected those that appealed to him, and contributed ideas of his own. As the conversation developed, Robert was progressively taking the initiative and developing his own storyline. Susan found the session rewarding, but also very demanding. She wrote:

I found it quite difficult because Robert was working on starting and planning his first draft so he needed a lot of help and attention. But Eleanor [Braunston Primary School] was writing the assessment of my story and wanted to ask questions on that. Their behaviour was excellent so that helped a lot. Having two pupils is a lot more difficult than having one. The situation ran alright though and I was in control. When I read my story Robert listened attentively but Eleanor tended to fidget. This was annoying, but after asking her politely not to she took notice and stopped.

Robert's discussion with Susan about his story, and the way he was exploring ideas, would have hit En 1/4c: '... take part as speakers and listeners in a group discussion or activity, commenting constructively on what is being discussed or experienced'.

Some of the Daventry School pupils described the process of drafting and editing in detail, often commenting sensitively on the perceptions that the children had of each other's work. Here is a typical extract from Mary's work diary:

Today we just worked in twos with our juniors. We both had had to write a story about the crash and what life was like on the island. I read my story to Veronica and then she read hers to me. I found that she's a very good reader and has some good ideas and a good imagination.

Veronica's story was very long but it wasn't boring. I suggested that she should make the first part shorter because it was over a page long and it was just about us playing games. Veronica had a lot more characters than I did and they were very good.

My story was about all four of us, Diane, Clare, Veronica and I, but Veronica's story just had me and her in it and some other man that we had met on the island. I'd never thought of having other people on the island but Veronica did and it was good. She had two men that lived in a hut where there were stolen jewels and four men came in an airplane and helped them to catch the two men in the hut.

I especially liked the part in her story where we found a chest and inside were some steps going down. We went down the steps into a little room where there was lots of jugs of water and lots of food and the stolen jewels. Veronica liked the part in my story where she had broken her leg and we had to make her some crutches out of branches.

The Final Versions

The stories of the Braunston Primary School pupils went through several drafts, and they were also helped by their own teacher. Unfortunately they didn't keep earlier versions, though the final results were usually very imaginative. For example, Felicity wrote a story in which the castaways discovered a cave on the island, and a very long tunnel which went to Egypt, and hence enabled them to escape. Veronica wrote an eighteen page story, in which the survivors of the air crash discovered treasure hidden on the island by English robbers, who were captured by the children. The main characters in these stories were the children who worked in groups of four.

Close consideration of the story by Emily (Daventry School) will show, typically, how working with partners at another school acted as an additional stimulus in the redrafting process. Emily had two partners from Braunston Primary School, Nina and Lucy. She read the first draft of her story to them, and then recorded their comments.

'The Castaways' by Emily: First Draft

The next morning we were all up early ready to discuss what we were going to do.

We nominated Pippa as the food collector as she was the tallest and most experienced!

Lucy would collect moss and grass for bedding in our new shelter and also berries to eat when we were hungry.

Felicity would look for materials to make our new shelter whilst I would start making the base of it using moss and grass for a flooring, palm leaves for a roofing and broken pieces of wood for support.

'What did you find today, Pippa?' I asked.

'Oh, I found some bananas growing on a tree just south from this point and there was a waterfall which runs into a stream containing fresh water,' Pippa said.

'Where was that?' asked Lucy.

'It's not far from here, which is very useful,' said Pippa . . .

After reading the first draft of her story to Nina and Lucy, Emily made notes on their comments:

Nina and Lucy thought that I could improve my first draft by bringing in more characters and making them more exciting.

More descriptions when we left the wreckage of the plane to explore the island.

Nina thought there should have been some illustrations, e.g. the island.

Lucy thought there should have been a picture of the plane when it had crashed.

They liked the ending and the beginning as they thought it was very descriptive.

No further improvements could have taken place.

Emily then added, after reworking the first draft:

Improvements made: more dialogue
                          characterization
                          description.

Second Draft

The next morning we were all up nice and early to have a meeting to plan a rota as we didn't know how long we were going to be kept, imprisoned on this island.

'Right, Pippa, I think you should be nominated as the "food-collector" because you're the tallest and most experienced, alright?' I said.

'Fine by me,' Pippa joked.

'Well, I think Lucy should collect materials like moss, grass for bedding in our new shelter,' debated Felicity.

'That's a good idea,' I replied.

'Now what?' questioned Pippa.

'Well we have got you and Lucy organized now there is just Felicity and I to decide for,' I said.

'We need materials for the shelter, don't we,' asked Lucy.

'Yes, good thinking Lucy,' said Pippa. 'Felicity can do that.'

'Well I can start on making a base for our new shelter,' I replied.

'Now remember, nothing fancy or elaborate, just plain but homely and secure if there are any strong winds coming. Lucy and Felicity don't forget, keep to a simple path and if there are any good spots for food or materials, mark it off with this red tape I have,' said Pippa in a mature way.

'Why do we have to mark it with tape?' asked Lucy.

'So we know where to find it when we are desperate, thicky,' replied Felicity.

'Now no cattiness or arguing, we have to respond in a mature attitude,' I told Felicity.

'Sorry Emily,' Felicity in her sympathetic voice.

'That's alright,' I said to her.

I though to myself — for the base I will use moss/grass bedding, palm leaves for roofing and broken pieces of wood for extra support.

'What did you find today, Pippa?' I asked.

'Oh, I found some bananas growing on a tree, just south from this point, and I marked them with a red cross so we know where to look if we need them next . . .'

It is clear how the second draft has been brought to life by the inclusion of extra dialogue, which convincingly develops the relationships between the children. This section of the story had been rewritten, largely as a result of Emily's discussions with her primary school partners.

Both groups of pupils completed their stories, turning them into presentation booklets for their partners. Most of the children took a lot of trouble over this; perhaps the most exceptional was Hannah, from Daventry School, who turned her story into an adventure game book, which ran to over a hundred typed pages.

This care over accuracy and presentation would have hit AT 4: Spelling, levels 3 and 4; and AT 5: Handwriting, level 4 (especially for the primary school pupils). Most of the booklets produced by the Daventry School pupils would have met AT 4/5: Presentation, level 5a–c; and level 6b–d.

Conclusion of the Project

We were able to arrange a final session in mid-July, near the end of term. The Daventry School pupils went out to Braunston Primary School, and all sixty pupils crowded into one classroom. The seniors found the chairs rather small and uncomfortable. However, a very good atmosphere prevailed; the pupils exchanged booklets and read each other's stories. We finished off with a quiz between teams of four pupils from each school; the result was a draw.

Afterwards Emily wrote:

It was a very good day and made a change as the Braunston Juniors always came to our school.

When we walked into the room, it reminded me of when I was at junior school; the small chairs, small tables, and the pictures and posters on the wall.

Rebecca wrote:

The booklet Veronica gave me was very good, the writing was neat and the spelling was good. It was a very long story but it was good and not just long and boring. I think everyone enjoyed the visit . . .

Pippa wrote:

> ... We went to Braunston Junior School today. It was really good to see Felicity again. She presented her brilliant booklet to me, and I presented my booklet to her ... Felicity and I get on really well. I think this is because we share the same interests.

Programmes of Study

Many elements in the Programmes of Study for the three Attainment Targets were covered by the project at KS 2 and KS 3. In AT 1, the project offered opportunities for all the pupils to engage in pair, group and class activities (either as participants or audience). For example, at KS 2, the preparation of the radio script would have enabled the pupils to learn (in part) how to 'work with or devise an increasing range of drama scripts'. The range of opportunities included 'the use, where appropriate, of audio and/or video recorders, radio, television, telephone and computer'; 'the preparation of presentations'; 'taking part in shared writing activities'; and 'role-play, simulations and group drama' (DES 1990a; pp. 24–25). For the older pupils at KS 3, the project gave them opportunities for activities such as 'giving instructions to others in a group'; and 'planning and taking part in a group presentation' (section 17; DES 1990a, p. 26).

In AT 2: Reading the study of holiday brochures by both primary and secondary pupils covered by sections 17 and 18 in the Programmes of Study, which deal with the study of media texts at KS 3 (DES 1990a, p. 32). Using the brochures to plan a holiday showed that the pupils had learned 'how to find and select information for themselves and use it effectively' (section 20; DES 1990a, p. 32).

In AT 3: Writing, pupils at both KS 2 and KS 3 developed their skills, such as writing for an intended audience; editing and redrafting; planning the structure of a story; and taking care over the presentation of the finished story (DES 1990a, pp. 36–39). Holiday diaries, project diaries and radio scripts were other forms of chronological writing (section 18; DES 1990a, p. 37). This selection of activities indicates the range of elements in the Programmes of Study which were covered by the project.

Follow-up Study

As a follow-up to the project, I interviewed a sample of nine ex-Braunston pupils a few months later, at the beginning of their first term at Daventry William Parker School. The pupils had all enjoyed the project, and had liked the attention from an older pupil. They felt more confident about coming to the comprehensive school, because they had learned their way round, and already knew somebody there.

Mostly the pupils interviewed had found it helpful to discuss their story with the partner, and to use that feedback when improving the first draft. Eleanor's comments were typical:

Eleanor: ... At first I thought the story was going to be easy just getting on a plane, going to Florida, that was easy, but when they said you're going to have a crash, that got hard. Rebecca gave me some ideas what it would be like because she'd been to Florida ... yes, she'd been to Florida, so she knew some of the things, so she helped me ... described the plane better.

Teacher: So Rebecca helped you with the descriptions?

Eleanor: She didn't tell me how to put it; but she told me what it looked like in the plane, things like that, and what it was like to be up in one, so I could write more about the plane.

Teacher: Did you agree that that would help to make your story better?

Eleanor: In a way ... because putting a plane together is easy.

Teacher: What do you mean by 'putting a plane together'?

Eleanor: I mean describing it, but the actual story, I needed some help on that because I couldn't ... I didn't know what it would be like up in a plane, so that helped me.

Other pupils also felt the project had helped them to improve their writing, as this discussion with Felicity, Bernadette and Ann shows:

Teacher: What did you enjoy about the project?

Felicity: I think writing up the last story we did.

Bernadette: Writing up the crash-landing on the island.

Ann: I liked writing up the first story that we did and deciding where to go ... planning the holiday.

Teacher: How do you think the project has helped you with your English?

Felicity: Some of it has been redrafting because before you just wrote a straight story and that was it, but we've sort of learnt how to redraft them. Some of the stories we did, we drafted three or four times.

Teacher: You'd not done redrafting before?

Felicity: No.

Teacher: Did you do more redrafting when you were back at school?

Felicity ⎤
Ann ⎦ Yes.

Teacher: Felicity, how many versions of your story did you write to get to the final version?

Felicity: Four versions. Pippa only commented on one of them. She commented on the first lot of notes.

Teacher: Were her ideas helpful?

Felicity: Yeah, she was the one who gave me the idea of the Egyptian tomb.

Teacher: Who helped you with the third and fourth versions of your story?

Felicity: I think I gave it to my teacher, and she sort of told me

> where I was wrong and where it could be improved on, and I just took it back to my desk and improved on it ...
>
> Teacher: But the way of working was not something you'd done before?
>
> Felicity: Yes.
>
> Teacher: Any other ways in which you felt working with Pippa helped you?
>
> Felicity: No, except when I came to this school, it helped me because Pippa kept talking to me. Everytime she saw me she said 'Hello'.
>
> Teacher: Did you mind doing all that extra work on your story, if you were used to only doing it once before?
>
> Felicity: No, it made it better and I felt more satisfied when I'd finished it.

The other pupils had enjoyed the range of activities also. In retrospect they felt that working with secondary school pupils had helped them to develop their ideas, to improve the quality of their writing through collaborative editing and redrafting, and to correct spelling and punctuation.

These responses were echoed in the results of the survey forms completed by the Braunston pupils who came to Daventry William Parker School at the beginning of Year 7. Most of the pupils felt that the project had made them feel more confident about transition, because they already knew somebody at the comprehensive school. All the pupils enjoyed working with an older child, and they liked writing about the 'adventure' aspect of the project.

Their teacher Anne Cottingham, whom I interviewed at the end of the project, felt there had been benefits in many areas. First, the liaison aspects, particularly developing a working relationship with an older child at secondary school. The project made her pupils see the need for planning from one session to the next. They thought more carefully about their work as a result, and it helped the majority with sustained writing. Those children who were academically weak found the project very motivating, because it forced them to talk through their ideas with the Daventry School partner, before starting to write.

The project also had cross-curricular benefits, for example in using holiday brochures to plan and cost the proposed holiday. This activity extended the more able pupils. Other activities included the design of the shelter, and the construction of a model, as well as planning maps of the island.[6] I felt that the project provided a stimulus that benefited the main language skills of all the children involved. By working in pairs or fours across the primary-secondary divide, the children gained a sense of audience which gave additional purpose to their writing. Apart from the many benefits for pupils, the project was also a creative activity for the two teachers. Liaison links between the two schools were improved, and the teachers gained a better sense of continuity in language work. The project would also have fulfilled most of the strands in levels 1–6 of the three main Attainment Targets for English. Furthermore, the collaborative nature of the project demonstrated that 'no man is an island'.

Notes

1 I am most grateful to Anne Cottingham, with whom this project was planned, and to David Thrower (Head Teacher, Braunston Primary School), for his support. I am grateful to both colleagues for their comments on an earlier draft of this Chapter, and to John Follett, Head of Daventry PDC, for his evaluation report on one session.

2 The NCC Consultation Report (1990) gives 'arrange an outing together' as an example for this strand (p. 27).

3 Examples for this strand are: 'Plans and diagrams, descriptions of a person or place, or notes for an activity in science or design' (DES 1990a, p. 12).

4 Examples include '... conduct an interview on a radio programme' (DES 1990a, p. 4).

5 Examples include '... Compile a news report or a news programme for younger children' (DES 1990a, p. 4).

6 The use of the island theme lends itself readily to cross-curricular work, particularly in a liaison context. An imaginative project involving a middle school, and its contributory schools, is described by Talbot, C. (1990) 'When the Talking Stops: An Exercise in Liaison', *Education 3–13*, **18**, 1, pp. 28–32.

Chapter 7

'Good Times, Bad Times'

'It was the best of times, it was the worst of times.' (Dickens: *A Tale of Two Cities*)

Introduction

In 1988–89 we decided to repeat our poetry project with Chris Challis, though with different groups of pupils. The priority was to involve juniors in Year 6 from the Grange Junior School, which had become our largest contributory school as a result of the reorganization of local schools. The school had three classes of top juniors (over ninety pupils), of whom seventy had decided to come to the new Daventry William Parker School in the autumn term 1989; the rest had chosen to go to the other comprehensive school in Daventry. We wanted this large prospective intake to have some experience of curriculum continuity work before transition.

Mary Linden's class at the Grange Junior School worked with my top English set in Year 8 at Daventry School.[1] We had a half-day liaison meeting at the junior school to plan the stages of the project, and to pair up pupils across the primary-secondary divide. Subsequently there were several meetings after school to confirm details.

The approach used was very similar to that described in 'Poetry in the Making' (Chapter 3). However, each project has a character of its own, given the different pupils involved. This chapter will consider in detail the opportunities for oral work, the editing and redrafting that occurred, and the ways in which the children's awareness of language was developed. These aspects of the project will also be related to the Attainment Targets of the National Curriculum.

The project started with two separate workshops conducted by Chris Challis with the pupils at each school, on consecutive days in mid-January. He talked to the pupils about his profession as a poet, reading examples of his work, and using photographs as stimuli for poems. After the workshops the children described their impressions. At the Grange Junior School, Gerald wrote:

I enjoyed Chris Challis's visit very much. But I didn't expect him to have long hair and thought he was going to be posh, but he was just normal. I liked the idea of writing a poem for a certain picture and it was a good thing that you had a choice. Chris Challis has got a sense of humour. I especially liked the 'School Bully' poem and 'The Hunchback of Notre Dame'. I chose to write a poem about a dog at the doorstep of a shop and I did it from the dog's point of view.

John (another pupil from the Grange Junior School) wrote:

When Chris Challis arrived, I was surprised because he had long hair. I had other ideas about his appearance. I had an excellent time, it was great fun. He told a lot of jokes. I liked him because he was not serious all the time. After he talked about himself, he showed us seven pictures for us to write about. He read us some poems. My favourite was 'The School Bully' and 'The Hunchback of Notre Dame'.

The Daventry School pupils had watched the video of the poetry project from the previous year. Most of them were looking forward to their first workshop with a practising poet. The session went very well, and the pupils' enjoyment was reflected in their work diary entries.
Sally wrote:

Today Dr. Chris Challis came and talked to us for two hours twenty minutes. He told us how he became a poet and what he did in his spare time. I thought it was very good because he read us funny and serious poems and stories, and I thought the best thing was when he gave us some pictures to base our poem on. I did 'The Tramp'. Overall it was very interesting.

Alison wrote:

Today we had our first poetry workshop with Chris Challis. He is a very interesting man and a very good poet. In the first half of the lesson he read us some of his poems which I thought were very good. My own favourite was a short, funny one about Quasimodo.
    In the third and fourth periods Chris Challis showed us some photographs of different scenes which could involve good times or bad times. I chose to write one about a Tramp which I was quite pleased about. He chose one about a lonely swan. In twenty minutes he had written a brilliant poem. I enjoyed today immensely and it was a very unusual experience and I am very much looking forward to meeting the children from the Grange.

This enjoyment was reflected in the discussion the class had the next day about the workshop; all the pupils had found it interesting. The following week the two teachers met after school to evaluate the two workshops, and to finalize the pairings for the first joint session of the two classes.

This took place at the beginning of February, at Daventry School, without the poet present. The pupils interviewed each other, and read and discussed their favourite poems with their partners. As in the previous year, the Daventry School pupils had prepared worksheets on the poems they had chosen from anthologies. Towards the end of the session the pupils started to write the first drafts of their own poems on the theme of 'Good Times, Bad Times', helping each other with ideas. At this session the pupils voted to donate the profits made from the sale of their proposed poetry book to the NSPCC, so this gave the outcome of the project a specific focus.

There was a good working atmosphere, and by the end of the session the majority of the pupils had started writing the first drafts of their own poems. Lively discussions took place about their favourite poems.

For example, Linda (from Daventry School) worked with two junior school pupils, Nancy and Marie. Linda had chosen three poems from *Voices (The First Book)* edited by Geoffrey Summerfield (1968). She started with 'Death of a Bird' by Jon Silkin, and the three children read alternate verses of the poem. Afterwards they discussed it:

Linda: What do you think of this poem?
Nancy: It told you everything: I think it's good.
Linda: I thought it's a bit sad!
Nancy: Yes, it is a bit sad.
Linda: I like it. What do you think, Marie?
Marie: It's a good poem because it explains what you feel when something's dead, or something like that.
Linda: Yeah, when our guinea pig died I used to feel just like that.
Nancy: [Inaudible]
Linda: When things die you often feel a bit angry with yourself and you think 'Perhaps I could have done something else', but ... I like this poem.
         [Nancy tells an anecdote about the death of a family pet].
Linda: There's another one here that I liked. It's called 'Cockcrow' by E. Thomas [she reads the poem]. What do you think of that one? D'you like it or ...?
Nancy: I liked it, but I thought ... some of the bits they tried to rhyme it a bit too much.
Linda: Yeah.
Nancy: I don't like the last line, they tried to rhyme it, so they just put that, to try to make it rhyme.
Linda: It doesn't really fit in with the rest of the poem '... the milkers lace ...'[2]
Nancy: No, I don't think so.
Linda: [To Marie] What do you think?
Marie: Yes, it's not as good as the other one.
Linda: So we're not so keen on that one?

Nancy: No, I don't think so.
Linda: If you gave it marks out of ten, what do you think you'd
          give it?
Marie: Five.
Linda: [To Nancy] Would you?
Nancy: Two ... [laughs] ... because I think that last line really
          ruined it.
Linda: Yes, it doesn't fit in with the rest ... Let's look at the
          poems you've brought.
Nancy: This is my absolute favourite [gives it to Linda].
          [Linda reads the poem 'I've got a dog called Spot'.]
Linda: Oh, I like that one! What do you like about it?
Marie: It's true, my dad's got a friend ... has a dog with a spot on
          its shoulder and he calls it Spot!
Linda: Are there any describing words? ... You like the way it's
          described. Which part do you like best ... 'its long pink
          tongue'?
Marie: I think that's best, because if they roll their tongues, they're
          really panting.

Marie and Nancy read a few limericks and other poems they'd brought,
and Linda read the first draft of her own poem 'Only a day' which the two
juniors liked. The children then started to write poems for each other on the
theme of 'Good Times, Bad Times'. Afterwards Linda wrote:

With Nancy and Marie I worked through the interview poems
worksheet and looked at the poems they had brought. They also
brought some of their own work. They are both nice children. Marie
is the quieter of the two and needed a little more help on the
interview sheet. Nancy has neater work and seemed to be a little
more outgoing. Although Nancy's work was well presented, I think
Marie's work was, if anything, a bit better, but they were both really
good ... I enjoyed the session and am looking forward to meeting
the girls again.

Marie (Grange Junior School) wrote:

... When we arrived we were paired up with our partners. I was
rather nervous and thought that I was going to be rather shy. Also
that I wouldn't speak much. When we were introduced I began to
feel like I was part of the school.
    Me and Nancy sat down, our partner was called Linda. She was
very nice. Linda talked to us a while and then gave us a worksheet of
questions so she could find out more about me and Nancy. While we
were filling in our sheets Linda looked at our work, she said it was
very nice. She asked us about what poems we liked.
    Linda read us some poems she liked, we commented on them.

While we were working on sheets about the poems, Linda had read ours. Then we did our work on good times and bad times. I wrote about the measles. All too soon it was time to go. I said goodbye and went to get my things. I had enjoyed myself very much. I am looking forward to going again.

The transcript of part of this session conveys the sorts of interactions that were taking place. The pupils were meeting for the first time, and were getting to know each other, as well as covering a lot of activities within the lesson.

Many language skills were being used, especially those described in AT 1 and AT 2. The reading of poetry, and the discussions that resulted, would have fulfilled several levels of AT 2: Reading. The contributions of all three girls would have hit (at least part of) En 2/2e: '. . . listen and respond to stories, poems and other materials read aloud, expressing opinions informed by what has been read'; En 2/3a: '. . . read aloud from familiar stories and poems fluently and with appropriate expression'; and part of En 2/4b: '. . . demonstrate in talking about a range of stories and poems which they have read, an ability to explore preferences.'

Linda's contribution would have hit part of En 2/5a: '. . . demonstrate, in talking and writing about a range of stories and poems which they have read, an ability to explore preferences'. The girls showed awareness and sensitivity about the way language is used in poetry, and how it can affect the reader, as their responses to the poem 'Cockcrow' by Edward Thomas showed. Thus knowledge about language was developed, thereby hitting En 2/5e: '. . . show through discussion an awareness of a writer's choice of particular words and phrases and the effect on the reader'.

The oral work that was generated would have hit several levels of AT 1: Speaking and Listening: For example, Marie and Nancy's contributions would have hit En 1/3c: '. . . listen with an increased span of concentration to other children and adults, asking and responding to questions and commenting on what has been said'; En 1/3d: '. . . give and receive and follow accurately, precise instructions when pursuing a task individually or as a member of a group' (e.g. when filling in a personal questionnaire; answering questions on a worksheet). They would also have hit En 1/4b: '. . . ask and respond to questions in a range of situations with increased confidence'; and En 1/4c: '. . . take part as speakers and listeners in a group discussion or activity, expressing a personal view and commenting constructively on what is being discussed or experienced'; Linda's mature and sensitive guidance of the session would have hit En 1/5b: '. . . contribute to and respond constructively in discussion, including the development of ideas; advocate and justify a point of view'; and possibly En 1/6a: '. . . contribute to group discussions, considered opinions or clear statements of personal feeling which are clearly responsive to the contributions of others.'

The success of this first joint session was reflected in the work diary entries of the other pupils. The children from the Grange Junior School had been nervous before meeting their partners, but found that they got on well. The following two diary entries are typical.

Steven wrote:

I felt nervous because it was the first time I went to Ashby Senior School [Daventry School]. I was introduced to Tom as he was going to help me with some poems. Before we started he asked me some questions like how old I was and so on. We read some poems out of a book, then I read some poems I had written for him, then I did a crossword. Tom helped me. I did not want to go because I had enjoyed myself so much.

Cynthia wrote:

When I walked in the door I felt scared because I thought people would laugh at me because I'm just a junior, but I was wrong. All the people were standing in a row waiting for their partner. By the name of Alix I thought my partner was going to be a boy, but it was a girl. She was very nice and helped me with my work all the time. The work was quite easy, first you had to fill in a sheet that was all about yourself, then you had to read some poems and do a crossword with all the answers on from the poem.

Alix told me to think of some sad words and some happy words while she thought of some too, then when we had enough words we started to think up our sad poems. My poem was about when my cat died. Alix wrote about when her dog died. The time fled by. It was soon time to go. A boy kindly thanked us for being here and hoped we would come again. I got my bag and coat, said goodbye to Alix and went out of the door with my partner I was paired up with.

It is apparent from these diary extracts that the children were involved, and enthusiastic about the project. The discussions about their poems, as they were writing them, also contributed to their awareness of the language, as when Cynthia talked to Alix about 'sad words' and 'happy words'.

The Daventry School pupils also enjoyed working with the juniors. For example, Karen wrote:

I had my first lesson with Gerald. At first I was nervous, after all he was a boy! What was I going to say to him? I thought he was very smartly dressed and well up to date in fashion. We sat down and he filled his questions in. I read some poems and he spoke quite freely about them, although he was a little shy. When I relaxed I began to enjoy myself. We exchanged poems and talked about them. He likes writing poems on animals. He was a good poet and bright too. We chose our ideas for our poems. Gerald was very nice and friendly. I look forward to the next lesson.

I discussed the session with my pupils at their next lesson; everyone said something positive about their experience of working with a junior school partner, and then the classes watched the video of the session. Subsequently, the pupils worked on their poems, discussing them with a neighbour, and improving them. Mary Linden's class at the Grange Junior School also discussed their experiences, wrote up their work diaries, and spent several lessons editing and redrafting the poems they had started during the workshop with Chris Challis, and the joint session with their Daventry School partners.

Editing Poems Together

The next joint session was a week later, when the pupils read the poems they had written to their partners at the other school. They discussed each other's work, and made suggestions for improvements. The relationships that had developed between the pupils were very good. Our intention is to focus here on the processes of editing and redrafting, by looking closely at the discussions of a few pupils. The cross-phase nature of the relationships enhanced the stimulus that the pupils gained from working with each other.

Linda continued to work with Nancy and Marie; she read the first draft of her poem 'A Gypsy Life' to them; and then the girls discussed it.

A Gypsy Life
Roaming round the countryside,
In a painted van.
Up and down the country lanes,
Pulled by Mary-Anne.

Doing what I want to,
When and where I like,
Running free in fields,
Jumping ditches, streams and dikes.

I never go to school,
Couldn't tell a C from Z,
What use are books to gypsies
We keep stories in our heads.

We gypsies live together,
But the caravan's my own,
For my mother's passed away,
And by myself I've grown.

Some people say I'm lucky
Not to have a mother,
To tell me what to do
And not to tease my brother.

I really don't agree
And wish she could come back
I could have saved her when she fell,
That day onto the track.

The horses couldn't stop
They really weren't to blame.

Their hooves big and clumsy
Came down again and again.

So I live alone today,
Apart from Mary-Ann,
But she is not much comfort
As she killed my only mam!

Nancy: I think that's good.
Linda: Do you think there's anything I could improve about it?
Marie: I like all the others except for that one (pointing to a verse).
Linda ⎤
Nancy ⎦ 'Dikes ...'
Linda: That's what I wasn't so keen on: 'Not to tease my brother'.
        I couldn't think what else to put.
Nancy: Mm. Put 'over ... mother ... brother'.
Linda: I got stuck there, so I ended up putting about my brother. I
        think I'd like to change that.
Nancy: I was watching a programme about gypsies and they do
        have a kind of caravan of their own, and the girls go and
        live on their own, and the boys go and live on their own,
        so you couldn't keep that ... I watched a programme
        about gypsies on Saturday morning, and they do live on
        their own past a certain age.
Linda: What do you like about it? Do you like it or ...?
Nancy: I like it because you've rhymed it and it hasn't ... you
        haven't put in things that make it sound silly as if you've
        just rhymed it for the sake of rhyming it.
Linda: The first one I did was about the train robbers, but I didn't
        get on too well with that. I was trying to make it sound
        like a rhythm of a train but I just gave up in the end.
        [Nancy reads Linda's poem out loud]:

Ronnie Biggs

We're the greatest of train robbers
Buster and me
We make a great team,
Buster and me.
We've stopped all the trains from here to the West,
Buster and me, partners in crime.

To steal from the trains we started at stations,
Just like ordinary men.
Then, when the engine set off,
We started a journey.
From carriage to carriage,
Hoping to reach the driver.

While I strangled the driver and punched at the fireman,
Buster controlled the train ...

Nancy: I think you're better off with that one ['A Gypsy Life']
because I don't really think ...

Marie: [Inaudible].

Nancy: ... I think this gets a bit monotonous 'Buster and Me,
Buster and me,' although it's sort of the sound of the train,
it still gets a bit monotonous.

Linda: What I was trying to do was change the 'Buster and Me'
line every verse, sort of change it so it would still have the
same rhythm, but it was different.

Nancy: Yes, you do get some poems like that, but you're a lot
better off with that ['A Gypsy Life'] because I think that's
a lot nicer. I like it especially where ... um ... you say
about your Mum.

Linda: I'm not too good at comical ones and ... so it's not quite
serious either, so it's sort of between ...

Nancy: In between ...

Linda: I know you [Marie] like comical, and you [Nancy] like
serious, so ...

Nancy: I like serious and comical, it's just that I can't write comical
... ends up sounding stupid.

Marie: It's a good poem and ... um ... [looks at poem] ... I
can't even find it. [Reads.] 'Up and down the country
lanes/In a painted van'. I liked that bit because of the
caravan.

Nancy: And you've got this picture [points to the photo of a gypsy
caravan], which makes it feel more real.

Linda: Yeah ... well after I'd decided not to do that ['Ronnie
Biggs'] I couldn't decide what to write. So I just got some
old photos out and I was looking through them till I found
this one. I thought ... that's the only one ...

We can see from this extract the lively and thoughtful way in which the
two junior pupils, especially Nancy, responded to Linda's two poems. The
session continued with Nancy and Marie reading the redrafted versions of
their poems, and discussing them with Linda. The responses of the two
younger girls to Linda's poems not only showed their interest in poetry, but
also their sensitivity to language as in the effect of repetition in a poem.
The girls were extending their knowledge about language again, and they
would have hit En 2/5e, and possibly En 3/5e.

Afterwards Linda wrote:

This was our second meeting with the Grange Juniors. We were to
discuss the first drafts of our poems. It was obvious that Mrs. Linden
had encouraged the children and helped them in class time with their

poems. Marie had already written 5 drafts of her poem and Nancy 3 drafts.

Their work was great. Both, strangely enough were on similar themes and both on bad times. Nancy's was an account of a personal experience, when she broke her wrist. Marie's poem was about someone with measles. Both poems were full of great ideas.

I helped them both change the odd line and they also helped each other. When it came to discussing my poem I did not find it much help for actually changing my work, but they reassured me on the parts I was not happy with. It was a good session and the 2 girls seem to be getting to know me better.

Other pupils also interacted well with their partners and the extracts below indicate the ways the children were responding to each other's poems. For example, Alice (from Daventry School) was working with her junior school partner, Gerald. First he read his poem, 'The Day I Was Born'.

The Day I Was Born

The nurses exclaim
'Congratulations, it's a baby boy!'
After all that hard work my mum gets the credit!
I've been stuck in a bubble of water for days on end,
And when I finally popped it and struggled out,
My mum gets congratulated!
It's not fair this life!
I think I'll go back to where I came from!
Oh no! The nurse is coming!
Aw! She's grabbed me with those fatal hands of hers!
Ow! She's dumped me on some scales!
Then the nurse says with that big mouth of hers,
'Ooh! Isn't he big!
He's nine pounds!'
Then she snatches me off the scales.
She's taking me in the direction of a bowl of water!
Splash! Oh no, not more water!
Uh! They're rubbing slimey stuff all over me!
She's wrenching me out!
Despite my crying protest!
Now the nurse is rubbing this awful piece of cloth on me!
She's picked me up again!
Now I'm on my mum's lap.
Here comes my gran.
'Coochy, coochy, coo!' How soppy!
She's tickling me!
All this is tiring!
Is this supposed to be the best day of my life?

Alice: That is very good. I liked the way you, sort of, set it out ... I think it's very imaginative, the way you've set it out as a story.

Gerald: What do you think the strong point of it is?

Alice: Mm ... I would say the bit when she's putting the baby on the scales ... you know ... all the details you know ... how big he is.

Gerald: Yeah.

Alice: How horrible a nurse she is, and all that lot. I'd give it ten out of ten because it's very well thought out ... This is supposed to be a funny one. [She reads her poem.]

A Day of a Baby's Life

I wake up screaming
Nobody's coming.
By the time they do
I'm gasping and fuming.

Then my nappy is taken off
And someone shouts
'Oi, who's boofed?'
My breakfast is plonked in front of me,
So I felt sick and did a pee.

Then my mummy took me to the park,
I began to scream until I heard a bark
So I saw this doggy and took a walk
I played with it and had a little talk

Then my mummy took me home
I felt hungry and ate a bone.
I fell asleep on my mum's tum
I felt something funny
But I figured out it was on my mum.

I woke up and set on a bottle of
Lucozade, this was fun
But I wonder what tomorrow will be like
'I know, I'll go to the Himalayas on a hike'.

Alice: What do you think of that?

Gerald: I think it's very good and true to life like the baby and that, and what happens to it in its mum's lap.

Alice: Any strong points in it?

Gerald: Yeah, about the baby and the park and that.

Alice: I tried to make it rhyme and it was pretty difficult, but apart from that it was OK.
[They discuss possible improvements.]

Gerald: Put more emotion in it!

Alice: And my spelling! [Pause] Do you think it would be better
          if I added more onto it and made it more like a story?
Gerald: I think it's enough, actually ...

It is clear from this extract how involve the two pupils were in reading, listening and talking about their poems. Afterwards Alice wrote:

... We both read our poems and it was much easier than I thought to get him to comment on my poem, so I told him to write his comments on the back of my sheet which he felt happy with ... I have learned how much and far you can go with a poem.

After Gerald returned to the Grange Junior School he wrote:

This was our second visit to Ashby Road School and I felt it had a better atmosphere this time, then we went into a classroom and I read my poem out to my partner and she gave me ten points out of ten and I gave my partner's poem nine points out of ten. My partner's poem was very good. It was about a day in the life of a baby and it was very imaginative.

Nigel, from Daventry School, worked with Vay Dan Chang, a young Vietnamese boy whose command of spoken English was rather limited. Vay's replies to questions were usually brief, and Nigel was very concerned to help him:

Nigel: Now Vay, you did a poem for me, didn't you?
Vay: Yeah.
Nigel: Yes, on Tuesday, no Wednesday's lesson ... well, you
        started one so you could read it out.
Vay: Yes. [Reads]:

It's Christmas Day

Hip, Hip, Hooray,
It's Christmas.
I can't wait to open my presents.
My thoughts turn to go out and play with my friends
We play something
After we have our tea
We have turkey for tea
'Father Christmas', says my mum.
'Father Christmas will come and give you a present.'

Nigel: OK then. Now I'll read my poem out. [Nigel reads the first
        draft of his poem 'We moan if it's too sunny ...']

Vay: So I'll read yours and you can read mine, and if you think there's anything wrong just say so and I can change it.

Vay: There's nothing wrong with this and there's ... OK.

Nigel: OK? Are you sure? Are you sure?

Vay: Yes.

Nigel: OK. I think yours should be changed a little because you go on from 'Hip, Hip, Hooray/It's Christmas Day' and it's presents, and then you're going out to play and then you go in for your tea, and then you go straight to bed.

The thing you could do between the first and second verse is to put in something about your dinner, about pulling crackers or opening your presents, and finding nice little sort of cards and all that lot, and you can say about playing with your presents and doing that.

And between the second and third verse you could put put about watching the television and, you know, writing with some pencils or pens that you got for Christmas, OK? So, you can get on with that, I'll write that out again in the second thing, improve it a little bit, so that ... and then hopefully we'll read it again, and then we'll be able to ... you'll be able to put in on straight ... OK?

Vay: OK. [Nigel switches off tape recorder for ten minutes.]

Nigel: After about five or ten minutes me and Vay started on our second drafts and these are them:

Vay: I'll read mine out [reads]

Christmas Day

Hip, hip hooray,
It's Christmas.
I can't wait to open my presents
I got a bike and a satchel and a pencil
And a football and a ten pound ... a hundred pound.
I got changed and go out to play with my friend
We are playing snowballs, and other new games
And we make a snowman.
After we have out tea
We have a turkey, and pulling cracker
Then we have a pudding after our tea
I play with my new games,
Then after I watch the film.

Nigel: OK, right, er ... I'll read mine out and afterwards I'll discuss it again. [He reads his poem.]

We moan if it's too sunny,
We moan if it's too wet,

But we don't think of other
Countries that suffer.

Drought, malnutrition,
Earthquakes, floods, hurricanes.
Why need we send money,
When we need it here for
Hospitals and major operations?

Hearts, lungs, kidneys are needed,
Sending money elsewhere can
Cost people's lives.

So why need we send money abroad,
When we need money here?

Nigel: Now, what do you think of this, my poem? Do you think it's good?
Vay: No, I like the way, I thought ...
Nigel: Did you like the way I changed a few little bits of it?
Vay: Yes.
Nigel: You liked that bit? OK. So, well, I liked the way you made it ... much more spread out, you said about Christmas and you said what you got for Christmas, and you were playing games and you made a snowman, and you had your tea and pulled crackers and had your pudding, and you played new games. You've spread it out much more better, than in, you know, just put it in a couple of lines ... Yeah, really spread out. I thought that is OK now, OK. So get onto our display copy, OK?
[They started work on their display copies.]

Afterwards Nigel wrote that he'd found the session interesting:

Although my partner's poem was a little jumpy and needed to be improved a lot ... My partner understood me better this lesson than the last lesson because he knew me better.

We can see from the extract above that both Vay and Nigel were trying hard, and that though Vay's spoken English was limited, he was able to respond well to Nigel's comments, and alter his poem, obviously benefiting from the one-to-one situation. Vay was clearly learning how language is used from the discussions about poetry with Nigel. Katherine Perera has summed up the linguistic value of such activities succinctly:

Quite apart from all the humanistic reasons for pupils writing stories and poems, there are sound linguistic reasons, because the activity gives them the opportunity to experiment with language, trying out forms they would otherwise never use. Once mastered through writing, these structures are available for use in speech if the occasion demands it, thereby increasing the power and flexibility of the oral repertoire (1987, p. 31).

The extracts from the children's discussions and their diary entries show that many language skills were being used. As in the previous joint session, these activities would have hit several levels in all three of the main profile components, but particularly AT 1: Speaking and Listening, and AT 3: Writing. For example, the discussions of the pupils about the first and second drafts of their poems would have fulfilled En 1/3c, 4c and possibly 5b (i.e. discussion skills in a pair or group situation). The editing and redrafting of poems would have fulfilled (at least in part) En 3/3e: '... begin to revise and redraft in discussion with the teacher, other adults, or other children in the class, paying attention to meaning and clarity as well as checking for matters such as correct and consistent use of tenses and pronouns'; En 3/4e: '... discuss the organization of their own writing; revise and redraft the writing as appropriate, independently, in the light of that discussion'; and En 3/5d: '... assemble ideas on paper, or on a VDU, individually or in discussion with others, and show evidence of an ability to produce a draft from them and then to redraft and revise as necessary.' The *qualitative* difference between the strands describing editing and red-rafting is not altogether clear; however, all the children were participating in these activities, at different levels. In preparing display copies of their work (eventually destined for the book), most of the pupils would have hit En 4/3d: '... in revising and redrafting their writing, begin to check the accuracy of their spelling'. Most pupils would have hit AT 4/5: Presentation, levels 5a, b and c.

Final Workshop

The next joint session was held at the beginning of March, with Chris Challis and both groups of children together. The session was held in the Library at Daventry School, and lasted all morning. In the first half, Chris Challis read as many of the pupils' poems as he could and discussed them (he had been sent photocopies of the poems well before the session). Towards the end of the first half he produced another selection of photos which he talked about. Pupils worked in their pairs again, and helped each other to develop their ideas for the poems. The interactions and discussions between partners reflected their involvement in the task of writing poetry together.

For example, Nigel was very keen to help Vay get his poem started. Nigel had been inspired by the photo of country graveyard. Vay had liked the photo of a rugby game.

Nigel: A country graveyard that he described or had an old yew tree or all the old cobwebs. Now what are you going to do?

Vay: Rugby.

Nigel: Rugby. So you're going to do one about the rugby game. You ... OK ... I told you about a thesaurus, didn't I? You can look up words and you can find it and I brought my dictionary, it's a children's one and you might find some good describing words. In rugby you do have all these weird words: 'drive' and 'squeeze' and 'tackle', and all those words. [Looks in the dictionary]. I'm looking for the really ugly word in a graveyard like 'stench' ... you know, 'orphan'.

Vay: So I could start Monday I'm joining clubs, and Friday I start.

Nigel: Yeah [nodding]. The person you're going to write about has joined a club and then he's had his first game. I'm just going to a person that's in the grave that has these shovels and picks and axes that are just knocking down trees and digging up graves and putting in graves and all the crying and sobbing and all that. OK?

Nigel and Vay were able to communicate well, and afterwards Nigel wrote that 'my partner worked well, he was also very well behaved'. He was also struck by the fact that 'teachers can teach to two different ages of child in one class'.

Jimmy was one of the more voluble members of the Daventry School class. He and his junior partner, John, liked the photograph of the graveyard. John decided that he would write a poem about the vicar of the church attached to the graveyard while Jimmy chose a supernatural theme.

John: My poem is about the vicar ... constantly saying words about people he doesn't really know are true, like 'they're nice people', but he can't possibly be right all the time.

Jimmy: Doing out of foresight [?] because of his job.

John: Yeah.

Jimmy: What I'm doing is about a sort of zombie coming out of his grave, disturbing the still of the night.

John: [Looking at Jimmy's poem]. I like the describing words in it, like 'eyes hanging on' and that ... and the face ...

Jimmy: It's just holding itself together ... by sheer force. It doesn't really want to hold itself together, but it's got to, to live. [Looks at John's poem]. About another dead body ... It's all right saying things like that, these people getting married and they're nice and everything, and wish they're going to be happy. Probably doesn't really ... new job, bit of money in the pocket, use of the church, more money for the service and everything. And when people die he says 'He was a good man ...'

John: 'To all his fellow men'.

Jimmy: Yes most probably a load of rubbish. Probably meanest man in the whole of the village. His wife was a nice lady ... say ... Think of all the baptisms he does, these little brats that can't stop screaming ... Something else you could put in. All the warts all over him, and that, and completely sick and tired of it. Let's read it, then.

John: [Reads] 'I think I'm going to retire', he says.

Jimmy: [Reads] 'Another dead body', claims the vicar.
     'I'm sick and tired of repeating using words
     About people that can't possibly be true.
     People want hundreds of people
     To tramp ... attend services.'

John: No, it should be 'to attend services'. It was going to be ... I forgot the corrections in that part because it doesn't sound right. 'People want hundreds of people/The couple ...' or 'the widow wants ...' or ...

Jimmy: The widows, yes ... The widow, sobbing all the time, then ready to rush off with the next bloke that comes through the door; the milkman or the fisherman come to the door in their vests or whatever it is. What do you think the title will be?

John: 'The Fed-up Vicar' or something.

Jimmy: Yes, I think something like 'The Sick Vicar' or 'The Vicar'.

John: 'The Sick Vicar'.

Jimmy: Yeah. What kind of church will it be? A city church in the middle of the city, or ...

John: A quiet church.

Jimmy: ... or a quiet country church like on the photo?

John: Yeah.

What comes across is the enthusiasm of both boys, quite apart from Jimmy's cynical views about institutionalized religion and widows. They were able to help each other in discussing and improving their poems and afterwards Jimmy wrote that he thought his poem was 'The best poem I ever wrote!' His poem follows:

In the Still of the Night

In the still of the night
There were little sounds
In the graveyard.
The only sounds were
The hooting of an owl,
And the sound of a thrush
Bashing a snail against a
Gravestone.
But suddenly the still was
Shattered by a rustling and
A snapping.

Something was appearing from a grave
The thing was horrific
Its face looked as though it was melting
Its eyes hanging on by a thread
Its body was almost non-existent.
It was just straggly bits of flesh
Clinging on to the bones like a limpet.

The zombie dragged
Himself out of his grave
In the graves all around it
Other zombies started appearing
There were big zombies,
Little zombies and
Middle sized zombies
But they all had the same
Distinctive smell,
Rotting flesh.

All the birds and animals had fled
Even the thrush
Though he reluctantly left his supper,
The snail, behind.

The Zombies had appeared
They Were Ready To
TAKE OVER THE WORLD

Linda (from Daventry School) continued to work with her two partners
from the Grange Junior School, Nancy and Marie. Linda and Nancy had
been inspired by the photo of a graveyard; Marie used the photo of a
monument to some soldiers killed in the English Civil War as the starting
point for her poem. The following extract shows the lively, confident and
intelligent way in which the three girls were able to discuss their work:

Nancy: I've done a poem about a smiling one [reads]:
        'The faces that are disintegrating'.
        I couldn't think what's next, sort of . . . 'soon its time
        to go to bed'? which I don't know . . . I mean it is funny,
        but I didn't know whether to put that. It might sound a bit
        silly.
Linda: I've done a poem about a graveyard as well, but I've done
        it . . . I've gone about it in a different way. More serious
        about the graves being forgotten and remembered, so
        they're quite different really.
Nancy: I don't think this poem will all be, sort of, matched be-
        cause some bits, I think I'm going to do it differently.
        Marie, what poem (is) yours about?

Marie: It's about a monument. Written about the beginning of a ... goes like this [reads]:
'Got shining buckles and swords at the front
Belonging to very rich Lords ...'
          Then I'm describing the bits about the Cavaliers and the dead bodies, and horses and many of them carrying troubled plights ... and then the bloodshot bodies ... [laughs] ... and I'm going to carry on until they come to the monument.

Nancy: I've put two verses in my poem, but I don't know whether I'm just going to keep the first verse, because the second verse seems as if it's just been rhymed ... it's silly because the second verse goes:

As they get acquainted,
The faces that are disintegrated
Begin to smile.

Soon it's time to go to bed
This is the deads' bedtime ...

          ... which I don't really think because that, this is the dead's wake, which is a bit of a joke. When they get buried, they have a wake, don't they? So I don't really know whether to put the second verse.

Linda: Well, I think ... I don't ... I'd keep the first verse as it is, work on the second verse and if it doesn't turn out, then you can just keep the first verse.

Nancy: Yes, I might do that actually. It's Chris Challis ... *Dr.* Chris Challis said ... he said ... I mean you can say it all in about five lines, you don't have to go into great detail, though you can say it in seven pages or whatever.

The extracts from the transcripts show how the pupils were developing their sensitivity to poetic language, and the ways it affects the listener and the reader. Knowledge about language, awareness of the differences between spoken and written English, grew as a result of the project. The transcripts also show that most pupils were able to improve the first drafts of their poems, after discussing them with their partners. For example, after this session Linda wrote:

... The first hour was spent listening to Dr. Challis reading and commenting on some of the poems we had written. Dr. Challis read out my poem and I found what he said about it quite interesting. He also read one of my partner's poems out who turned quite a nice shade of pink.
    Then Dr. Challis showed us some photographs of a pop concert, a monument, a churchyard, a smithy and two others. Our task

Figure 7.1 'A Monument', by a pupil at Grange Junior School

was to write a poem about any of these pictures. We discussed our work with our partners and each produced our own poems ...

... Nancy wrote about the graveyard, Marie about the monument and I about the graveyard also. All our poems were very different. Then some people read their poems out.

At the very end I had to thank Chris Challis on behalf of everybody for coming. Mr. Tabor said a few words before me and said exactly what I was going to say, so very quickly I made something else up. I don't think anybody noticed!

I am really getting to know the two girls now and I enjoyed the session.

Marie (from the Grange Junior School) wrote:

When we got to Ashby Road (i.e. Daventry School) I was over-flowing with excitement. I said 'Hello' to Linda, then we all sat down to listen to Chris Challis while he read some of our poems out. I sincerely hoped he did not read mine. He read out Linda's and

Figure 7.2 'Gravestone Secrets', by a pupil at Daventry School

Nancy's, they both went red. Then he did a lot of talking, it was very interesting.

In break we all chatted together about Chris Challis, and the way he read the poems. After break we started on some poems. It was very disappointing that it was the last time. I did enjoy myself very much all the times we visited Ashby Road School. It was very exciting.

This sense of excitement and enjoyment was reflected in the work diaries of the other pupils. For example, Jane (from Daventry School) wrote:

... For the first half of the lesson Dr. Challis read out some poems from the Juniors and our English set. I was really surprised at the high standard of poems there were. Chris Challis read out my poem 'Swinging of Moods', he said that it described reaching the age of thirteen well, and he had enjoyed it.

He also read out my partner's poem. 'Third Born', all about her little brother. He said that in the nine lines it was written in, it said all about the good times and bad times of having a little brother ... I chose to write a poem about the churchyard because it looked so

Figure 7.3 'Swinging of Moods', by a pupil at Daventry School

pretty. We spent the last half hour writing our poems. During this project I have learnt a lot, and enjoyed working with the Grange Juniors.

The pupils gained greatly from this session, in terms of developing social skills, language skills, and stimulating their interest in poetry. The pupils' oral work would have hit several levels in ATs 1 and 3. For example, the discussions about each other's poems would have hit AT 1, levels 3c, 4c and 5b. The editing and redrafting that took place would have hit AT 3, levels 3e, 4e and 5d.

The session was observed by the Head of Daventry Teachers' Centre, as part of his independent evaluation of our curriculum continuity projects. Afterwards he wrote:

This session was a follow up to some recent poetry stimulus work that Dr. Chris Challis had done with this group. Pupils from both phases were present and Dr. Challis spent this session reading out a selection of the children's poetry which was a result of earlier work already referred to.

He totally captured the children's attention in the way he presented and analyzed their work. His choice of the children's poetry

was such that both groups of children were represented in his selection. His analysis was superb and his sensitive choice of language
was such that he made his comments in a way that was not seen as
talking down to the children, yet they were able to understand what
it was he was trying to convey. I am sure that the work which
followed this session, but which I was unable to stay and observe,
was of a very high standard and this way of working has a great deal
to recommend it.[3]

The writing of work diaries, and the completion of self-assessment
sheets after the sessions, were a valuable part of the project, since the pupils
were required to evaluate their own performance, as well as describing their
thoughts and feelings. The Kingman Report (1988) advocated self-assessment
because it is helpful for pupils' language development (2:28), and contributes
to the improvement of standards (5:12). Dorothy Heathcote also emphasized
the importance of increasing pupils' self-awareness:

> If you cannot increase reflective power in people, you might as well
> not teach, because reflection is the only thing in the long run that
> changes anybody ... Reflection is what makes the knowing some-
> thing that can be touched on and assimilated for later use (quoted in
> Howe 1988, p. 102).

The work diary entries quoted in this chapter will, it is hoped, have
demonstrated how the pupils benefited by reflecting on their experiences.
After the session described above, the pupils in each class completed their
display copies of the poems, and the two teachers made a selection for the
book. The PTA of the Grange Junior School donated £50 towards the cost of
producing the book.

In the summer term the Daventry School pupils organized a dramatized
presentation of some of their poems in small groups. These presentations
involved the use of costumes and music, as well as drama. The show lasted
about half an hour, and was compèred by two pupils. It was presented
to the residents of the local old people's home, at an assembly of pupils in
Year 7. This activity would have hit En 1/4d and En 1/5d, which describe
the group planning of a presentation.

By July the book of poems had been printed, and a final joint session
was held at Daventry School, with all the pupils and Chris Challis. The
Daventry School pupils staged the presentation of their poems for the
juniors, and then everyone received a copy of the book. It was a satisfying
end to the project.

The elements in the Programmes of Study for KS 2 and KS 3 which the project
covered were similar to those described in Chapter 3. The dramatized presentation of
the poems by the pupils from Daventry School would have fulfilled 'planning and
taking part in a group presentation' (etc.), thereby achieving En 1/6c (section 17; DES
1990a, p. 26).

Follow-up Interviews

Towards the end of that summer term, a number of pupils from the Grange Junior School were interviewed, to find out what they thought about the project. Most of the pupils admitted that they had felt nervous about going to Daventry School for the first time, and meeting their partners. However they had all enjoyed working with the older pupils and had gained much from the workshops with a practising poet, as the following transcript shows:

Teacher: What did you enjoy most about the project as a whole?

Nancy: I thought being with an older person, and experiencing working with an older child.

Gerald: I agree with Nancy, working out our poems together and getting our ideas.

Teacher: What did you think about the workshops with Chris Challis?

Nancy: I thought it was very interesting, only he didn't just speak like we were really small. He gave us his point of view, and that's what I found most interesting about it.

Gerald: Yeah, he did make us feel equal to him ... um ... I mean he progressed, he explained drafts and rough drafts to us ...

Marie: ... I thought he helped us a lot in learning how to write a poem and to draft it up, and I thought he was good.

Nancy: ... I liked the way he took the photos, I thought that was good. It gave you something to think about and also the way he thought ... he taught us how to get our poems, to get it to perfection.

Paul: ... I thought the pictures were helpful, they helped me a lot to do the poems because I had something to write about.

Marie: I thought Chris Challis helped us to choose the pictures by telling us the story to go with each one.

Teacher: Why did you like the story that was attached to each photograph?

Marie: Because I thought the story fitted well with the picture and I thought if you just left the picture there and told us to get on we'd have no idea what it was about.

Teacher: Very good ... Did you find working with your partners was helpful?

Nancy: I think it was another person's point of view, and it was someone else to help you ... like an older person, knowing different words. That's what helped with someone else older working with you ... they [the seniors] treated us as equals which helped us to a higher standard, really.

Teacher: How do you feel the project helped you with your English?

Nancy: I think ... to use some better words, because in most poems that I've written before I've used words like I'd use out in the playground, but we've actually got to know about new words instead of just saying, um, 'happy', we would say 'overwhelmed', and before I'd just have said 'happy' or something. And I think that's what happened.

Teacher: Where did you get the word 'overwhelmed' from?

Nancy: Well, when we were talking to Chris Challis or our partners, like if we just put 'happy' down, that's not really using emotion, and you've got to try some better words, really try and think, you know, think, and use dictionaries, and so that where instead of saying 'happy' you could say 'overwhelmed', and that's where I think I got it from, using better words.

Gerald: I liked it when he said 'Use more emotional and describing words', but it sounded as if it's more real to life when you read the poem out ...

Paul: Well, I've learned more about the poems, and I've learned more words to describe different things.

Marie: Well, I thought that as I was using more new words I would also be able to use the dictionaries and get other words, and the dictionaries helped me a lot, because I never usually use dictionaries for words.

Susan: ... I thought the best part [of the project] was when you actually saw your own poem being published, and I like the way they [the seniors] did the plays about the poems.

John: ... I thought he [Chris Challis] was great fun, and he had a good personality, and he was very friendly with everyone ... he wasn't snappy, and he always told you a lot about himself, which I liked ... My partner, Jimmy, was helpful. I read my poem out to him, and he told me a bit about it. He said 'It's good, but you've got to make it more understandable.' because I had it ... not like a poem, but just a dead-end thing and he helped me with that.

Martin: I gained a lot of confidence with Jane and she helped me a lot with my poems, and she told me what was right and wrong.

Teacher: Do you think there is a right and wrong with poems?

Martin: Yeah, you can change words about to make them more exciting, you know.

These extracts from the follow-up interviews indicate the range of benefits that pupils considered they had gained from the project. They all felt more confident about going to the comprehensive school in September, because they knew their way around, and had already got to know a few of the older pupils.

Their teacher, Mary Linden, made the following observations:

> ... The children found the project very valuable, both in terms of language development, and in a confidence-building exercise in their move to secondary education. The experience of working with older children was very enriching. In this project the most enjoyable part for the children was in having their work valued by their peers, the older pupils, and Dr. Chris Challis.
>
> ... I gained in experience in preparing such an event; I got to know the secondary school better, and some of my colleagues who work there.

In the first half of the following autumn term (1989) a survey was conducted among the pupils in Year 7 at Daventry William Parker school who had taken part in the curriculum continuity projects. The survey was intended to find out how, in retrospect, the pupils felt about the project, and how it had helped them to settle in. The replies showed that the pupils had enjoyed drafting and editing the poems, working with a practising poet, and seeing their poems published in a book. Their sensitivity to language had also been developed. For example, one pupil wrote: 'It helped me to use more adjectives'. All the pupils who completed the questionnaire wrote that the project had helped them to settle down at the new school, and feel more at home, because they already knew some of the older children.

This account of the project has been detailed, drawing at length on the written and spoken words of the pupils involved and concentrating on the opportunities that the project offered for oral work, and for editing and redrafting. As we have seen, a range of levels in the three main Attainment Targets were hit by the project. At the same time, liaison and curriculum continuity were developed. The work diary entries show how much the pupils had enjoyed the project. One hopes that they will remember it as among 'the best of times' from their years at school.

Notes

1 I am most grateful to Mary Linden for her help in the joint planning of this project, and for suggesting improvements to the earlier draft of this chapter. Thanks are also due to Terri Lifford (Headteacher, Grange Junior School) for her encouragement and support, and to the PTA of the Grange Junior School for financial help.

2 The last line of the poem is: 'The milkers lace their boots up at the farms.' From the transcript it would appear that the girls did not understand what this line describes.

3 I am grateful to John Follett, Head of Daventry Professional Development Centre, for his evaluation of this session.

Chapter 8

The Space Project

Introduction

The Space Project[1] was an ambitious attempt to combine a cross-curricular approach to the study of space (for the primary school pupils) with a series of workshops with science-fiction writer Ian Watson. The project involved Alison Gadsden's fourth set for English in Year 9 at Daventry School, working with Madeleine Warren's class of juniors, who were in Years 5 and 6 at Barby Primary School, one of our country primary schools. The primary school pupils were 10 and 11 years old; the Daventry School pupils were 13 and 14 years old.

The planning for the project took place in the middle of November 1988; Alison paid a half-day liaison visit to Barby, when the structure of the project, and the range of activities, were decided. Subsequently, any further planning took place over the telephone or after school. The range of activities was intended to stimulate and motivate both groups of pupils in their interest in space, through creative writing, art and design, as well as developing the social or personal links across the phase. Both groups of pupils worked in project folders; the Daventry School pupils kept work diaries, though the primary school pupils did not.

The joint activity for the first session was senior-junior pair work on a poem about space. When the Daventry School pupils were told about the project, and the activity planned for the first session, they were interested and intrigued. Jack (who lived in Barby) wrote:

> ... I am looking forward to tomorrow. I know most of the children and hope to enjoy myself working with them. Also I am fascinated about space, so there will be another fascinating thing in it. Overall I am pleased and looking forward to it.

Michael wrote:

> ... The work we are going to do which is poems are very good because I enjoy it and the subject Mrs. Gadsden has given us seems like it is going to be exciting ...

Jane wrote:

> ... I've heard what we are doing with the Barby School and it
> sounds very interesting. It is going to be a good challenge marking
> their work. It will be good to work with different age groups. Also,
> it will be a very good practice with the written work.

First Encounters

The next day the Barby pupils came to Daventry School with the poems
about space which they had already started. The pupils worked in pairs
(which the teachers had predetermined) on the poems. The younger children
had started to make 'Space mobiles' out of cardboard at their school, on
which they were going to attach the completed poems. This first activity was
both part of the project, and an 'ice-breaking' activity. The pupils responded
very well to each other, and were able to complete their poems within the
hour session. For example, Stella (Barby Primary School) worked with
Martin (Daventry School) and wrote the following poem:

The Moon, The Sun and the Comet

The sun went down
The moon came up
All the planets have
Come awake.

The sun shines bright,
In the afternoon light
The moon shines so bright
Like a brilliant light.

The comet shoots through the night
Its tail glittering with golden light
Shouts of wonder from the crowd below
As the sky lights up with a golden glow.

The language of the poem is simple but effective, and it also enabled the two
pupils to work together, and to get to know each other.

Paula (from Barby) worked with Jack, from Daventry School. Their
joint poem reflected their shared interest in aliens.

An Alien World

An Alien World is far ahead,
The stars are whizzing past
A journey to the alien world
Mars, I think, or past.
We are shooting through space
I'll hope we'll land soon

> What's this? I think we're landing
> Oh! We're on the moon.
>
> I think I'll look out of the window.
> Wow! We have come far.
> I'll press this little button
> and just step outside
> What's that, a green blob?
> I shall go and meet him.
> I shall take him back to earth
> Where all my friends will meet him.

Afterwards Jack wrote:

> ... I enjoyed working with the younger children. I worked with a
> girl called Paula Cook, whom I already knew, as I live in Barby too.
> We worked quite well together, but making and changing the
> second verse took us a long time, so we never got to finish the
> presented finished version, but I thought the poem was quite good.
> We both suggested ideas, and were happy with the chosen ideas, and
> overall it was enjoyable.

This enjoyment was reflected in the work diaries of other Daventry
School pupils. For example, Mary wrote:

> ... I found the lesson fun, I enjoyed it. First we read the poem
> which was very good, then we thought of some words to make up
> the second verse. Then we altered a few things in the first verse, and
> began on the second verse. We got on very well together, we talked
> about it, we improved it, and then wrote it out neat and she [Sarah]
> has just got to decorate it now.

Darren wrote:

> I think the project went pretty well on Wednesday. I worked with a
> boy called Peter Brown ... I thought his poem very good and had
> plenty of detail. He worked pretty well with me ... It was a pity
> that we weren't given a lot of time, and I would of liked to carry on
> with this work. It was exciting, interesting and enjoyable. I cannot
> wait till we meet next time and work together again.

The activity of this session satisfied AT 3: Writing, levels 3e, 4e, 5d and possibly
6d, where pupils have to revise and redraft their work through discussions with the
teacher, other adults or another pupil. The discussions between the pupils also
fulfilled several levels in AT 1: Speaking and Listening, e.g. level 4c: '... take part as
a speaker and listener in a group discussion or activity, commenting constructively on
what is being discussed or experienced.' The participation of the Daventry School
pupils in these discussions would also have hit AT 1: levels 5b, 6a, and possibly 7a.

The follow-up work for the Daventry School pupils was to design a space machine of some sort, with instructions for use to accompany it. They also had to devise questions on the machine for their primary school partners to answer. Their teacher felt that this was the most successful activity of the project for the older children. They demonstrated considerable imagination and artistic ability in inventing and designing their machines. The pupils had to write instruction manuals, describing the design and functions of the machines, how they worked, and the materials used.

Many pupils produced vocabulary lists (often including specialized technical words) to accompany their machines. The worksheets they devised on the machines tested the younger children's vocabulary skills through anagrams, questions, crosswords and word-searches. The machines were often ingenious, and some could be lethal. For example, Alan designed 'The Anti-Assault Protection Vehicle' for use in 'dangerous situations'. He described it as follows:

> ... The Army series: from titanium tyres, aluminium and titanium body; windows thickened perspex and darkened. Titanium is a bullet-proof metal but when heated it goes soft but flexible and still bullet-proof.
> *How It Works*: The computer; rapid fire guns on front; two types of missiles, heat-seeking and computer-guided missiles. Radar detracts approaching missiles, flares detract approaching heat-seeking missiles.

Mary had a more domestic approach, and her machine, called the 'Slip-in, Slip-out', was intended to be labour-saving and practical. She wrote:

> ... My machine is a washing machine, a tumble dry[er] and an iron all in one with piece in between that joins the washing machine and the tumble dryer together.
> ... Its use is to wash, dry and iron clothes automatically without you have[ing] to keep changing them from machine to machine, and then instead of you standing to iron them they will iron themselves ...

Other pupils looked into the future, and saw the possibility of a nuclear holocaust. For example, Michael designed a 'war tank', which would enable twelve people to survive the aftermath of such a war. Robotic hands, thick armour-plating and laser guns protected the survivors inside.

Jack was inspired by a computer game set in the future to design a futuristic police car, called the 'Techno-Cop 72'. He described the car as looking

> rather like a more streamlined Audi, with a spoiler and guns, and a big engine sticking out of the bonnet. It has five exhausts, as the engine is fast. It has a special aerial for picking up high frequencies,

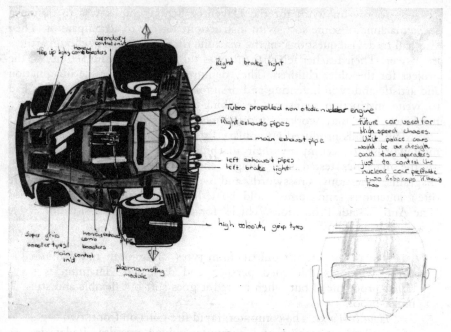

Figure 8.1 *'Techno-Cop 72', by a pupil at Daventry School*

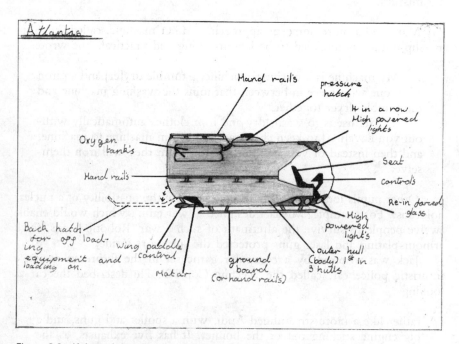

Figure 8.2 *'Atlantas', by a pupil at Daventry School*

and extra-thick tyres that cannot be worn as easily as normal tyres. The tires have steel grids, for less chance of smashing ... Machine guns are revealed when the number plate is opened, and can shoot out.

The body is made of a thick but light metal, which a grenade cannot penetrate. This is called 'Aluron', a cross between aluminium and iron.

Jack went into considerable detail, describing special features of the car, such as the tear gas gun, machine gun, tyres, compact radar, signal box, etc. This selection illustrates the range and variety of machines which the children invented.

The planning and designing of the space machine, with the accompanying written commentary, would have fulfilled AT 3: Writing, levels 4a, b and c, and possibly levels 5d, 6d and 7d (i.e. redrafting of a range of writing, including a description or report). The invention and use of technical terms reflected the pupils' awareness of language, and this would have hit En 3/5e: '... show in discussion the ability to recognise variations in vocabulary according to purpose, topic and audience and whether language is spoken or written, and use them appropriately in their writing.' (Examples include understanding the place of technical vocabulary; NCC 1989, p. 48).

In January 1989 the second joint session took place at Daventry School, when the Barby pupils were shown these designs by their Daventry School partners, and had to answer questions on them. The pupils enjoyed renewing the contact from the previous session, and working together again. The following conversation between Gaynor, from Daventry School, and Nina, from Barby Primary School, illustrates the sort of interactions that took place. Gaynor had explained what her machine was used for, and wanted to find out how much Nina had understood.

Gaynor:	We've been talking about my machine of the future. I call it the 'Revision Machine' ... Why did I call it the 'Revision Machine'?
Nina:	Because it helps you with ... to revise.
Gaynor:	Can you play games on it, yes or no, and why?
Nina:	No, you cannot play games on it because it hasn't got a place to put the pictures on.
Gaynor:	What is it made of, basically?
Nina:	A small computer.
Gaynor:	What do Revision Machines do?
Nina:	It helps you to revise things for exams.
Gaynor:	Why is it needed?
Nina:	[Pause] It is needed to help you with exams like GCSE ...
Gaynor:	What does it do if you get some questions wrong?
Nina:	It ... um ... it goes over and over again until you've learned it properly.

Afterwards Gaynor wrote that she'd found the work

... really interesting ... I think I have learnt quite a lot because we discussed our work ... When the time was up you had to give the pupil our puzzle, and we had to give them a piece of paper so they could start to design their own machine of the future.

This sort of discussion clearly fulfills En 1/4b: '... ask and respond to questions in a range of situations with increased confidence ...'

The other pupils also enjoyed the session. Afterwards Jack wrote:

... Again, I enjoyed the project, but much better than before. I worked with the same girl, and we worked a lot better than before, as there was more talking and helping going on. We only did the questions and half a drawing, so there was quite a bit of work left out, but I think we worked hard.

Mary reported:

This lesson was better than the last lesson because I had met my pupil once so I was a little more talkative with her, and she would talk to me, if she was finding something a little bit difficult she would ask for my help, or if she could not read a word or did not understand how to do something she would again ask for my help, but she only needed it two or three times. We got on with the work quite well and quite fast. She read the report very fast, and had no trouble reading it.

Then I gave her the word search. She found that very easy and the questions and anagrams she found easy. When we had done all the work, we copied out the poem and my invention. I have not quite finished her poem, and she has a little bit to do, but did not quite get it finished.

The writing of work diaries would have hit part of En 3/4b: '... produce other kinds of chronologically organized writing'. The Daventry School pupils also filled in self-assessment sheets after each session, and this would have hit En 3/4c: '... organize non-chronological writing for different purposes in orderly ways'. (Examples include recording in writing as aspect of learning; present information and express feelings in various forms; DES 1990a, p. 13).

In parallel with these activities, the Barby pupils were also engaged on a project about the planets. They used reference books to find the basic information, which they wrote up in their folders. Each pupil chose a planet to do a detailed mini-project on, as well as designing their own space vehicles. The language work connected with this part of the project included compiling a space glossary, doing a cloze test about aliens, and writing about the American space shuttle.

Thus the younger pupils were already developing their knowledge about language (anticipating En 3/5e), and using reference skills as described in En 2/5f: '... use appropriate information sources and reference books ...'

After the previous joint session, both classes prepared for the visit of science-fiction writer Ian Watson. Each pupil had to prepare a list of questions, which they would use when talking to the writer. The Daventry School pupils had also undertaken individual studies of a science fiction story. They discussed these texts and produced written reports on them.

These activities would have hit En 2/4b: '... demonstrate, in talking about a range of stories and poems which they have read, an ability to explore preferences', and part of En 3/5a: '... write in a variety of forms for a range of purposes and audiences, in ways which attempt to engage the interest of the reader.'

Ian Watson spent half a day at Daventry School at the beginning of February. During the first half of the session, he talked about science fiction and his writing, and he answered pupils' questions. In the second part of the morning he asked the pupils to choose three words at random from a dictionary, and use them to develop a science-fiction story. The pupils helped each other with their stories, working in cross-phase pairs. Ian Watson and the two teachers present circulated among the pupils. Most of the stories were completed after the workshop.

The session would have enabled the pupils to fulfill En 1/4b: '... ask and respond to questions in a range of situations with increased confidence'; En 1/4c: '... take part as speakers and listeners in a group discussion or activity, expressing a personal view and commenting constructively on what is being discussed or experienced'; and possibly part of En 1/5b: '... contribute to and respond constructively in discussion, including the development of ideas ...' Writing the science fiction stories would have hit several levels in AT 3, e.g. levels 3c and 4b.

The pupils found the workshop stimulating, as the diary entries by the Daventry School pupils showed. For example, Mary wrote:

> The science fiction writer Ian Watson came to school to talk to us about how to write science fiction stories, and told us things about himself, like how long he has been writing, why he started writing and how he started writing. Then we looked after our pupils at break-time, then went down to the library. We chose our words, then we wrote things that we would base on for our words, then began to write the story which we both did quite well.

Darren wrote:

> I was excited to meet Ian Watson, but when I did I didn't expect him to be as he was. I rather thought he would be a bit like Roald Dahl, but he wasn't at all. He gave us a talk which was very interesting. We then asked him some questions, then looked at some of his books and magazines, that he had brought with him. We went to the library after break and had a go at writing our own story.

Jack wrote:

> On Wednesday, an author by the name of Ian Watson came in to tell
> us about himself, how he writes his stories, and help us write our
> own story. The Barby children were there. Dennis and I worked
> with a Barby pupil called Alison, and we helped her start the story
> off. I thought it was good fun, and it was great talking to the author.

After the session the pupils continued working on their stories in class,
and each teacher made a selection of stories, which were sent to Ian Watson
for his comments.

A few weeks later the final joint session, with the writer and both
groups of children, was held at Daventry School. Ian Watson went through
the stories he had been sent, reading out extracts from them, and commenting in detail on them. In some cases he suggested how they might be
improved. Towards the end of the session the pupils again picked three
words at random from a dictionary and started writing another story. As
before the pupils worked in pairs, helping each other to start their stories.
Afterwards the pupils either revised or improved their first stories, or worked on the second one. As in the previous session, the discussions about first
drafts, and the redrafting that took place, would have hit AT 3: levels 3e, 4e
and 5d (the strands which describe the processes of editing and redrafting).

The session had been valuable and stimulating, and this was reflected in
the work diaries of the Daventry School pupils. Alan wrote:

> We wrote a story to send to Ian Watson. He came in to give us ideas,
> this was very good. He had some very good ideas that I hadn't
> thought of. We picked three words out of the dictionary and joined
> them together to get the story-line. I wrote my story, it was sup-
> posed to be the best we had ever done, but mine wasn't very good.

Jane wrote:

> I enjoy writing stories, I think I did better with Ian Watson's help.

Both groups of pupils completed their stories and turned them into
booklets. In March the pupils met again, and read each other's booklets, and
commented upon them. The opportunity to read each other's stories provided an enjoyable way of rounding off the project.

The project motivated both groups of pupils. It is only possible to give a
few extracts to illustrate the range of written work produced. The class of
Barby juniors was mixed ability; the Daventry School pupils were in the
lower ability range.

Jane, from Daventry School, wrote a story entitled 'Two Worlds',
which had an imaginative opening, describing how three children from an
alien world visited Earth two million years ago. The children got caught up

in a time-travel experiment from the year 4089 AD, and were transported to that time, and saw what the Earth looked like in the future. Jane started with a vivid, dramatic description, which set the stage for the development of the characters and their relationships:

Two Worlds

Two million years ago the planet Earth was empty but one dark and dusty night dark came upon the Earth, then suddenly lightning struck which brought flashes of light in the sky. Three people came out from a screen, they came on to land, they were asleep so they did not realize where they were.

Morning had arrived, the sun had risen but the sun had not reached the people because blocking their light was a machine; it was all made out of metal with one big button.

The one and only girl started to wake as she opened her eyes, she looked around, she was confused and looked puzzled. She patted the two boys on their backs and shouted 'Wake up, wake up'. The two boys stretched and yawned and opened their eyes. 'Where are we Harry?' said Bleg. Bleg was quite handsome boy with a bit of intelligence, not like Harry, he made no sense. Zara was quite a bossy girl.

Zara shouted 'I'm hungry! What can I've to eat? Bleg you said you've got the brains so tell me'. Bleg replied, 'This green stuff.' It was all over the ground.

Zara grabbed a handful, she described it as a long piece of green cloth with juice covering it. She tasted a bit, she thought it was nice.

After eating they started to explore the earth. They saw the machine, they looked at it but didn't touch it in case anything happened. It was sort of built into a point at the end so they decided to give it a name. 'Pointer'.

Night came, the stars started to glow and the sun had died down. All three of them just sat near to the machine in silence and deep thought of what the machine could possible be. Could it send you out of space? Would it be able to provide you with food? What? They had no ideas of what it could be, soon they began to get tired and soon they had drifted off to sleep . . .

An effective aspect of the story was the way Jane described something familiar (e.g. grass) from the aliens' point of view.

David was in the Daventry School class, and he had been highly stimulated by the project. He produced the first chapter of story about two children who came across a mad scientist who threatened to destroy mankind. The way David developed his storyline, and the wealth of descriptive detail, showed considerable imagination. The final version was produced on his computer at home.

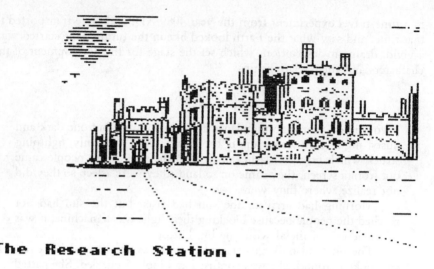

The Research Station .

Figure 8.3 *'The Research Station, illustration for 'The Beasts of Valhal' by a pupil at Daventry School*

The Beasts of Valhal

Chapter 1. The Beginning

He walked down the street past broken drains and windows. He stopped and stared at the once magnificent buildings which were once the pride of the nation. Many years ago this place was the centre of the future, many experiments were carried out here, but twice they ended in disaster. No one still living ever knew the nature of the experiments, the population were moved out of this area, which was sealed off after the second experiment ended in disaster.

Sam moved carefully towards the perimeter fence where he could see a large hole. On the other side poking out of a bush was the wheel of his motorbike, he was about to mount his bike when he saw a computer disc inside a clear box, he picked it up and read the words 'PROJECT VALHAL', putting the disk in his pocket, he started his bike and rode towards the new town.

When he reached the apartment building where he lived he got off his bike went to the outside lift and inserted his security card. The lift doors opened and Sam proceeded up to the seventh floor, he steped into his apartment through the lift doors and went straight to his computer consol. Sam inserted his computer card to gain access to the computer memory banks, he inserted the disc and typed in four numbers, the numbers which were on the disc. The words 'PROJECT VALHAL SECTION 2 CLASSIFIED INFORMA-TION' appeared on the screen.

Sam knew that his knowledge was insufficient to gain access to the program so he turned to his communications consul and punched in the co-ordinates of his close friend Sara, who had majored in computer studies at the town's universtiy. A small-faced girl with hazel eyes appeared on the screen, 'Hello Sam, I thought it was about time you called it's been very quiet around here. Where have you been lately?' Without any form of greeting Sam answered, 'Sara, get over here now I need your help, expect you in ten minutes,' and broke the connection.

Sam was still huddled over the computer when the lift doors opened to Sara who had her own pass card as she often used Sam's extensive computer equipment. 'What's the panic?' she exclaimed. 'Look at this I can't get into this program,' Sam replied. Without any more talk Sara slid into the seat and studied the display. 'OK Sam, make a big pot of coffee and let me get to work.' A hour or so and many cups later a cry of triumph came from the bowed head at the computer. 'I've broken in', Sara exclaimed. 'But I don't like what I'm seeing.'

Sam looked over her shoulder and saw a screen full of printing scrolling away, he punched in the printer and the machine started belching forth masses of printout. Sam grabbed the first page off the printer and started to read, his face turned white as the full horror of what he was reading dawned on his brain.

Chapter 2

Sam read with growing dread the printout which was coming from the printer.

Project Valhal

These are the last words of Dr. Ivan Streggoff the world may ever see. For many years I have been working on experiments with DNA and I have at last found ways of changing the structure of the human body whilst the body still lives, during the first few years of these experiments my colleagues and I encountered major problems, the human DNA structure did not respond to the chemicals which had been developed. The results of these experiments were deformed human monsters which were destroyed to prevent discovery by the world. After further lengthy experiments certain substances were discovered which led us to believe that we were on the right track, I tried these substances on myself and at first I was aware of increased mental alertness and increased physical prowess. Much later the changes became difficult to control. Mental and physical deterioration began, and I am devolving into a beast. I am dying as I write these words and I curse HUMAN KIND and all who is not as I.

I, Streggoff condemn the human race to suffer the same fate as me unless the human race can find two people who will risk their lives to prevent what I have set in motion, I have built a device that will release the compounds which are destroying me into the atmosphere on the first day of June 2010. In this computer program are three problems to solve at the complex failure of any one part will result in premature release of the DOOMSDAY DEVICE.

Solving the problems will result in further information being released and although I have made it easy for any one with computer knowledge to start this disc I have made sure that no one will be able to hack into this program any further.

If you wish to proceed enter your names now.————————

Sam and Sara looked at each other and back to the screen ...

Jack, one of the most talented pupils in the class, produced a poetic piece of prose, about a person in the future, who was changed into another life-form.

The Story With No Name

Once, at the beginning of time, they came to Earth. The sun's strength was running so low, they couldn't absorb any of the sun's heat, as their planet was too far away.

So they came and left because of man, he adventured and destroyed half of the population how is unknown. So they fled leaving their way of communication behind. It was a living plant, of which somehow, they could communicate to each other. They left it on the only suitable place for them on this planet, in tropical America, the Savannah.

Roxanne was a citizen member of Technocity in a time where computers ruled. But for some reason, her city was being bombed by something. With her telepathic powers, she tried to communicate but couldn't picture anything, though she was sure whatever it was, was trying to help her.

She had urges to stay out in a neutron bombing of something else. She thought it was them making her, but she knew what would happen.

Suddenly she felt anger and rage, she felt a bombing coming near, and her wristcom warned her, but she threw herself off the building. She felt herself being lifted into the sky, it was like a dream.

There was no city noise, no shouting, just beauty and grace.

The birds singing in the clear blue sky. All bizarreness had disappeared. Then, she felt herself being dropped.

She was in the most beautiful meadow. Red and pink roses, it was like a paradise to her. She looked into the middle and saw a different plant. She recognized it as a lady's bedstraw plant, and it was dying.

Paradise disappeared.

She was alone, on a plain. It was hot. The mud was burning her feet.

She felt the plant reaching nearer. They wanted her. She wanted to know who it was.

She knew exactly how to use it, but had no previous knowledge about it, as if it was in her blood.

Her head tingled and the plant pulled her nearer.

She heard a voice in a language she understood but had never heard before. She felt a warm reception as if her mother and father were there, but they were dead.

She turned around and there they were. They spoke their language, but didn't move to talk. That was their way.

'Come back with us, you are of our blood. We want you back, we need you to help.'

She couldn't feel herself think.

'You have gone through your stage, you are ready.'

Her skin started moving, fiercely she ripped off her clothes, her body split and she came out, changed. She was ready for the beginning, for this was the end of the beginning, and the beginning of the end is about to begin.

The pupils from Barby Primary School were also stimulated by the project. For example, Rosemarie wrote a story about herself, and her friend Gemma, going on an important space mission to the planet Squash. The story reflects some of the work they had done on space (e.g. the way both girls disappear into a Black Hole), and there is an echo of *Alice in Wonderland* in the cake labelled 'Eat Me'.

Donna (also from Barby) wrote a story about going on holiday to Japan in 1972, with her Daventry School partner, Tina. There they met three aliens, and visited their planet in flying saucer. The story didn't have any dialogue, but it was a sustained piece of writing, and Donna was able to develop her ideas and express them fluently.

The Alien World

It was February 1972 and I was in Japan for a holiday. It was very sunny and I felt quite hot. My new friend and I were out for a walk in the country. It was very quiet and the trees were rustling in the slight breeze. Suddenly a light started flashing in the bright blue sky. The big flashing light was coming nearer and we started running out

Planet Squash!

Me and my friend Gemma were excited, and ready to go on this important space mission to the planet squash. The space ship was called "SQUASH DISCOVERY II". We put our space suits on ready we carried our helmuts and walked to the ship. Our boots were heavy but we got used to it. When we were in the ship count down started "10,9,8,7,6,5,4,3,2,1 blast off" and we shot up like a fire ball. First of all I got confused with all the buttons but then I remembered. Two weeks had gone but we couldn't see planet ~~squash yet! then something came in sight it was squash~~

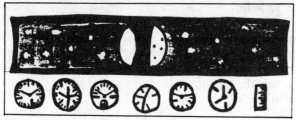

It looked a rather dull yellow planet but it was exciting we landed and got out of the ship with our helmets on and picked up rock from the ground for samples then the planet started shaking we laid on the floor and waited. When it had stopped shaking we stood up and instead of the planet being covered in rock and dust it was like a rain forest I ran to the ship to get my camera and took pictures of the trees and flowers. There was a lovely lake and lots of animals then BUMP! BUMP! there was a big hairy spider like a giant. I pulled gemma and we fell into the lake. After a few minutes all the fish and sea creatures started to hold on to us then we were sucked down a hole and we fell asleep. When we woke up Jewells were every where. I ran up to them but When I tried to touch them they disapeared then on the floor I saw a cake and on it it said "EAT ME." Gemma ran over and said "should we eat it? and I said "O.K" so we did.

We ate and ate until we were full. Then we fell asleep. When we woke up we were back in our space ship so I woke Gemma up and said "should we go back to earth." and Gemma said "Yes" so we did. On our way back we came across a black hole we tried to get away from it but it was to strong and our ship went flying. Soon our oxygen ran out and we could hardly breathe then we fainted and we were never seen again.

Figure 8.4 'Planet Squash!' by a pupil at Barby Primary School

of the country. All of a sudden we realized what the flashing light might have been. It might have been a flying saucer from another planet. We stood still and stared at it. It was a flying saucer and it was also very big and round. Then it landed on the floor. It was making ever such a lot of noise. We couldn't get away quick enough so we just hid behind a great big tree.

The door of the flying saucer flew open and a queer alien walked out followed by two more. They looked very ugly and mean but really they were very nice aliens. They were green and hairy with ten fingers on each hand and ten toes on each foot. Tina and I were very frightened but we just kept still. We watched for a few minutes and when I turned round to whisper something to her she was gone and when I looked back to see where the aliens were they were gone too. I was starting to panic when I felt myself disappearing. Then suddenly I found myself inside a kind of round thing which had lots of buttons and levers. Then I realized that I was inside the aliens' flying saucer and it was then I realized I was invisible.

Then I heard the door of the flying saucer open. The aliens walked in and they had Tina with them. Then all of a sudden my head was coming back and gradually my whole body appeared again. Tina saw me and she came up to me and stood by me. All of a sudden the three aliens started talking in very queer voices that neither myself or Tina could understand. Then they started pressing lots of buttons and pulling lots of levers and then the flying saucer flew into the sky. Tina and I didn't say anything we just stood in the corner of the flying saucer. After about five hours we landed on a kind of green planet with lots of green aliens on.

The door on the flying saucer opened and the aliens walked out onto the green planet. Then the door closed again. Then we thought that the only way to get to the earth was to make the flying saucer go back to where it took off. So we looked at all the buttons and levers and we slowly pressed and pulled a few. Then 'Whoosh' we flew off into space and then the next thing we knew was that we were back in the country standing right where the adventure first began.'

These five examples of pupils' work show the range of the stories that were produced as a result of the cross-phase workshops with Ian Watson. They would have fulfilled En 3/3a, b, c and e; En 3/4a, b and e; and part of En 3/5a: '... write in a variety of forms for a range of purposes and audiences, in ways which attempt to engage the interest of the reader'. The editing and redrafting which took place would have hit En 3/4e, and perhaps En 3/5d. The redrafting of the older pupils might also have hit En 3/6d and En 3/7d. Writing stories for the primary school pupils would have enabled the Daventry School pupils to fulfill En 3/6a, for which the example is: 'Write an illustrated story which is suitable for a younger reader' (DES 1990a, p. 14).

The care that both groups of pupils took with the accuracy and presentation of the final versions of their stories would have hit AT 4: Spelling, levels 3 and 4. All the

pupils were concerned with neatness i.e. AT 5: Handwriting, level 4; and A
Presentation, level 5a–c (5c does not apply to those pupils who typed their
versions on word processors).

It is clear from the diary entries quoted above that the Daventry School
pupils had enjoyed the project, and were stimulated by it. Workshops with
a practising writer had motivated most of the pupils, particularly as their
stories were written for a specific audience. As Allen (1987) has argued,
teachers should pay more attention to the process of writing, and

> ... from knowledge of how experienced writers behave, develop
> classroom practices which allow children to behave like real writers.
> This has to involve giving the children more responsibility, more
> control over what they write and how they write it. At the heart of
> being a good writer, an author, is having *authority* over what is
> produced (p. 24).

As with our other projects, the Space Project fulfilled many elements in the
Programmes of Study for ATs 1–3 at KS 2 and KS 3. For example, as part of AT 2,
the Daventry School pupils read a range of science fiction texts before Ian Watson's
visit. This would have been part of the variety of genres which pupils are expected to
read at KS 3 (section 14; DES 1990a, p. 31). The primary school pupils' projects on
space involved the use of reference books, and learning how to find information
(section 10; DES 1990a, p. 31) When the Daventry School pupils designed machines
of the future, they used (or invented) technical vocabularies, thereby developing their
knowledge about language (section 21; DES 1990a, p. 38).

Follow-up Interviews

Follow-up interviews were conducted with about half the primary school
pupils and their teacher in the following term to discover what they thought
about the project.

Initially the juniors had felt apprehensive about meeting and working
with older pupils. However, the majority had got on very well with their
partners and had enjoyed getting to know them. All the juniors said that the
project had made them feel more confident about going to the secondary
school, and more confident about their ability to cope with English there.
The pupils had also enjoyed the range of activities, such as joint work on the
space poems, designing machines of the future, meeting Ian Watson and
writing stories, the art work associated with the project, and pursuing their
individual projects on the planets. For example, Keith felt writing the stories
'helped me to imagine more' by using a wider range of vocabulary: '... It's
given me a wider area or view of working ...'

Tina felt she had learned

> ... about writing stories ... How to end stories and how to begin
> them, and what sort of things happen in the middle, and describing

137

things more ... Something new. My partner didn't give me a lot of help ... I got quite a lot off Ian Watson ...

Ruth felt that the project had helped her to become more interested in the presentation of her work. Peter got on very well with his Daventry School partner, who helped him a lot with his poem. Peter also felt he gained a lot from the workshops with Ian Watson: '... [he] helped me to think about stories ... I didn't really put a lot of thought into my stories, but I do now.'

Janice said, '... I like the idea of space ... and we've got a telescope at home. I've never looked through it. Doing the project made me ask my dad if I could look through it.'

Paula felt that the project had helped to improve her ability to write stories and the quality of her presentation:

> ... I think it's great how the teachers came up with such a fun project. It wasn't boring ... I found it helped me with my writing a lot ... it gave me more ideas, and I learned about the planets.

This short selection of extracts from the interviews is representative of how the pupils felt about the project, and the benefits they thought they had gained from it.

Their teacher also felt that her pupils had benefited greatly from the project, though they had been apprehensive to start with: '... going down on the coach on that first morning some of them were very white ...' After the initial ice-breaking activities, good relationships developed, and both groups of pupils helped each other successfully.

Their written English had also improved, particularly with punctuation and presentation, because the juniors had the older pupils to guide them. Ian Watson's talks had been excellent, though at times some of the juniors found him difficult to follow. However his suggestions about the structuring of stories (e.g. 'beginning, middle and ending') and other advice helped the pupils, though it took them a long time to produce their final drafts. Most of this work was done after the joint sessions, or for homework. The follow-up work in class had been mainly on the solar system, and the pupils were also encouraged to read a lot of science fiction. In general, the project gave the pupils responsibility and maturity, and made them feel important.

Their teacher thought she had gained professionally through planning the project with her Daventry School colleague, and through contact with the older pupils during the workshop sessions. She felt that this experience had stretched her, and that it had been stimulating.

The Daventry School teacher also felt that initially her class had been apprehensive about working with the juniors, because they were worried that their work wouldn't be up to standard. As a result, they made a big effort, and particularly enjoyed designing the space machines, with the accompanying instructions, as well as the worksheets for their partners to do. However the seniors were also motivated by the knowledge that Ian Watson would be commenting on their work. Ian Watson's reactions to their first drafts were very useful in helping the pupils to redraft their stories. He went round and talked to the pupils individually and the fact that they were writing for someone *other* than the teacher was very important. The pupils also took more care with the presentation of their final versions, and did not want to have any spelling or punctuation mistakes in their work. The pupils also gained in terms of developing their social skills. In general, the teacher felt that her class was not the easiest to motivate but the project kept them motivated for a whole term. At a professional level, she had enjoyed planning the project with her colleague at Barby Primary School, and the organization had gone very smoothly.

In the autum term of 1989, the survey we conducted among the new pupils in Year 7 confirmed the impressions recorded in the summer. The ex-Barby pupils felt that, in retrospect, the main benefits of the project had been in helping them with their writing, in learning to work with older pupils, and in getting to know something about the secondary school. All the pupils felt that the project had made settling into the new school easier because they already knew some of the older pupils and teachers. As we have seen, the project would have fulfilled a wide range of levels and strands in the Attainment Targets for English, and it offered several opportunities for cross-curricular work, particularly in the primary school. In addition, curriculum continuity in English, and liaison were developed between the two schools.

Note

1   We are most grateful to Ian Watson for his commitment to this project. I am grateful to Alison Gadsden and Madeleine Warren for allowing me to use their pupils' project folders, and for discussing the project with me in detail. They have read an earlier draft of this chapter, and I have incorporated their suggestions into the final version. I am also grateful to Joan Tapsell (Headteacher, Barby Primary School) for her support and encouragement.

Chapter 9

The Newspaper Project

... I've only to pick up a newspaper and I seem to see ghosts gliding between the lines (Henrik Ibsen, *Ghosts* (1881), Act 2).

Introduction

The Newspaper Project took place in the spring term of 1989. It was somewhat misnamed, because though the teachers concerned had intended that the pupils would produce joint newspapers, the majority of groups chose to make magazines. The project involved the second English set in Year 8 at Daventry School, taught by Sybil Herlihy, and Bob Cotter's class of juniors (in Years 5 and 6) at Welton Primary School. This is one of our smaller contributory schools, and is situated in the nearby village of Welton. The juniors were 10 to 11 years old; the Daventry School pupils were 12 to 13 years old.[1]

The initial planning for the project took place during a half-day liaison visit which Sybil Herlihy paid to Welton Primary School in November 1988. The dates for the first two joint sessions were arranged, as well as the groupings of pupils. There were nineteen juniors in the project, and they were divided into nine groups. As a result, some of the Welton Primary School pupils had more than one senior partner to work with.

The initial hope had been that the pupils would use the 'Newspa' computer programme on the Daventry School computer network. However, due to the numbers of children involved, and the rigidity of timetabling at Daventry School, this was not possible.

Getting Started

The first joint session took place in the middle of January 1989, in the library of Daventry School. The children had not been told anything about the project in advance, except that they would be working in groups with pupils from the other school. At the start of this session the pupils were given their brief by the two teachers, and allocated their partners and groups. To start with the children interviewed their partners (in pairs), and then went into their groups to decide on the type of newspaper or magazine they wanted to produce. The session was lively, and the pupils got on well together, though the majority of children from Welton Primary School were shy at first. At this first session the Daventry School pupils tended to dominate the decision making. Each group decided on the type of newspaper or magazine, and the individual tasks, so each pupil knew what he/she had to prepare for the next joint session.

Simon, Dennis and Linda (from Daventry School) worked with James and Lily (from Welton). After the session Simon wrote:

> ... We started to talk about what sort of project we should have in our newspaper. We decided it would be a children's newspaper, and we should write and draw pictures of our school. We decided what we were doing. Lily was the main person to do all the deciding. She and Linda decided on all the subjects we should do in the newspaper. James was quiet to start off with, but then settled in slowly. We got to know each other quite well at the end of the day.

Dennis wrote:

> We all agreed to do a newspaper about Welton School and Daventry School. We put things about e.g.:
> Jokes
> Plans of each school
> Writing about the schools
> Cooking
> Birthdays
> Questionnaires
> Interviews, etc.
> Then we talked about who was doing what, by then, time had passed very quickly, and it was time for them to go, it was 3.20 p.m. After they had gone our class talked about what we did, and what we are doing.

Lily (from Welton) had also enjoyed working in this group. On her self-assessment sheet she noted that she'd learned 'how to get on with boys' and she had clearly benefited from the contact with older pupils: 'I think it is very good to get other friends.'

Jenny, Stephen and David (from Daventry School) worked with Karen and Tim (from Welton). After the pupils had interviewed each other in pairs or threes, they got into their group. Afterwards, Jenny wrote:

> We decided to do a newspaper on 'ghosts'. So we talked about who was going to do what before we meet again in two weeks time.

> When we decided that they only had a few minutes left so we talked
> and argued a bit. They went at 3.20 p.m. to catch a bus ... I
> thought it [the session] was good, but I felt a bit shy at first, till I got
> to know the people we were working with ...

On her self-assessment sheet Jenny commented that she had learned 'how to
mix with strangers and find out about them ... It's good working with
younger people, as they learn from it.'

Karen (from Welton) had found the session interesting, though she had
wanted to do a newspaper on sport, especially riding, though she accepted
the group's decision. Afterwards she wrote '... I have learned a lot from my
partner [but] I would rather do riding than ghosts because they give me the
creeps!' By the end of the session it had been decided in this group that the
two Welton pupils would do the art work, and the Daventry School pupils
would research the stories about local ghosts.

The fact that most of the Welton pupils were shy at first, was understandable. Some of the Daventry School pupils were clearly aware of this,
and did not want the younger children simply to agree with them. For
example, Felicity, Diane and Martin from Daventry School worked with
Rachel and Mark from Welton. The children got on well together, though
Felicity felt the Daventry School pupils tended to dominate. Afterwards she
wrote:

> ... we all decided on a project called 'Rock Pop and Fashion'. The
> only problem we had was no-one wanted to do fashion, so we all
> decided to all do it. One other thing is they [i.e. the juniors] agreed
> with us, instead of disagreeing with us, which is what we want ... I
> was satisfied with my own work because we helped the younger
> children.

Rachel (from Welton) responded enthusiastically when filling in her self-
assessment sheet afterwards. She thought the project was 'good fun, educational', and her comments on the first session were 'good fun, easy, new
friends, brilliant'.

Whilst most of the children worked in groups of four or five, Philip
(from Daventry School) and Alice (from Welton) worked as a pair, without
becoming part of a larger group. Both felt awkward to start with. During
the initial pair interviews Philip felt that:

> [Alice] ... was quite shy to start with and I was conducting the
> conversation, which was quite taxing and annoying at the same time
> ... [When the teacher said that they were not going to join a larger
> group] ... I felt a bit left out. We then went off to a different part of
> the library and discussed the possible topics for the newspaper. Once
> again I felt that I was conducting the conversation to a certain extent.

Alice had also found the session difficult at times. Afterwards she wrote that the project was '. . . quite good, but I think I would like it better if my partner Philip liked horses. And I would think it better if he took more interest in Nature.' However she felt that she'd learned that 'boys are not so bad after all', and overall, she had been satisfied with the start of the project. Thus, the first session had enabled the pupils to meet in pairs and groups, and to make the initial decisions about the nature of their magazines or newspapers.

A great deal of oral work took place, which would have hit several levels in AT 1: Speaking and Listening. All the pupils would have met En 1/4c: '. . . take part as speakers and listeners in a group discussion or activity, expressing a personal view and commenting on what is being discussed', and possibly En 1/5b. The writing of work diaries would have fulfilled En 3/2b: '. . . structure sequences of real or imagined events coherently in chronological accounts'; part of En 3/4b: '. . . produce other kinds of chronologically organized writing'; and part of En 3/5a: '. . . write in a variety of forms for a range of purposes and audiences, in ways which attempt to engage the interest of the reader.' The completion of the self-assessment sheets would have also (in part) hit En 3/4c: '. . . organize non-chronological writing for different purposes in orderly ways'; the examples for this strand include 'present information and express feelings' (DES 1990a, p. 13). It will be apparent that the social benefits, in terms of the development of relationships, were also very important.

Work in Progress

The pupils had a fortnight to prepare materials for their magazines or newspapers, and at the beginning of February they met again in their 'editorial groups' at Daventry School for an hour. There was much lively discussion; pupils looked at the drafts of each other's work, and made further decisions about the contents of their magazine. For example, Dennis, Simon and Linda from Daventry School worked with James and Lily from Welton Primary School.

James: I'm doing a ghost story.
Dennis: You can do the writing first, then you can think of the heading, Yeah?
James: Yeah . . . what shall I . . . how shall I do the heading?
Dennis: Typing . . . I'm writing about Daventry School . . . I've done a plan, I've done about the future . . . um . . . I'll tell you what we're doing [other children giggle]. Doing jokes; about Welton School, Daventry School, puzzles, cooking, cartoon strips, problem page, star signs.
Lily: I'm doing that.
James: What page?
Lily: About fashion really, and the future.
Dennis: And the newspaper is called 'Weldav', half of Welton,

	half of Daventry [Schools] ... and Dennis ... in London.
Linda:	Dennis of 'The Express'!
Teacher:	Do you know what you're going back to do after today?
James:	Yeah ... look!
Teacher:	You could have another piece of paper and write it on a proper piece of paper. Do you ...?
Dennis:	It's doing all the things I've ... everything that is main in school like the library, that's the main thing ...
Teacher:	Do you know how it's going to look, your newspaper?
All:	No.
Teacher:	You ought to decide in the next ten minutes, because when you next meet you've got to actually put your things on a sheet or whatever. You've got to know ...
Dennis:	I know, we could use a piece of sugar paper.
Simon:	No, no, no.
Teacher:	You must decide on the size, come on ...
Dennis:	We're having a book, yeah, a book.
Teacher:	What size?
Dennis:	A ... 3, A3.
Teacher:	A4.
Dennis:	A3, A4.
James:	A4.
Teacher:	A3, folded in half.
Dennis:	Yeah ... Tell you what, we could put our thing together, put a card strip folded over, like that, like a book.
Teacher:	Will you write on the back of the pages?
Dennis:	Yes.
Teacher:	Have ... have you criticized each other's things?
Dennis:	Yes.
Teacher:	... Or are you just going to copy them out as they are, or are you going to read? ... I mean are ...
Dennis:	We're going to read everything.
Teacher:	If it's in a magazine, it's got to be in sections ... You've got to organize a contents page.
Dennis:	Yeah ... Linda's doing the contents page aren't you?
Linda:	Yes.
Dennis:	We've got it down here.
Teacher:	The other thing is ... every page must be full, so you must decide if somebody else's article goes at the bottom. [inaudible].
Dennis:	Right, we'll all ... I know what you could do [to James] ... that could go down there. I know what you could do, right, instead of that [i.e. puzzles] on that page, you could do it on here, so you can go, answers of all the puzzles of page ... number.

James:	I think we can do it all on page eight ... er ... three.
Dennis:	I think you can put all the answers on there, can't you?
James:	Yeah, all right.
Dennis:	So you can write ... just leave that.
James:	I'll have to Tipp-Ex that out.
Dennis:	You can put answers on page ... and put the page number there... so and so.
James:	We'll have to number the puzzles.

The pupils were helped and prompted by the teacher's intervention, but this extract shows how they had to talk through issues amongst themselves before reaching decisions about the format and content of their magazine.

Their oral work would have hit En 1/3c, 4b, 4c, and possibly 5b. These particular strands refer to group discussions, and asking and responding to questions.

Dennis took a dominant part in the discussion transcribed above. He also spent part of the time drawing a plan of Daventry School, and writing about it. Afterwards he wrote that he'd found the work of the session interesting, though by the end '... we ran out of ideas ...' Simon (also from Daventry School, and part of the same group) also found the work interesting, and felt that he'd learned how to work and communicate with younger children. Lily (from Welton) enjoyed working with the older pupils and reading their work. Afterwards she wrote: 'I am very satisfied with my work, and so is my group.'

'The Ghost Times' group continued to plan the contents of their magazine and to look at the first drafts of each other's work. David (from Daventry School) thought the session was 'interesting in the way the younger pupils had taken to it'. Karen and Tim (from Welton) were the younger members of this group. Karen wrote a funny story about ghosts for the magazine, and afterwards wrote that she'd found the work '... easy, but there are not much books to look in and I do not know much ghost tales.' Tim wrote 'I have learnt the difficulty of putting a newspaper together ... Some pieces [of my work] I was satisfied with, but others I thought I could do better.'

Seven out of the nine groups were working on pop or teenage magazines, with considerable enthusiasm. 'Rock, Pop and Fashion' was a typical mixture of articles, interviews, puzzles, etc. After this session, Felicity (from Daventry School) wrote:

First the Welton children came into one classroom and settled down whilst the teachers spoke to us. Then half of us went into another classroom, whilst the others stayed in the one everyone was in. We all discussed each other's work, and they picked out our faults. And we did the same. After that we carried on with our project. Before they went we made sure that we all knew what we was going to do. At least they made a comment on our work.

Alice (from Welton) and Philip (from Daventry School) found the second session much easier, and they were able to be more relaxed with each other. Afterwards Alice noted that the session had been '. . . great fun, and this time the time flew by very fast.' She thought it was enjoyable reviewing each other's work, and seeing what her partner had done during the preceeding fortnight. Alice also felt more confident 'This time I was not embarrassed but friendly', and she had learned that 'boys are good fun to do work with.' Her Daventry School partner, Philip, also felt that the work 'was easier now I know the person [i.e. Alice] better.'

Two more joint sessions were held — the third in the middle of March, and the fourth and final one at the beginning of May. The pattern of the sessions continued in the manner described above; the pupils reviewed and discussed each other's work (which had been prepared since the previous session), suggested how it could be improved, and planned what had to be done for the next session. The editing and redrafting which occurred would have hit En 3/3e, 4e and 5d. By the end of the fourth session all the magazines and newspapers had been completed.

The Conclusion of the Project

Seeing the finished product gave all the pupils considerable satisfaction. Ruth (from Welton, and part of the 'Flash Gazette' team) thought producing the magazine had been '. . . interesting to do, and at first I thought it looked like a long path.' Looking back at the project as a whole, she felt it was a '. . . good way of mixing older people, and a good work experience', and that she had learned '. . . what kind of things they do at the big school.'

Ellen, from Daventry School, was part of the 'Gazable' team. She wrote that the project had been '. . . very enjoyable but hard work.' One of her Welton partners in this group, Helen, wrote of the project: 'If it is as good at Daventry School as it was on this project, then I am glad I am going.'

The previous sessions had been recorded on video. At the end of the final session, after the pupils had completed their folders, and looked at each other's magazines, they watched the video of the project. This was an enjoyable way to round off the project.

The finished magazines were bright, colourful, and full of variety. The two most original ones were 'The Ghost Times' and 'The Dinosaur Times'. The former contained a number of stories about ghosts, e.g. the ghost which haunted Warden's Lodge (part of the old grammar school in Daventry), and stories about ghosts in Denmark, Australia and Germany. These articles were written by the Daventry School pupils, though the two pupils from Welton in the group contributed some funny stories about ghosts, and a legend. They also did some of the art work.

'The Dinosaur Times' was clearly the result of a lot of planning, and background research, and the finished magazine was very well presented. It had been produced by Dorian and Susan (from Daventry School), and Cynthia and Jeremy (from Welton). Language work was evident in the two 'prehistoric wordsearches', which tested the reader's knowledge of words such as 'carnivore', 'herbivore', 'fossils' and 'dinosaur', and anagrams that made the names of three dinosaurs. This was an example of how the project helped to develop the pupils' vocabulary and knowledge about language (e.g. En 3/5e). There were several pictures or short articles about dinosaurs and a questionnaire. An article about 'Plant Eaters', and a story about an explorer who discovered a dinosaur's egg in the jungle had been written by Cynthia, while Jeremy contributed several cartoons. The rest of the magazine had been written by the older pupils.

The group consisting of Dennis, Simon and Linda (from Daventry School) and James and Lily (from Welton) produced a magazine called 'All Sorts', which was appropriate in the circumstances. The girls had contributed lengthy 'teen' articles on beauty care, make-up and cooking. The pupils' original idea, for a joint newspaper called 'Weldav', was represented by several articles about the two schools, and an interview with the Headteacher of Welton Primary School, conducted by one of his pupils. There were also puzzles, cartoons and a horoscope. Thus while the magazine may have lacked a consistent style, it was colourful, with varied content.

Most of the groups had been influenced by the format and content of teenage magazines such as *Just Seventeen* or *Smash Hits*, and they were used by several groups as sources of ideas during the joint sessions.

'Flash Gazette', by Charlotte, Gillian and Susan (from Daventry School) and Ruth and Clare (from Welton), was typical of this genre. The magazine started with an article about the Lockerbie air disaster but the rest of the magazine had articles about Jason Donovan, the television series *Neighbours*, Michael Jackson, Kylie Minogue, hair care, teenage fashion, cartoons, etc. The magazine also contained an article about Helen Keller, and a section on horses, reflecting the different interests of the pupils. The other magazines conformed to a similar pattern. They were all very colourful and attractively produced, reflecting the enthusiasm and commitment of the pupils involved.

In terms of Attainment Targets, it is clear that oral work (AT 1) was very important. However the preparatory and follow-up work between sessions also involved Attainment Targets 2 and 3. For example, the use of reference materials (particularly by pupils working on 'The Dinosaur Times' and 'The Ghost Times') would have hit part of En 2/3f: '. . . use appropriate information sources and reference books'; and levels 4d and 5d (which also describe the use of reference materials, etc.). Surprisingly, there is no mention of responses to media texts (which the pupils were using, e.g. magazines) before level 5.

Most of the pupils were involved in the writing of stories and other articles, and editing and redrafting. These activities would have hit En 3/3a-e, En 3/4a-d, and En 3/5a, b and d. In addition, the care taken with accuracy and presentation would have hit AT 4: Spelling, levels 1–3; AT 5: Handwriting, levels 1–3; and AT 4/5: Presentation (e.g. levels 6d and 7d).

The project contributed to the pupils' awareness of the media, and the nature of magazines, though the emphasis was on creative work, rather than analysis. However, the pupils were drawing on and refining their knowledge of different types of magazines, when they came to make choices about their own. Implicitly the children were learning about genre and audience, and the use of appropriate styles. The project could have been part of a Primary or Lower School programme of media studies. The range of activities involved in the project, helped '. . . to widen the range of children's understanding and use of language, and to develop their skills in it' (Cox Report, section 9.4).

The project gave the pupils extended opportunities to experience many elements in the Programmes of Study for AT 1 at KS 2 and KS 3. Planning the newspaper/ magazine would have included 'assignments where specific outcomes are required'; and 'taking part in shared writing activities'. The role-play, as members of an editorial team, would have fulfilled in part the element describing 'role-play, simulations and group drama' (section 8; DES 1990a, p. 25). The older pupils often took a leading part in these discussions; at KS 3 they are expected to take a more responsible role in group work (section 18; DES 1990a, p. 26).

Reading teenage magazines, and taking ideas from them, involved the study and use of media texts (AT 2: sections 17 and 18; DES 1990a, p. 32). Pupils edited and redrafted stories for their magazines at KS 2 and KS 3 (DES 1990a, pp. 37–39), and experimented with layout, and combinations of text and illustrations (section 18; DES 1990a, p. 37).

Follow-up Interviews and Survey

Towards the end of the summer term of 1989, follow-up interviews were conducted with eleven of the pupils at Welton Primary School, drawn from Years 5 and 6. While they had felt nervous before meeting their partners at the start of the project, they had all got on well with the Daventry School pupils. They had enjoyed group work on a newspaper/magazine, as this had been a new activity. The project had involved quite a lot of follow-up work, usually in their own time. A few representative examples will illustrate how the pupils felt about the project: Robert said:

> I liked doing it with the other school . . . you could do what subject you liked . . . I have a choice . . . Our group decided what the newspaper was about ['Graffitti'], and then I decided what I was going to do.

Cynthia said:

> I liked it each week when we decided what we would do then. We didn't do actual work in their classroom, we talked about what work we were doing away from the classroom . . . I did writing about the herbivore cycle . . .

The other children interviewed also said that they had enjoyed taking part in group decisions about their magazine, deciding what their individual contribution would be and looking at each other's work. Some of the pupils enjoyed doing the research for their articles. The social aspect of the project had been very important; all the children felt they had learned how to get on with older pupils, and this had given them greater self-confidence.

This was particularly important for the juniors in Year 6, who were going to Daventry School in the following September. Most felt happier about making the transition, because they already knew their way around the comprehensive school, and the older pupils had been friendly. For example. Nigel admitted that he was still nervous about going to Daventry School, but as a result of the project he felt:

> ... a lot better, because I was worried about that I would find people I wouldn't know, and wouldn't like, and they wouldn't like me, but now I can go there and feel all right.

Helen said:

> Well, I feel better because you've seen the school; we've been there quite a bit, so you know some people there already.

In the first half of the autumn term of 1989 we conducted a survey among the pupils in Year 7 who had participated in the curriculum continuity projects in 1988–89. The returns from the ex-Welton pupils showed how much they felt they had benefited from the project. All of them wrote that they had enjoyed working in a group with older children, planning a newspaper and writing articles for it. A number of pupils also felt their English had improved as a result. For example, Alice felt it had helped her to write 'more creatively'. Karen wrote 'I read a lot more and could spell better.' Robert felt that he had learned 'what it was like to write an article for a newspaper.'

Looking back on the project, the pupils could see how it had helped to make transition easier. For example, Rachel wrote: 'It made me feel happy about coming to Daventry School', and the project '... made it easier because I [had] worked with different children in a school I was going to.' A number of children wrote that the project made them feel more confident because they already knew a few pupils, and could find their way around. Alice wrote that the project '... made me more excited about coming', and settling in at the secondary school was easier 'because everyone was very kind and helpful towards me'. Eleanor wrote that the project had made her excited at the prospect of going to the secondary school: '... I was looking forward to it.' Robert wrote that the project had made him feel 'more confident' about coming to the new school. These examples are typical of the ways the pupils evaluated the benefits of the project.

Their teacher, Bob Cotter, had been interviewed at the end of the summer term of 1989. He felt that the project had benefited his pupils in several ways. First, in terms of liaison, because the project had given the children some familiarity with the new school, and introduced them to secondary education there. Secondly, the work had been varied and interesting. It had given the pupils a lot of preparatory work to do between sessions, and they had spent a lot of their own time on it, both at school and at home. Thirdly, the self-evaluation sheets (used by both classes after each session) had been a valuable new activity. Each joint session was followed by a discussion in class. Filling in the self-assessment sheets afterwards made the pupils think about how they had behaved, and what they had achieved.

Bob Cotter felt the work had been testing and varied, but his main reservation was that the older children tended to dominate the decision-making in the early stages. As a result most of the magazines had a 'pop' format, and this largely determined the sorts of activities that took place in the subsequent sessions. The younger children were a little overawed to start with, but as time went on they became more assertive with the Daventry School pupils.

The project fitted in with the spring term's scheme of work, which included a unit on newspapers. But the project was still an 'extra', largely because of the extra time required to bus the children to and from Daventry School. Bob Cotter felt such a project would fit in with the demands of the National Curriculum, but the main problem was the pressure or demands from other subject areas. However many of levels 1–3 in the three main Attainment Targets for English were met by the project, as well as several levels in some of the other subjects.

From the point of view of a small country primary school there were also organizational problems. His class contained pupils in Years 4, 5 and 6, and alternative arrangements had to be made for the pupils in Year 4 during the visits to Daventry School. The rigidity of the comprehensive school timetable was also a restriction. He wanted to do a similar project again, but time, and the demands of other subjects in the National Curriculum, would have to be taken into account.

Sybil Herlihy, the Daventry School teacher, felt that her pupils had gained many benefits from the project. The main disappointment was that the original idea of group newspapers was not realized and that the pupils were not able to use 'Newspa'. Sybil Herlihy wrote:

> We had agreed at our first meeting not to impose our ideas, after the initial input. In the event all, except one group, opted to produce magazines rather than newspapers. These tended to be lively, but fairly repetitive.

On the positive side there had been:

> ... much delight in the process ...
>   ... After initial shyness on the part of the juniors, and dominance in decision-making from the second years [i.e. pupils in Year 8], the groups settled to amicable discussions on equal terms.
>   Most of the children put in a great deal of time and effort, and all responded well to others' comment and criticism, and were eager to share their experiences. Lots of enthusiastic involvement in both

planning and execution. Cross-phase friendship and mutual respect was evident — most gratifying!

Note

1 I am grateful to Sybil Herlihy and Bob Cotter for allowing me to use their pupils' project folders, and for commenting on an earlier draft of this chapter.

Chapter 10

The Drama Project: Fear and Suspense

It should be noted that children at play are not playing about; their games should be seen as their most serious-minded activity (Montaigne, *Essays*, XXIII).

Introduction

The Drama Project took place in the first half of the summer term of 1989, and involved David Williams' low ability English set in Year 8 at Daventry School, working with Neil Richards' class of juniors from Years 5 and 6 at Falconer's Hill Junior School (the adjacent junior school). Some of the juniors in Year 6 had participated in 'Poetry in the Making' and several of the other pupils in Year 5 had taken part in the story-writing project during the previous academic year. Thus many of the junior school pupils had already been involved in a project with older children. The juniors were 9 to 11 years old; the Daventry School pupils were 12 to 13 years old.[1]

The planning for drama project took place during three short visits paid by David Williams to Falconer's Hill, when it was decided that the project would be drama-based, that the theme would be 'fear and suspense', and that the children would be expected to write and produce their own plays for performance (to the other children) at the end of the project. In total, sixty children took part in the project. The teachers did not want to dictate how the project would develop in terms of content, but rather to provide an initial idea, and an overall structure, with which the pupils could work.

The project extended over six weeks, with weekly joint sessions, either at Falconer's Hill Junior School, or in the hall or drama studio of Daventry School. In describing the progress of the project, the work of a few groups of pupils will be examined in detail, to show the opportunities for oral work, writing and performance that occurred.

First Encounters

The first session took place in the middle of April at Falconer's Hill Junior School, when the pupils from both schools met for the first time. The teachers explained the scope of the project, and told the pupils who their partners were.

Meeting new pupils (particularly if they were of the opposite sex) could be the source of a lot of anxiety. Diane, from Daventry School, was typical of a number of older pupils who felt self-conscious about meeting her partner for the first time. After the first session, Diane wrote:

> ... As we all walked into the hall I glanced around the hall, wondering who I was going to pair up with. Then we sat down on a bench, and we were face to face with the other children, still trying to figure out whether I was more nervous than excited. Then a boy had to stand up, and his partner from my school. My heart went out to the boy, and then my name was called out. I was shocked, I had to stand up and walk to the end of the aisle, and stand by my partner. We were both embarrassed because people were laughing at us. I didn't feel as embarrassed when I saw other people were getting paired up with people of the opposite sex.
>
> Soon everyone was matched up, and then my partner had to choose another friend [to make up the group], and he chose a boy. We then were told what rooms to go in, and we were to go to the classroom. I didn't know where to go, so I just tagged along.
>
> We reached the classroom and sat down, and began to fill in a sheet. Then we exchanged sheets and I learnt their names are Mark and Gerald.

One of Diane's partners, Mark (from Falconer's Hill Junior School) wrote:

> ... I went down to the hall to meet our partner. I got picked out first. I felt scared. When I met her we came back to the classroom. We filled in a sheet, her name was Diane ... we are writing a story on fear.

Feeling scared was an emotion also shared by older pupils. Thus Deirdre (from Daventry School) felt 'a bit scared' at the prospect of meeting her two junior partners, Luke and Robert. However, the three pupils were able to discuss ideas for their play, and by the end of the session, Deirdre wrote that she '... felt much better when my best friend told me Luke Taylor was her brother'.

Each child had to fill in a personal questionnaire about him/herself, and swap it with his/her partner, so that they could learn about each other. As part of the 'ice-breaking' activities, each pupil wrote three paragraphs about his/her experiences of fear, suspense and excitement, and relief (when tension or suspense was relaxed). The pupils shared these experiences with their partners and then in groups started to discuss what sort of play they wanted to write. The session was successful, and by the end most groups had reached a decision about their play.

Jill, from Daventry School, worked with Peter and Martin from Falconer's Hill. Afterwards she wrote:

> ... When we got into the reading room we started filling in the questionnaire. The first thing I said was yes, I have got 56 pets, because Peter didn't believe me. After that we got talking and discussing ideas for the play. We decided that we would have a haunted hotel and ghosts in it. I said who I would like to give worms and things like that to eat. I then thought of Michael Jackson so that's why he's in our play as the main character.

Peter clearly enjoyed meeting and working with an older pupil once he had overcome his initial anxieties. He wrote:

> I expected to have a very stupid person. But I got a bright girl (trust me!). We went to the reading library. I was really scared. Her name was Jill Butler. She came from Berkshire. Jill was a good laugh. She has got 56 tropical fish.

Developing Ideas

The five following sessions occurred at weekly intervals, on Wednesday afternoons, because this was when the Daventry School pupils had English and the juniors were able to do the project. The second session also took place at Falconer's Hill Junior School, and it was clear that the pupils had overcome the embarrassment and shyness of their first meeting. The pupils were very involved in discussing and planning their plays, and the two teachers circulated among the groups, providing help and encouragement.

The success of the session was reflected in the pupils' work diaries. Peter (from Falconer's Hill, and a member of Jill's group) enjoyed the session, and afterwards he wrote:

> ... Yesterday the seniors came over again to do some more on fear with us. I was not as scared as last time. But we wrote half the script and acted it out in rough a couple of times, it turned out very good. I play a butler, a ghost and a cook. Martin plays Michael Jackson looking for his great-grandfather's will.

Christopher, from Daventry School, was an ex-pupil of Falconer's Hill, and he worked with two junior school girls, Kate and Paula. He felt that his group had worked productively on their play, which was about two professors who discovered some beautiful cave paintings — and the caveman who had painted them! Christopher wrote:

> We sat down and started to talk about what we were going to do. We started to do the first scene and Kate dominated that scene, and we started to talk about the props and so on, and Paula was a professor with Kate, and I was the silent caveman that turned nasty and started on them. After, we all went on with good work, and enjoyed ourselves thoroughly.

Gordon, from Falconer's Hill, was pleased with the way his group had worked. He wrote:

> ... We met with our partners, I was looking forward to seeing my partner. We went into the library. We had to write a kind of scary situation, and then mix our ideas together. We wrote who played who, and where the scene is. I really enjoyed it. I am looking forward to the next time we meet again. Our title was 'The Midnight Caller', it is about a man who keeps phoning up and giving threats.

The oral work generated by the first two sessions (and the succeeding ones), would have met several levels in AT 1: Speaking and Listening. For example, the juniors would have met En 1/2a: 'participate as speakers and listeners in a group engaged in a given task'; En 1/2b: '... describe an event, real or imagined, to the teacher or another pupil'; and En 1/3a: '... relate real or imaginary events in a connected narrative which conveys meaning to a group of pupils, the teacher or another known adult.' The involvement of all the pupils in planning the plays would have fulfilled En 1/4c: '... take part as speakers and listeners in a group discussion or activity, expressing a personal view and commenting constructively on what is being discussed or experienced.' The older pupils would have hit En 1/5d and En 1/6c, which include the planning and organization of a group presentation. The writing of plays which took place as a result of the group discussions would have hit several levels and strands in AT 3: Writing.

The majority of plays were about ghosts and hauntings, though other themes were also used. For example, there were several murder mysteries, a bank raid, a play dealing with animal rights, and a play about boxing called 'Bruno's Revenge'. As well as writing the scripts the children were planning their stage sets, props, costumes, sound effects, and other requirements for a successful production.

Work in Progress

The following week, when the third session took place, most groups were finishing off, or revising their scripts, and starting to rehearse the entire play. The groups of pupils had 'gelled' and the children were working well together.

Gordon, from Falconer's Hill, planned out the stage-set of his group's murder mystery, and the children rehearsed their play. In his work diary, Gordon sketched out the set, and labelled it. He wrote:

> ... We met our partners for the 3rd time. We now had to do our play. We got our stage stuff: blocks, benches and chairs. We were filmed ... our play is a scary play. I am the baby and a girl, and Philip Andrews is my dad and the killer.

At this stage the groups were discussing their scripts, revising and improving them, and thinking ahead about the performance. Andrea, Joanne and Sally from Falconer's Hill Junior School, worked with Daniel and Simon, from Daventry School. Their play was about a bank raid carried out by two robbers. In the following transcript, the children discussed the beginning of the play, and the sound effects (created by a drum and cymbal) needed to make the performance more dramatic, as the robbers burst in. Each child was writing a copy of the script, as the discussion proceeded.[2]

Joanne: First there's the drum and cymbal going off.

Andrea: First there's a drum [to Daniel] and then you come in, and the drum goes off.

Daniel: Yeah.

Joanne: Drum, cymbal, drum.

Daniel: We say 'everybody down', yeah?

Andrea: [To Joanne] Write 'drum, cymbal, drum', so we know what instruments ...

Joanne: No, just put 'Everybody down!'

Daniel: 'Everybody down', then you say ... 'they walked over to the cashiers.'

Joanne: Drums, cymbal, drum... what else do we need? ... Drums, cymbal, ... do we want the bongos?

Andrea: No, just put that for now ... [to Daniel] Right, what are you going to say?

Joanne: [Interrupts and reading the script.]
'It was a quiet Saturday night, where we join Charlene and Catherine cashing up in Barclays Bank in Northampton. Catherine went to lock up. Two guys burst through the door and said.'.. and when they burst through the door it's drum, cymbal, drum. [To Daniel] What do you say again?

Daniel: 'Everybody down!' You could say 'they walk over to the cash desk.'

Joanne: They walk over to the cash desk.

Daniel: 'Everybody down!' Yeah ... 'or else we'll shoot'. [All the pupils write this down.] You could say 'they walked over to the cashiers and fill their bag-ba-ba-ba-bags' [the girls laugh].

Simon:	No, 'put money in the bags quick' [the pupils write].
Joanne:	Walked over ... to the cashier [writing].
Daniel:	'Cashier' will do.
Joanne:	Yeah, I know, Cashiers.
Sally:	Everybody then has to do this?
Simon:	Yeah, they do, then they know what they're doing.
Joanne:	Then what do you say?
Simon:	'Fill the bags up and quick'.
Joanne:	'Fill 'em and quick'.
Simon:	Yeah, 'fill 'em and quick'.
Andrea:	No, put 'fill the bags and quick'.
Joanne:	No, 'fill 'em and quick'. No ...
Simon:	Yeah, it sounds really neat.
Joanne:	'Fill 'em quick!'.

This transcript shows how involved the pupils were in working out their ideas together, and how they were concerned about the language that was used in the script.

The editing and redrafting which took place would have hit several levels of AT 3: Writing, as the extract quoted above illustrates. For example, En 3/3e: '... begin to revise and redraft in discussion with the teacher, other adults, or other children in the class' and En 3/4e: '... discuss the organization of their own writing; revise and redraft the writing as appropriate, independently, in the light of that discussion.' Some of the pupils would also have hit En 3/5d, 6d and 7d (which also refer to editing and redrafting).

Sensitivity to the effect of words when spoken was shown (for example) by Simon when he said 'Yeah, it sounds really neat' to Joanne's suggestion for an alteration to the script. Awareness of the differences between spoken and written English, even it not explicitly expressed, was developed as the pupils worked on their scripts and planned the performances. As a result they would have hit, at least in part, En 3/5e: '... show in discussion the ability to recognize and choose variations in vocabulary appropriate to purpose, topic and audience and according to whether language is spoken or written.'

After the session described above, Andrea (from Falconer's Hill) wrote:

> ... We started to work on our script. Joanne and myself were cashiers called Catherine and Charlene. Daniel and Simon were the badies called Bill and Ben. We were going to do a play for the radio, but we didn't, we are now going to do a play [for performance] instead.

Simon (from Daventry School) was also pleased with the work of this group. He wrote:

> On this day we decided to work in a group of five. We thought of more ideas, and I came up with the title 'Trapped in the Bank'. We all decided on that, and we started to write the script. After that we started to act a little out.

This is the final script that the group produced (with minor spelling and punctuation corrections):

Trapped in the Bank

Cast:	Sally — Narrator	Daniel — Bill
	Andrea — Catherine	Simon — Ben
	Joanne — Charlene	

Part 1

Narrator:	It was a quiet Saturday night where we join Charlene and Catherine cashing up in Barclays Bank in Northampton. Catherine went to lock up. (Drum, Cymbal, Drum.) Two guys burst through the door.
Chatherine ⎤ Charlene ⎦	Ah!
Bill:	Down, else we'll shoot.
Narrator:	The cashiers froze and did nothing. They walked over to the cashiers.
Ben:	Fill these up and quick.
Bill:	Come on, hurry up, go a bit faster.
Narrator:	They fired the gun three times. (Drum, Drum, Drum)
Catherine ⎤ Charlene ⎦	Ahhh (Cymbal back up.)
Narrator:	By this time the police had surrounded the building, there the story begins.

Part 2, The Building

Bill:	Cops.
Ben:	What?
Bill:	I said the cops are here.
Ben:	What, the cops?
Bill:	Yes, you daft fool.
Ben:	We'll have to take them hostage.
Bill:	OK that sounds good, we've got nothing to lose.
Ben:	Right, sit down over there at the back of the room. NOW!
Narrator:	Once again they fired the gun but this time out of the window.

Part 3, Going Upstairs

Bill:	Right, let's get some card and string. Write out 'Hostages'.

Ben:	I'll take them upstairs onto the roof.
Charlene:	Help! Help! Help!
Bill:	Take her downstairs and shut her up.
Ben:	You get downstairs with the other girl.
Catherine:	(In a frightened voice.) OK.
Ben:	Sit down over there again.
Catherine:	I'm frightened.
Charlene:	So am I.
Catherine:	I hope this don't go on for much longer.
Charlene:	If only we could get to the window.
Catherine:	I've got a plan.
Charlene:	What is it? Right, go.
Catherine:	OK I'll tell you.
Bill:	Wow, what's going on?
Catherine:	Hiyah! Quick, get out of the window.
Charlene:	Hhh ...! (the girls escape).
Catherine:	Phew, that's over!
	(The police catch the robbers.)
Narrator:	But when they got to prison they didn't stay there long because they escaped. So look out for them or it might be you in that frightening and scary position one day.

The script is simple, but it was the result of considerable group work, and it gave the pupils the opportunity to develop their own talents later in performance.[3]

Preparing for Performance

By the fourth session most groups felt under pressure, because they had a week, or a fortnight at the most, to get their plays ready for performance. Deirdre, from Daventry School, worked with her group on a supernatural play called 'The Whistling Wood'. After the fourth session she wrote:

> ... We started to think about how we was going to set our play out. I wrote down the script but we didn't read it, we learned it off by heart. We finished going through it, acting it out, not in front of everybody, though next week we have to rehearse.

Christopher (from Daventry School) rehearsed outside with his partners, Paula and Kate (from Falconer's Hill). The girls played two professors who were transported into another dimension, where they met a caveman. The transcript shows how the pupils worked through part of the script, discussing their movements and delivery.[4] The play starts when the girls have just entered the cave. Kate and Paula read from their scripts.

Kate:	'I'm extremely tired.'
Paula:	'What have you done, what have you done?'
	[Christopher whistles, because in the play one girl accidently presses an alarm concealed in a cave.]
Christopher:	Go on, drop to the floor, drop to the floor, holding your ears.
Paula:	Oh!
Christopher:	You've got to, you've got to, right. Then when you hear me die you can get back up, go out of the cave, and then you sort of try to explore all round there [points].
Paula:	I'll get my thing [turns page in her folder] where it says what we've got to do. [To Kate] Turn over the other page where ...
Kate:	Your one ... Oh yeah, right.
Paula:	OK. Great! [Girls walk off, to start next scene.]
Christopher:	Right, so you start to explore outside the cave, right? 'Where are we?' [The girls look around.] You've got to say 'Where are we?' You turn and see a strange plant on the floor. Act as if you're in a different dimension. [Points to a large advertising balloon over Daventry.] Pretend that balloon is a dinosaur and you go, 'Oh my God!' You're in a different dimension, act like it [inaudible]. Go round and try to explore [pointing] — All right?
	[Christopher moves away; the girls start to walk, reading the script with Christopher watching].
Paula:	'Where are we?'
Kate:	'I don't know.'
Paula:	'Well, you got us into this mess.'
Christopher:	Aagh! [Waves arms up in air, intending to imitate a pterodactyl. Girls laugh and continue.]
Kate:	'What's that noise?'
Christopher:	[Makes dinosaur noises.] Come on go back round here [pointing as if to a cave.]

Afterwards Christopher wrote:

... We got to work straight away, and started to rehearse outside. It was going along quite well, Paula and Kate are very good actors. Mr. Richards [from Falconer's Hill] recorded us outside [on video] and we are looking forward to presenting our play on 23rd May in the Drama Studio.

The oral work involved in planning and rehearsing the performance (as this extract shows) would have met several Levels in AT 1: Speaking and Listening. For example, rehearsing the girls' movements and delivery would have hit En 1/3d: '...

give, and receive and follow accurately, precise instructions when pursuing a task individually or as a member of a group'; En 1/4c: '... take part as speakers and listeners in a group discussion or activity ...' etc. and En 1/5d: '... contribute to the planning of, and participate in, a group presentation'; and possibly En 1/6c, which also describes the planning and presentation of a group performance.

Preparing for Performance

The fifth session took place in the dance and drama studio of Daventry School, and the pupils were under considerable pressure to get their plays ready for the final session, when they would have to perform their work. However, a couple of groups were able to present their plays at the end of this (fifth) session.

Hannah (from Daventry School) was a member of one group which acted its play out. Their play was about a haunted house in a wood, and the performance went quite well. Afterwards Hannah wrote:

> As I am going on holiday next week we had to perform ours. So our group asked if we could do ours this week, and we did. We got our props and really got stuck in, it was exciting. Next we were ready to be filmed, we all had butterflies in our stomachs.
>
> We started, we all stumbled on a few words but it was not really bad. But when the ghost appeared to me he was meant to say 'I am a ghost and I will haunt you', but he did not say that. He forgot to say that so I said it for him. It sounded stupid, but I think it went quite well overall. I really enjoyed myself, it was exciting and also nerve-racking. We [also] watched Jeffrey's group, that was really good.

Christopher (from Daventry School] radiated his customary enthusiasm. His group spent the first half of the session in the drama studio rehearsing and then with the other pupils, they watched two of the plays. He wrote:

> ... We arrived at the Drama Hall ready to start rehearsing, and we set out some blocks and mats, and got our scenes ready and started. We were finished pretty soon and we went to the props store and found some wigs. None suited the caveman and we could not see what was there for the professors, so we went through it again, but was stopped because some people wanted to film theirs so they did.
>
> We liked the play, it was about a boy who knows there's a ghost in the house, but no-one believes him. And another play went on when a boy and two girls break into a school, and they look at where they used to have their classroom. The school is haunted, what will happen to them? But afterwards, we went away knowing that next week will be the filming time for us.'

Final Session

The sixth and final session of the project took place in the drama studio of Daventry School at the end of May. All the remaining groups acted out their plays, or played the recordings they had made. The session was highly successful, and enjoyed by all those present. A few diary entries illustrate how the pupils responded.

Jill (from Daventry School), had written a play about Michael Jackson with her junior school partners, Peter and Martin. Flexibility was required, because one of the group was absent. Jill described the session thus:

> ... Today we met in the drama studio for the last time that we will be working on the play. Martin again was away as he has meningitis, and is in hospital. So instead of John we had James doing Martin's part as Michael Jackson. We rehearsed the play for the last time, and for the first, last and only time for James.
>
> We didn't bother with costumes as it would have been hard for James to dress up as Michael Jackson. It was soon time to act out the play in front of the audience and also be filmed.
>
> I felt like I did the first day, meeting Peter and Martin. Yes, again I felt really embarrassed, but this time more than before. The play did go wrong in a few places, but it didn't show as it did work out alright in the end, and I think that James was clever being able to learn the script so quickly as he had less than an hour to learn the whole thing, including the words, actions, and where and when to come in.
>
> All in all, I think I got on well with all four of the people I worked with. Everything went well and I enjoyed myself, as I hope everyone did.

Diane's group acted their play 'Lost in the Ghost House'. Afterwards she wrote:

> As the other groups were performing their plays, and they were very good, it was very nerve-racking to think that we were to perform next in front of the other groups, and what would they think? Although the play could have been better, but nothing or nobody was perfect. I enjoyed the project on the whole, and I especially enjoyed mixing with the young children.

Christopher (from Daventry School) had been looking forward to acting in his group's play with Paula and Kate (from Falconer's Hill). After their performance he wrote:

> ... We went through our play and the girls acted excellently, and then we were well rewarded by the cheerful claps at the end. The best thing was when I had to dress up in a dragon uniform and fur

coat, and all the running around doing different people and things. I thoroughly enjoyed it, and I hope that we can do something like this again.

The plays were all filmed, and three weeks later a party was held in the drama studio for all the pupils involved. The video was shown, and light refreshments were provided. Pupils were able to renew the friendships with members of their group, and share in the enjoyment of their plays. Afterwards Deirdre (from Daventry School) wrote:

> ... I think my performance and play were very good, because it had scary things in, and I like scary things in plays or films ... I think the visits to the Juniors were terrific. I thought it was ace, I'd like to go again.

The performances would have met En 1/4d: '... participate in a presentation', and possibly En 1/5d and En 1/6d as well. All the pupils kept work diaries, in which they recorded their feelings about the project, and assessed the progress they had made. These diaries and the revised play scripts, would have hit several levels and strands in AT 3: Writing. For example, the writing of the work diaries would have hit part of En 3/4b: '... produce other kinds of chronologically organized writing' (other than stories). The scripts, with their colloquial dialogue, would have met part of En 3/5c: '... demonstrate increased effectiveness in the use of Standard English (except in contexts where non-standard forms are needed for literary purposes) and show an increasing differentiation between speech and writing'. (Examples: 'Understand that non-standard forms for literary purposes might be required in a dialogue, in a story or a playscript ...' DES 1990a, p. 13). The writing of some of the scripts would have hit En 3/7b: '... produce well-structured pieces of writing, some of which handle more demanding subject matter; punctuate their writing so that meaning and structure are clear to the reader.' (Examples: 'Devise a news broadcast of topical interest or develop a playscript from an improvisation. Go beyond first hand experience.' DES 1990a, p. 14). In fact, most of the strands in AT 3: levels 1–5 would have been met by the writing that was generated by the project.

This account of the project has focused primarily on the process, whereby the pupils from two schools worked together in small groups. Neelands (1984) has described the value of this sort of approach:

> The purpose of process-centred learning is to enable children to discover, *for themselves*, new meanings — not to inculcate tired, well-worn meanings as is the case in content-centred education (p. 4).

The playscripts which were produced were not great literature; rather they provided a skeleton or framework which enabled pupils to develop their ideas, and their dramatic talents, through performance.

The project gave the pupils many opportunities to experience the elements described in the Programmes of Study for AT 1 and AT 3 at KS 2 and KS 3. For example, the project enabled the pupils to 'work with or devise an increasing range of drama scripts, taking on a variety of dramatic roles' (section 6; DES 1990a, p. 24); 'allow pupils to work in groups of various size', and 'enable pupils to talk with wider audiences' (section 7; DES 1990a, p. 25). At KS 3, a strong contribution to 'planning and taking part in a group presentation' is considered to fulfill En 1/6c. The editing and redrafting of scripts took place at both KS 2 and KS 3 (DES 1990a, pp. 36–39). Discussions of the scripts as they were being written and revised, and consideration of their likely effects in performance, heightened pupils' awareness of the differences between written and spoken language at KS 3 (AT 3: section 28; DES 1990a, p. 40).

Follow-up Interviews

Follow-up interviews were conducted with fourteen pupils from Falconer's Hill, and the teachers involved in the project, at the end of the summer term of 1989. The pupils were from Years 5 and 6, and they all admitted they had felt very nervous when first told about the project by their teacher. Many had been anxious at the prospect of meeting their partners for the first time, but all enjoyed working with the older pupils. A few children felt that the older pupils had been bossy, and tried to dominate, but in most cases decisions about the plays had been reached by the whole group. A few typical examples illustrate how the children felt. Sally said, 'We all put some ideas together, and decided what we were going to do ... We was all involved in making the decision.' Jane said,

> Well, I was sitting down, we was all writing things, ideas. I said, 'Why don't we do "The Haunted Courtyard"'? So we all started doing it, and we was arguing over which bit we was going to do and that, so we then ... David writ one bit, I writ the other, and Sally writ the other ...[5]

Sally said,

> Simon [from Daventry School] kept making all these noises, and then Mark goes, 'Why don't you, why don't we do a hold-up in a bank or something?' It was funny trying to act it all out, because you didn't know where to go next, but it was enjoyable. We writ the script, then we acted it out. We decided what we were going to write together. Stella gave most of the ideas.

James felt that he had not been fully involved in the initial decision-making. He explained,

> Oh well, Richard Chambers [from Daventry School] just said, 'We're doing something, a radio play', and we all had to agree on it. We done a script, right, in a group. When we done the group [discussion] we got it all written down, we practised it out a lot, we didn't do any sounds [special effects] and after that we all agreed on

it, we had to, then we all practised it out, and I kept getting it all wrong. I kept saying 'loomstick' instead of 'broomstick' ... I laughed.

The pupils felt that they had learned a lot about drama, and that they had become more confident about performing in front of others. Working with the seniors had enabled them to learn how to work with older children, and how to reach decisions in a group. For example, Paula felt that she had learned how to compromise, through accepting other people's ideas and reaching an agreement, and not just having everything her own way. A number of pupils said they had learned how to give and take in the group situation. Several had enjoyed the process of writing the play, and learning their lines. Most of the pupils said the project made them feel more confident about going to Daventry School and that they were looking forward to doing drama there.

Neil Richards, who taught the pupils at Falconer's Hill, felt the project had benefited his class in several ways. He was impressed with the freedom that the project had given to the children, and the creative use they had made of that freedom, to produce some very good drama work. Once the project had been set up, the children were excited and enthusiastic about it and the two teachers were virtually superfluous. One result of the project was that the children developed a great interest in drama. They often volunteered to do an improvisation in small groups, which they showed to the rest of the class. The pupils gained a lot of confidence ... Neil Richards said,

> They can say what they feel, and they know that they're going to be listened to, and they can express themselves clearly. They can decide what their work will be.

Creative writing also improved as a result of the project. Through working on a script with others, the pupils became more aware of how to follow the threads of story, and make it more complete. Most of them learned that a story or play should have a beginning, a middle and an end:

> ... They've come to this themselves very much so, because they see others finishing things properly, so they think 'we will', it's a knock-on effect ... The creative writing is one aspect of the work they do in school, and so is the drama, it all helps with ... Whether they're describing a science project or talking about what happens in PE. I'm very pleased with the project.

This positive appraisal was echoed by David Williams, of Daventry School, though he felt the pre-planning would have been better if it had taken place in one extended session, rather than three short liaison visits. The allocation of pupils into pairs and groups was made on the basis of pupils' social attributes and how they would complement their partners and other group members. For example, a pupil with a forceful personality might be placed with a child who needed encouragement. Similarly, a bright child, who was capable of responding quickly to a drama stimulus, would be placed with a weaker child. The pairing was usually boy-girl, across the primary-secondary divide, so that the children would be drawn out, and gain more confidence.

The main benefit was a sense of social integration, which was especially evident during rehearsals: David Williams said

> It would be foolish to think there was a great artistic achievement at the end, but there was a very enjoyable sense of enterprise, and a sense of achievement for many of the children, who are surprisingly self-critical.

David Williams felt that the project suggested further possibilities, in terms of what could be achieved in a more extended period of time. He was impressed by Neil Richards' enthusiasm and energy, which gave the younger pupils the confidence to start working with the Daventry School children. The older pupils had not shown much social unity previously, but during the project they learned to apply 'admirable self-control and maturity in their partnership with the juniors'. Working with the juniors provided an excellent stimulus, and the spin-offs were improvements in oral work, and in all forms of writing.

Clearly, the pupils gained greatly in terms of relationships, increased self-confidence, and the development of language skills. These benefits were aptly summarized by McGregor *et al.* (1977), in the context of a general discussion about the value of drama:

> ... Drama revolves around social interaction. Through drama the child can explore his actual social relationships at a real level, and an unlimited number of hypothetical roles and attitudes vicariously, he may experience a growth in self-confidence both in his ability to formulate and challenge ideas and in communicating and exposing his views to others. Through experiencing other people's drama he may find out more of their perceptions and interpretations of the world (p. 24).

The Cox Report (1989) highlighted the importance of drama at both primary and secondary levels. In the primary school it is central '... in developing all aspects of English ...' especially practising varieties of language in different situations; helping children to make sense of different situations or points of view through role play, helping children to evaluate choice or dilemmas, and accustoming children to take account of audience and purpose in planning a play (Section 8.5). Thus drama '... is not simply a subject, but also — more importantly — a method; it is both a creative art form in its own right and also a learning tool ...' (Section 8.6; repeated in slightly different words in Sections 8.14).

At the secondary level drama was considered important '... as a means of developing and broadening pupils' verbal communication skills ...' (Section 8.10), and it could help pupils to experiment with a wide variety of language styles (Section 8.11), especially through role-play (Section 8.12). The joint-school approach described above, working across the primary-secondary divide, met many of the recommendations made in the Cox Report for drama. At the same time, continuity and liaison between the two schools were strengthened, and a powerful stimulus was provided for the development of language skills.

Notes

1   I am grateful to David Williams and Neil Richards for allowing me to use their pupils' project folders, and for reading the first draft of this chapter, and commenting on it. I have corrected the spelling and punctuation of childrens' work used in this chapter. I am also most grateful to Colin Hughes-Rowland (Headteacher, Falconer's Hill Junior School) for his support and encouragement.

2   I am grateful to Michael Jones for help in checking the accuracy of this transcript.

3   Two of the other scripts will be found in Appendix 3.

4   I am grateful to Christian Hirons for help in checking the accuracy of this transcript.

5   For many local children, 'writ' is used as the past tense of 'write' in everyday spoken English.

Chapter 11

'New–Forged Bond': An Example of 'Horizontal' Continuity and Liaison

---

What's in a name? that which we call a rose
By any other name would smell as sweet.
(Shakespeare: *Romeo and Juliet*)

Introduction

The reorganization of education within Daventry was a traumatic experience for everyone concerned. The proposal was first made in the autumn term of 1986, when a Section 12 notice was issued by the Secretary of State for Education. Though the majority of townsfolk, teachers, parents and pupils were opposed to the change, the final decision to go ahead was taken by the LEA in December 1987, with the support of Mr. Baker. The three 11–18 comprehensive schools in Daventry were to close in July 1989. In September 1989 the Grange Comprehensive School would reopen as a 16–19 Tertiary College, and its pupils would be absorbed into the two remaining secondary schools. These would be transformed into enlarged 11–16 comprehensives. The rhetoric of reorganization was that all three institutions coming into existence in September 1989 would be 'new', and that 'old thinking' would be inapplicable to the reorganized structures.

During the spring, summer and autumn terms of 1988 the teachers at the three comprehensive schools in Daventry had to decide which of the new institutions they wanted to join. Reapplication for one's old job (though at the 'new' institution), or an application for a post at one of the other institutions, was a stressful process. The situation was particularly demoralizing for staff at the Grange Comprehensive School, many of whom had been there since it opened in 1978. Those that chose to go to the 'new' Daventry School or Southbrook School, felt that they were, on the whole, being expected to 'fit in' to pre-existing structures.

There was some upward movement, and a number of staff obtained promoted posts at the new institutions, but others were disappointed. As always, there were winners and losers. A few older staff, who had been at Daventry School for many years, chose to leave or take early retirement. By

December 1988 virtually all the appointments at the new institutions (to take effect from September 1989) had been made.

The pupils in Years 8 and 9 at the Grange Comprehensive School in September 1988 had to decide whether they wanted to transfer to Daventry School or Southbrook School in the following year.[1] This chapter describes a poetry project involving selected pupils in Year 9 at Daventry School and the Grange Comprehensive School, who chose to go to the 'new' Daventry William Parker School in 1989/90. The project was intended to stimulate their interest in poetry, and to help the integration of new pupils; it also provides an example of 'horizontal' continuity and liaison.

Reorganization: The Background to the Project in 1988/89

Towards the end of the Easter term of 1988, pupils in Years 8 and 9 at the Grange Comprehensive School visited Daventry School and Southbrook School, to enable them to make a decision about which school they wanted to transfer to. By the spring term of 1989, these pupils had decided, and they had to fill in a form, 'Your New School', giving personal details about their families, best friends, hobbies and interests etc. The form was sent to the pastoral staff at the school of their choice, and it helped in sorting pupils into new tutor groups for the next academic year.

At Daventry School, the pupils in Year 8, who would be moving into Year 9, were put into eight tutor groups; the pupils in Year 9, moving into Year 10, were put into ten new tutor groups. Staff at the Grange Comprehensive School suggested which tutor groups their pupils should be put into, so that friendships would be maintained. At Daventry School this information was used as the 'core' around which the new tutor groups for Years 9 and 10 were constructed. The approach used was similar to that employed for drawing up tutor group lists in Year 7 (see Chapter 1).

Activities were planned to help the integration of new pupils in September 1989. Two consecutive 'Industry Days' were held in April, for pupils who would be together in Year 10, in the next academic year. Pupils worked in their new tutor groups, with their tutors, on a range of tasks, and local industry was involved. Two 'Problem Solving' Days were also organized for the new tutor groups in Year 9. These activities were highly successful, and greatly enjoyed by the pupils.[2] In the summer term, two afternoon discos were held for the pupils. These opportunities for the pupils to work together, and to meet socially, undoubtedly contributed much to the smooth start of the academic year in September 1989 at the new school.

As part of the rhetoric of the 'new' institutions that were about to be created, the two surviving schools decided to change their names. Southbrook School changed its name to Danetre School, and a new logo was designed (Danetre was the old name for Daventry). After much consultation, Daventry School changed its name to Daventry William Parker School. William Parker was the local benefactor who founded the Grammar School in Daventry 400 years ago. The new name showed our continuity with the original school in the town. A new logo, featuring the founder, was designed by a member of the Art Department.

Daventry School was formerly split between two sites. Since September 1986 it has occupied one of the sites, on Ashby Road. Within Daventry, the school is always referred to as 'Ashby Road' (as in 'My son's at Ashby Road'), or 'the Ashby Road School'. Pupils at the school initially reacted adversely to the proposed new name, saying that it was snobbish. The new name and the modified school uniform, were gradually accepted by pupils and parents, however.

The Poetry Project: 'New-forged Bond'

In January 1989 we were fortunate in being offered the services of two poets, Maggie Holmes and Barrie Wade, through the Poetry Society's 'Poets in Schools' scheme.[3] We decided to use this opportunity to help the integration of pupils, coming into Year 10 in September 1989 at Daventry William Parker School, as a result of reorganization.

After consulting closely with the English Department at the Grange Comprehensive School, we chose twenty pupils in Year 9 from each school. The selection was taken from across the ability range, and each pupil was allocated a partner at the other school.[4] The pairings were made so that the pupils would complement each other, socially and academically. Two groups of twenty pupils were formed, a suitable number for a workshop with each poet. The remainder of this chapter describes how the pupils responded to the workshops, and how their enjoyment of poetry was developed. Follow-up interviews, conducted in the next academic year, show how the project helped the pupils to integrate at the new school.

We had an ice-breaking session at the beginning of the summer term with all the pupils so they could meet their partners before the first workshop with the poets. The approach used was similar to that employed in our curriculum continuity projects with the primary schools. The pupils interviewed their partners, and using photographs as stimuli, wrote some poems. They decided that the anthology they were going to produce would be sold to raise money for cancer research.

Though many of the pupils were apprehensive at first, they got on well, and were able to work successfully together, as these typical diary entries illustrate.

5th April 1989
When I had met my partner I relaxed a bit and as we filled out the interview on each other we both became a lot more friendly. All the other Daventry pupils were friendly and helpful too. The first piece of work we were given was to find a poem about school or food. This was fun to do, we searched through the book provided but could only find one or two which were both about school.
Then we read them out, it was good to listen to the poems other

pairs had picked. My partner read ours out. After that piece of work we went on to writing a poem.

We were given a group of photos which we had to pick one from and base our poem on it. (This was not in pairs.) I found it hard to pick a photo at first but as soon as I saw this one photo I picked it. I started my poem straight away. It is called waiting. The picture I had, had a man sitting reading a newspaper alone in a wine cellar full of barrels.

In my poem I tried to give a feeling of slow impatient waiting, alone and bored. Then, at the end, the feeling of 'what's it all for?' The time seemed to fly past in the afternoon. I had just finished my poem when we had to pack up and go home.

So far I have thoroughly enjoyed this poetry project and I am looking forward to meeting the practising poets, Barrie Wade and Maggie Holmes and the next poetry session.

*   *   *

Today was our first meeting with the Grange pupils. When I met my partner, Angela Lane, we had to go and interview them. After we had finished that we chose several poems and read them aloud to each other, and then in front of our group.

After we finished that we selected a photograph or picture and studied it, we then had to write a rough draft about it. We could either write a poem describing what we saw or just write a poem on what the picture told us. We then had to read some aloud to everyone.

This gave me a chance to get used to other people from different schools and I really enjoyed it.

I look forward to our next meeting, with the poets, Maggie Holmes and Barrie Wade, soon.

*   *   *

Today we filled in our personal information sheets. Nina and I didn't talk much to start with, but when we did we got on quite well. We began to look through books to choose a poem on food or on school. We found one on school dinners and another on an apple tree. We chose the apple tree because it was longer. Next we had to choose a picture and start a poem using it. I found it difficult to start with, but once I'd got the poem started it came easy.

First Workshop

In the middle of April we had our first workshop with both poets. This took place in the afternoon; initially all the pupils were together, and then they divided into their two groups. Maggie Holmes and Barrie Wade quickly established a rapport with their groups, and stimulated them to write. The positive responses of the pupils were reflected in their diary entries, as these extracts show:

17th April 1989

Today we worked once again with our partners from the Grange. However we also met our poet for the first time. His name is Barrie Wade. He is very nice and is good at what he does. We all learnt what a Haiku poem is.

I got on well with my partner, again, and I look forward to seeing her and Barrie Wade again next time.

*   *   *

I really enjoyed today. Maggie Holmes was really nice and made us feel at ease right away. She made the poems make sense and it was good fun to read them. We had to look at a box and imagine what was in it. I imagined an old house. I am looking forward to enjoying the all day session.

*   *   *

We got to Daventry School a bit earlier than the first poetry session and got started a lot quicker. We were split up into two big groups. One group went with Barrie Wade and stayed in the library with Maggie Holmes. I felt at ease and was getting to know the pupils for Daventry School very well.

Maggie Holmes started by playing some game so we could get to know her and her to get to know us. We had to say our name and a fact about ourselves, it was good fun and you found out what people like. Then Maggie Holmes talked to us about herself and her work.

This was interesting and educational. We were then given a question sheet each and we had to note or tick things if we agreed with them. An example of the statements are: Poetry is boring. Poetry's for the intelligent. Poetry is Fun. Anybody can write poems, and poems can describe the way you feel.

After that Maggie Holmes brought out a small box and asked us to imagine what was in it and write a poem about it. For some reason I instantly thought of a gold diamond ring. We had to write a poem within three minutes or try and get as far as we could. I found this very hard to do but I had a good go at it.

When we had finished that we formed groups of about four and made a list of as many different words for 'together' as we could. Then we had to pick one of the words and write a poem to do with it. I picked fusion, I found it very hard to get the poem started but after that it was easy.

At the end of the afternoon Maggie Holmes read us one of her poems. It was very good. We then packed up and went home.

I enjoyed this poetry session and had great fun. Maggie Holmes was great, she was fun to work with and very interesting. I now like poetry more than I did before I started the course and I appreciate it a lot more. I am looking forward to seeing what we will be doing in the next session (which is for a whole day.)

*   *   *

Not surprisingly everyone was far more talkative today than at the first meeting. I found myself talking to them as if I had known them for years. The poet, Barrie Wade, was a fascinating person. He was older than I expected. He brightened up the session, made it worth while and educational.

The pattern for the rest of the project was that Maggie Holmes and Barrie Wade would each hold an all-day workshop with their group. Barrie Wade conducted his workshop at the beginning of May. I was fortunate in being able to participate in both all-day workshops, and write poems as well. Other colleagues in the English Department at Daventry School joined when they were free. The workshops also provided a good opportunity for us to work with the two colleagues from the Grange Comprehensive School, who were going to join the English Faculty at Daventry William Parker School in September 1989.[5]

The pupils working with Barrie Wade wrote a lot of poems during the course of the day. They worked individually, and in small groups. The following diary entries are typical of how the pupils responded.

Thursday 4th May
I found the work interesting, and it has improved my poetry skills. My behaviour was very good, and I co-operated well in my group, and gave some ideas for a group poem. I have learned to write poems properly and in a given time. I wrote some poems which were quite good. I enjoyed the whole day, and we got to know Barrie better.

       *   *   *

Today was our last day of poetry. We did poetry work all day with our poet, Barrie Wade. We did quite a few poems in groups and on our own. The best part of the day for me was when we were allowed out onto the field in the sun to do a poem on anything. I really enjoyed this as I could think up fresher and new thoughts being in a different place.

       *   *   *

The 'I wish' poem was not very good, but the other poems I thought were good. I did not like writing the poem about myself! But I did like writing the poems about other people. Our group worked well together when writing our poem, and we finished it outside in the nice weather!!

       *   *   *

The working atmosphere was really great. The poet, Barrie Wade, was good fun to work with. I wish we were given more time to complete a poem though. We really got talking to the Grange pupils!

A few days later, Maggie Holmes held her all-day workshop with the other group of twenty pupils. They gained a great deal from the day, as these diary entries show:

8th May, 1989

This session was really great. I really enjoyed it. This was the best session and we could spend time to think about what we are writing.

* * *

Today's session was all day and the Ashby kids were very good to us. At the start Maggie Holmes said just one word 'rock' and gave us five minutes to write a poem. Mine was about an ordinary rock that drew comparisons with a callous old man. We had to write limericks and find something outside to write about. Mine was a dandelion. Then we had lunch, which was very good of them, and returned to the library. Oh yes, with Jodi I wrote about a twig. In the afternoon we went out to write a Haiku and a Riddle which I did not finish. Then we just had to generally clean up our poems and write them out neatly.

* * *

After a brief introduction, we started straight away on a poem. We had five minutes to write one on the basis of the word 'rock'. These were then read out. The next exercise was an observational one, where we were allowed the freedom of the school (within reason) to find and focus carefully on an object and write a poem about what came to mind. I chose a low sprawling fern that seemed to be reaching down for the earth but the way the poem developed, it became about roots. After second break (time flew) we were read a series of limericks we wrote out for ourselves. These were then shared with the class. Then again, an observational exercise, we picked another object, this time with our partners, and wrote a poem on it, either together or separately. We did ours separately. We picked the cover of a book which pictured a golden coloured cat walking out of the mist. I immediately focused (as usual) on the idea of a magical, fantasy poem, which I write best, while Robert picked a more 'down to earth' portrayal, of a runaway cat, out on the moors. This made quite a contrast, and we read the poems out together to show this. I think this was probably the best poem I wrote that day, titled 'Nothing has been Proved.'

After lunch, we had two tasks, a riddle, in which I portrayed the light of the tree, and a Haiku poem, which I found very difficult. The remaining time was spent on copying up and discussions on the use of lighting, music and drama to add to the poems. By the bell, I was whacked!

After the workshops, the pupils completed their poems, and made neat copies of the ones they liked best. The English teachers at both schools made a selection for the poetry anthology. There were three half-day rehearsals in the dance and drama studio at Daventry School, in preparation for our joint Poetry Evening for parents and friends in July. Each pupil had to present a poem, or participate in a small group presentation. Maggie Holmes and Barrie Wade attended, and read some of their poems as well. Afterwards

Barrie Wade commented that from the quality of the poetry and presentations, one could not tell which pupils were the 'high-fliers', and which were not.

Barrie Wade wrote (in his preface to the anthology):

It is always a pleasure to help young people to find their voices in poetry. Poetry is for speaking and all young people can write it, given encouragement. When youngsters find their voices, they can astonish with originality, power and freshness and the poems in their book show. Even though it may be difficult to get a start, the end results (after alterations and additions) can leave you breathless with admiration. I've tried to say that in the following poem.

The Writer

She is the one who sits and thinks.
When Miss says *write* our pens race into gear,
twist through letter loops and word chicanes
with minds tight-bunched and hammering to overtake.
It is as if in pole-position she has stalled.
Her brow is radiator furrowed.
She judders at her desk
and I can see that Miss is trying not
to lean across to give a push.
By the lesson's end her littered page
shows fragments of tyretread
patterned into asphalt
and yet

She is the one who stands and reads
next day while we sit breathless,
whose words splash coloured images
brilliant as petrol spilled in puddles
that we passed along our way.

Maggie Holmes wrote:

As a writer I go into schools with two sublime beliefs. Firstly, that poetry is accessible to everyone. Secondly, that anyone who wants to, can write poems. I also believe that poetry, besides being hard work, can also be fun.

The group of third years that I worked with reinforced these views. In the one and a half days I was there, I was delighted to see a great deal of embryonic poetry, with a quality of writing and honesty of feelings that was refreshing.

I was full of admiration for the level of commitment to find ideas, struggle with words, and complete the poems. Would that my own output were that prolific!

I look forward with pleasure to the production of the anthology, bringing together the work of two individual groups, and two schools.

The Wine and Cheese party was an enjoyable way of rounding off the evening. The anthology 'New-Forged Bond' went on sale then and subsequently at both schools. Almost £30 was raised for cancer research from the profits.

Follow-up Interviews: Pupils' Attitudes

A year later I interviewed over half the pupils who had taken part in the project. I wanted to find out what they felt about the project, and how it had helped their integration at the new school since September 1989.

Most pupils had experienced mixed feelings when first told that they were going to take part in the workshops. Many pupils feared that it would be boring, because they didn't like poetry — a sorry reflection on the effect that we (as English teachers) have in the classroom. However most pupils looked forward to meeting new people, even though some were apprehensive about this. The pupils at the Grange in particular welcomed the opportunity to work at Daventry School. The following extracts are typical.

Philip: When I first heard about it, I thought I would enjoy it a lot, as it meant coming down to Daventry School and meeting new people.

Belinda: I didn't want to go for the poetry, but I wanted to go for the new people.

Kevin: I was surprised at being picked and ... I just didn't think I'd get picked for something like poetry. I'm not particularly good at English or anything along such lines, so I was surprised. But I was glad to go, the chance to see the new school we were going to.

Charles: I was quite interested to see what was going on, what we were going to be doing.

Robert: At first I thought it would be boring, because I thought, oh poetry ... it's not very exciting, but I'll go along with it because it looks like fun, and I'll get to meet all the Grange pupils.

John: ... I wanted to look at the school, and to get to know some of the people, and I was interested in poetry as well.

Peter: I thought it would be really hard because I'm not really good at poetry ... I hadn't done much before, and I felt intimidated by the thought of trying to write poetry.

All the pupils enjoyed the workshops, and found the poets very stimulating to work with. Most pupils were surprised to find that they could produce good poetry themselves, and they enjoyed working with pupils from the 'other' school. Many said that the Poetry Evening had been fun. The following extracts indicate the range of responses.

Laura: I enjoyed hearing other people's works, and being able to write with other people, and being able to produce something quite good.

Belinda: It gave me greater enjoyment of poetry, because I had thought of all of it was really boring ... I learned to write in different ways.

Kevin: I enjoyed working with Maggie Holmes. It was interesting to see what she had to say about the subject, and I enjoyed writing the poems in the group.

I did find that I was able to write some poems. I was surprised really. I wrote quite a few and got some in the book at the end.

Robert: At first I couldn't do poetry at all, but after this, because we wrote so many poems in one day, it was very quick. I found I could write well in such a short space of time.

John: I liked the practising poets. I was in Maggie Holmes' group. She was very good, and some of the poems I wrote ... I'm very impressed with what I've done ... She explained everything so well, and she presented it in different ways, a variety of ways, like doing a poem off a picture ... I've got a wider range of knowledge about poetry, and listening to other people's gave me ideas, and I was able to criticize some of theirs as well. They criticized me, and helped me along a bit.

Peter: I liked the way Barrie Wade made poetry seem easy to us, sort of, we can make poetry out of the things around us, not just these weird things in the mind ... everything can be to do with poetry ... I enjoyed the Poetry Evening with the parents, it showed what we could do.

Jane: We learned different ways of doing poems from Barrie Wade, like Haikus.

Susan: We were outside with Maggie Holmes, and using our imaginations. It was really good! ... Now I can look at poems and see different meanings in them as well, instead of just thinking they're boring. I just like poetry more now.

Alison: I enjoyed it because I learned a lot about poetry from Barrie.

Simon: I think the best thing was that it was completely open-ended. You weren't told exactly what to do. That way you could bring out your own talents in it, which in a lesson is difficult to do, because you're told what to write about. So that's why I enjoyed it most, I think.

The social aspects of the project were also important for all the pupils involved. They had appreciated the opportunity to work with pupils they would be together with at the new school in the autumn term of 1989. The following examples are typical:

Philip: I liked working with my partner and making new poems. I got on very well with my partner. He's in my Tutor Group now, so I know him. It was a good way to get to know him.

Kevin: I met some people from [Daventry] School I didn't know previously. I was glad to know them. It helped when I came here at the beginning of the year.

Charles: It helped a lot when I moved to the school. I knew people ... it helped with new people ... it helped with new lessons. You knew people and were less tense.

Robert: I got to know a lot of people that I wouldn't have got to know before, and I talk to them now, because of the poetry project. If I hadn't met them during the poetry project, I might not know them now.

John: I was nervous at first about working with Daventry School pupils, but I thought it was a good way to get to know them. I started to make friends. The group I was in worked together very well ... We started some good relationships up with people, that when we came to this school we wouldn't have known at all.

Peter: We learned to work together well ... helped each other. I was apprehensive about meeting new people. Some of the people that came here [in the autumn term] I already knew them because of the project, so through them I knew other people.

Alan: I got on fine with my partner, though before the project I was nervous that Grange and Daventry pupils wouldn't get on. The project helped at the beginning of this year, because if you know one person in a group of people, you get to know the rest.

Jane: I made friends with quite a few of them [from the Grange] and several friendships grew out of the project.

Sandra: It broke the ice between you. I didn't think 'Oh, no, we've got the Grange people coming'. We really got to know them.

The poetry project was thus one of a series of activities that helped pupils to work together, and to start friendships. More generally, I wanted to know how the ex-Grange pupils felt about the move, which was far more traumatic for them than the ex-Daventry School pupils, who had stayed in the same buildings. The ex-Grange pupils in the sample felt they had settled in well, but several admitted to missing their old school.

Nina: It's like changing schools all over again, when you move up a school. We'd just made friends with everyone at the Grange, and now we had to make new friends all over again. Me and Alice made friends through the move, but we're still 'ex-Grangies'.

Teacher: How do you see the pupils who were here before?

Alice: Ashby Road! ... They're in their groups as well, and they don't really want to split up with the friends, and let us fit in.

Laura: We're just where we were before, in our old groups ... When we came it was good to know that some teachers were here that we already knew, and it was good to know that we could go to them if we needed help or anything.

Belinda: I thought it would be horrible, splitting up with friends from the Grange. When I came here I thought people weren't going to be really friendly, but they were. The teachers are friendly too, but a bit stricter.

 I don't hang round with the friends I had before. I hang round with the people in the fourth year that used to go to this school, and I hang around with a few that used to go to the Grange ... We're all friends together, so it doesn't matter.

Kevin: It's better than I expected, but I still miss my old school ... all the people and teachers I left behind. We're still stuck in our groups — I am. I don't really go round with the people I know now.

Philip: I have made new friends.

Charles: We seem to have merged together into one whole school now.

Teacher: Do you still see yourself as an 'ex-Grangie'?

John: No, I've forgotten all that. I felt like that at the beginning. There was one group, and the other, but they're mingled now. This mingling started about a month after the beginning of the year, though my closest friends are from the Grange.

Edward: Sometimes I've been called an 'ex-Grangie' by some of the kids in my Tutor Group. I sit with an ex-Grange pupil (in the Tutor Group) because I know him. In other lessons I generally mix.

Kate: I'd always been to the Grange since ... for ages, and I'll always look on it as my school, I don't know why.

Eleanor: As soon as I go past the Grange I say 'That's my school'. I feel upset about it in some ways, though here I've made more friends, and we're all mixed.

David: In big groups, like in the playground, I think of myself as ex-Grange. In sport, I think of myself as part of Daventry

> William Parker School together. It depends on how you feel.

The ex-Daventry School pupils didn't have the same feelings of loss, and in general felt that the social mixing had been successful in Year 10, as these extracts illustrate.

Robert:	I feel that we've come together very well. At first we were saying with the lads: 'We'll beat them in', and all this, but we didn't. In the end we all mixed well together.
	At the beginning of this year we were very separated, but now I hang around with people that are all from the Grange. I don't hang around with anybody who used to be at this school, anymore. I never think about whether they're ex-Grange.
Susan:	Though we were split up at first, everyone is now friends.
Alan:	Some of the Grange [pupils] stay in their group, but mostly we mix quite well.
Jill:	Everybody mixed in well at the beginning of the year. People still comment on it. Some of the ex-Grange pupils say 'Wish we hadn't come here', but underneath ... everyone gets on really well. I think they feel they're the same as everybody else.
Alan:	There's no longer any feeling of 'ex-Grange' or 'ex-Daventry School', we're all mixed together.

It was clear that the integration of pupils in Year 10 at the new school had been successful, and the poetry project had played a part in helping this process. In addition, the pupils involved in the project had been stimulated by the workshops with the practising poets. There are parallels with our efforts to establish continuity and liaison between primary and secondary phases. The activities outlined above would also have hit many of the same levels in the Attainment Targets and covered the elements in the programmes of study for Key Stage 3, as described in Chapters 3 and 7.

Reorganization successfully created teaching structures at the three new institutions within a year or so. The development of a new ethos at Daventry William Parker School, reflecting the blend of teachers from the three original local schools, and pupils from two of the schools, will undoubtedly take much longer.

Notes

1 From September 1988, primary pupils who would have gone to the Grange Comprehensive School, transferred to either Daventry School or Southbrook school.

2 These activities took place at Southbrook School as well, planned by small committees of staff drawn from both schools. The organization of the Industry Days was coordinated by Mark Twyford, Pastoral Coordinator (1989–90), and Head of Lower School, Daventry William Parker School from September 1990. The planning of the Problem Solving Days was coordinated by Debbie Hollister, Head of PE, Daventry William Parker School.

3 I am most grateful to Maggie Holmes and Barrie Wade for their inspiring contributions to the workshops; and to The Poetry Society and W.H. Smiths booksellers, who sponsor the 'Poets in Schools' scheme.

4 One of the differences in ethos between the two schools was that teaching at the Grange was predominantly mixed-ability. English was taught in mixed-ability groups in Years 7–11. At Daventry School, English and other core subjects were 'setted' from Year 8 upwards.

5 I am grateful to Maureen Meguer and Pauline Drake, formerly at the Grange Comprehensive School, for their help in the planning of this project. I am also grateful to Jo Cumberland-Harper, Ann Bunce, Mark Twyford and David Bradford for help with the organization, and to colleagues in the English Department for their support.

Student Poetry from 'New-Forged Bond'

ME

Artificial additives on hair and face.
Is that the real me?
Always trying to keep up with others,
Is that the real me?
Laughing about cruel jokes, hurting others,
Is that the real me?
Lying to save myself,
Is that the real me?
Showing off to impress,
Is that the real me?

The real me lacks confidence
I need the additives,
Always wanting to be part of the crowd,
So laughing about others makes me belong,
Deceiving to get out of trouble
Or so not to get embarrassed
I have to lie.
At home I am sensitive, caring, kind,
Why do I need to be two different people?

ME? OR WHO?

I suppose that I'm really quite hard to explain.
Sometimes I'm friendly and sometimes cheerful,
But I am sometimes upset.
My moods change like the weather.
I like to say what I think,
Even if it upsets some people.
If I don't like people, I show it,
But if I like them I am a good friend.
I like to laugh and have fun,
I try to look different and I like to stand out in a crowd.
Being normal is not what I go for.
When I'm with people I don't know I'm quiet.
But my close friends think I'm mad.
I hang about with a few boys,
You can trust them better than girls.
I think I'm different from others,
Maybe I'm an alien.

Figure 11.1

BLIND DATE

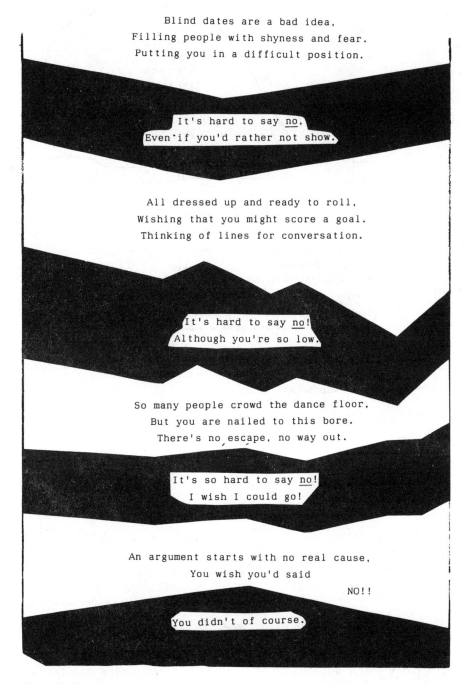

Blind dates are a bad idea,
Filling people with shyness and fear.
Putting you in a difficult position.

It's hard to say <u>no</u>,
Even if you'd rather not show.

All dressed up and ready to roll,
Wishing that you might score a goal.
Thinking of lines for conversation.

It's hard to say <u>no</u>!
Although you're so low.

So many people crowd the dance floor,
But you are nailed to this bore.
There's no escape, no way out.

It's so hard to say <u>no</u>!
I wish I could go!

An argument starts with no real cause,
You wish you'd said

NO!!

You didn't of course.

Figure 11.2

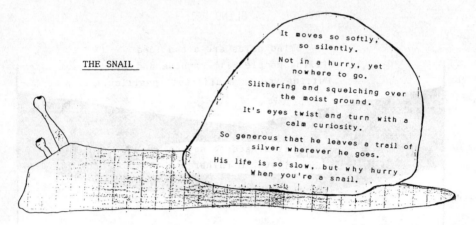

THE SNAIL

It moves so softly,
so silently.

Not in a hurry, yet
nowhere to go.

Slithering and squelching over
the moist ground.

It's eyes twist and turn with a
calm curiosity.

So generous that he leaves a trail of
silver wherever he goes.

His life is so slow, but why hurry
When you're a snail.

THE PREDATOR BECOMES PREY

Soaring through the air,
Changing direction,
This way, that way, no this way.
Gliding, diving and swerving,
Looking for flies, worms and other small insects.
The sparrow lands and pulls a big, long, juicy worm
                                            out of the ground,
Take off, back to all the flying again,
But wait, there's something following it,
      What is it?
      Eagle?
      Kestrel?
      Hawk? Yikes it thinks , a hawk!
Soaring behind the bird, not more than a few meters
      CRUNCH!!
      CRACK!!
      SNAP!!
The sparrow disappears, and the kestrel soars off into the
                                              distance.

Figure 11.3

```
        There it sits
Limp and lifeless
Grey and black
As if it were dead
But is it dead?
The lines are roads.
Roads to where?
The sea, the sky, the moon, the stars.
```

A Dark Metamorphosis

Based on Tolkein's Book 'Lord of the Rings'

```
They craved.
They were enslaved.
Once they had a home,
And now they were sworn,
To the power of the rings.

Onwards they came,
Minds tortured, insane.
They possessed no mortal choice,
Their lips held no mortal voice,
Just a whisper, the names of the rings.

To an immortal master,
They drew on, faster,
Contorted, all humanity gone,
The black riders, rode on,
They were bound, bound to the rings.

The dark Lord summoned,
The empty, cloaked shapes,
That straddled black, mindless horses.
He summoned, his shadow-finger pointed,
And they rode into Mordor, to the master of the rings.

To the room in the tower,
To a prism of power.
To the walls they receded,
Nine archways, until needed.
When the Dark Lord called to him,
His invincible,, dead slaves,
The nine, dark wraiths, below only to one.
The zenith of power.  THE RING.
```

Figure 11.4

CLOCK IN THE DISTANCE

There's a clock in the distance

Far away,

I hear it's chimes every day.

The steeple is tall

It touches the sky.

On the clock face

It is 3 o'clock.

I wonder if it is right.

In my mind time stands still.

I hear bells, wedding bells,

I wonder what her dress is like,

I wonder .....

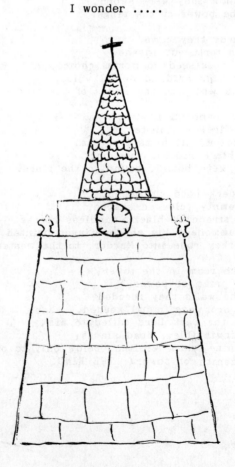

Figure 11.5

Chapter 12

Curriculum Continuity Continued

In 1989/90 seven joint projects with six of our contributory schools took place, involving over 420 pupils. The planning occurred in the autumn term; the projects ran in the Easter term, though some went over into the first half of the summer term. There was a considerable diversity of topics. The projects included writing stories and poems on 'myself', cross-phase writing on the theme of 'the journey', linked to RE, planning the amenities for a village which was to be developed; making television news programmes; a multi-media project with a practising writer, which resulted in the production of a book; a drama-based project on energy; and a project on Dracula, involving IT. I am grateful to Jackie Turner (Head of English, Daventry William Parker School) for describing the latter project below, and for providing a National Curriculum web and a planning chart of some of the activities.

Count Alucard

Jackie Turner

Serves and fears
The fury of the many-headed monster,
The giddy multitude
(Massinger, *The Unnatural Combat 1639*)

National Curriculum

The 'giddy multitude' could well serve as an accurate description of the current state of the teaching force in England and Wales. There have been so many new initiatives, (and so many new initiatives which have lost their way) that it quite easy to feel we are serving a 'many-headed monster'. The intention of this chapter is to demonstrate, in a small way, how the National

Curriculum statutory orders can be used to serve English teachers, and not the other way around.

A curriculum continuity project undertaken with one of the feeder junior schools in the Daventry area is used as a focus for discussion. The 'Count Alucard' project formed the basis of half a term's project with a 'bright' enthusiastic, second year group (Year 8) at Daventry William Parker School; working with a mixed ability top class (Year 6) of juniors from Grange Junior School.[1]

Details of the Project

The best ideas often emerge quite by chance; the 'Count Alucard' project proved to be no exception. Jude Eddon, the junior school colleague with whom I was to work, had discovered a rather battered worksheet lying around in the staff room. We used this worksheet as a basis for our ideas, believing it to offer interesting and stimulating opportunities for pupils to write in a variety of non-chronological forms.

The nurturing of a good personal relationship with our junior school colleagues is a very important aspect of curriculum continuity work. Secondary teachers and junior school teachers need to work together to jointly plan the project, in order for ownership of the project to be shared. In order to achieve this, half-day liaison visits are an integral part of the planning process.

Having previously worked together on a curriculum continuity project, Jude and I knew each other very well on a personal level and appreciated each other's sense of humour. We also knew that each other's teaching style was compatible and, perhaps most importantly, were aware of the pitfalls of undertaking such a project. Our last attempt, whilst successful in some areas, had been rather disappointing overall!

Having learnt from mistakes made in the previous year, Jude and I were conscious of planning a realistic project with specified outcomes. Jude was keen to develop the pupils' limited experience of Information Technology and, in addition, prepare them for a future residential experience incorporating the use of computers. With limited access to computer resources in the primary school, an opportunity to work on a Nimbus computer network, comprising twenty stations, was not to be missed. I was also keen to develop the computer work prevously undertaken with my group.

The project was aimed specifically to provide pupils with the opportunity to:

1 work as a member of a group in the planning and production of a range of non-chronological forms, including notes, lists, menus, and invitations;

2 use a computer to assist in the production of the above forms;

3 record their thoughts, capture immediate responses and collect and organize ideas so that they are available for reflection.

The primary/secondary liaison also offers many other important opportunities for pupils of both ages. Many of these have been well documented elsewhere and are not the focus for this chapter. Writing for an audience, other than the class teacher, was however a very important part of the 'Count Alucard' project. The project sessions can be summarized as:

1 Three joint sessions in the computer network room, with pupils working in mixed groups producing a range of non-chronological writing forms.
2 Separate sessions. Horror stories and poems written individually by pupils for their junior school partners.
3 A joint presentation session. Display of junior and secondary pupils' work. Oral presentations from Daventry William Parker School pupils to Grange Junior School pupils.
4 Individual written evaluations of entire project.

Throughout the project, pupils were asked to keep a diary of their experiences and these were completed at the end of every session.

The account of the 'Count Alucard' project is written from a secondary school perspective and this is reflected in Table 12.1, indicating Key Stage 3 Programmes of Study and Attainment Targets. Table 12.1 could just as easily have reflected the Key Stage 2 level of Attainment Targets. The table is currently being used by members of the staff in the English Faculty at Daventry William Parker School, as a means of planning the curriculum delivery and relating it to the English National Curriculum Programmes of Study and Attainment Targets. The notation used in column three is based upon the standard description of Attainment Targets advocated by SEAC. Column three seeks to identify the range of Attainment Targets which could be achieved by the pupils on each of the activities. Whilst it is very important that assessment is built into the curriculum, the starting point for planning should always be the Programmes of Study. The brainstorming web (Figure 12.1) illustrates the various opportunities for Speaking and Listening, Writing, Design and Information Technology work involved in the 'Count Alucard' project. The intention was not for every pupil to experience all of the various forms, neither to assess all the pupils on the various different forms; the individual writing aspect of the project, for example, offered pupils a choice of writing a poem or a story.

The Joint Computer Sessions

There were three joint, one hour sessions planned in the computer network room, with approximately sixty pupils involved each time. The large number of pupils involved, and the use of Information Technology, necessitated close attention to practical details. Pupils had access to a large network, with twenty Nimbus stations, and an adjoining classroom. The Newspa program was set up on the computers, but the pupils were only provided with access

THEME TITLE: CURRICULUM CONTINUITY PROJECT

© JAT. 1990.

DETAILS OF ACTIVITIES	PROGRAMMES OF STUDY	ATTAINMENT TARGETS	ASSESSMENT OPPORTUNITIES	RESOURCES
SESSION 1 ▲ Pupils divided into groups of 4, with pairings of one GJS pupil and one D.N.P.S pupil. "Count Alucard" information sheets distributed to pupils. Groups to brainstorm ideas for: 1) Invitation 2) Menu 3) Party Games 4) Entertainments ● Pupils to decide upon responsibilities. ▲ Pairs begin to sort at computer stations or tasks, using PAINTSPA. ▲ Pairs begin to draft ideas on paper.	**AT1 SPEAKING + LISTENING KEY STAGE 3** Pupils should be given the opportunity to: ● express and justify feelings, opinions and viewpoints with increasing sophistication; ● present their ideas, experiences and understanding in a widening range of contexts across the curriculum, and with an increasing awareness of audience and purpose; ● give increasingly precise instructions; ● communicate with other group members in a range of situations; ● assess and interpret arguments and opinions with increasing precision and discrimination.	EN 1/3c EN 1/4c EN 1/5b EN1/6a EN 1/3b EN1/3d EN1/4b EN 1/5c EN1/6b	**ORAL** Individual within group situation. Individual contributions at computer screen.	'Count Alucard' information sheets. Computer-Network with at least 20 stations, loaded with PAINTSPA program. A4 lined paper A4 unlined paper A4 coloured paper A4 card Scissors Glue Felt-type etc. Curriculum Continuity folders.
	AT3 WRITING KEY STAGE 3 Pupils should be helped to recognise explicitly the different stages in the writing process - using a computer. Pupils should have opportunities to: ● write in a range of forms, including annotations, menus, lists etc; ● write for a range of purposes including giving instructions, explaining etc, produce writing and proof-reading in a word-processor; ● organise and express their meaning appropriately, for special audience, etc on screen, but designed and paced, use appropriate methods of presentation so that finished work is presented, displayed clearly and attractively for their readers.	EN 3/3d EN 3/3c EN 3/4c EN 3/4c EN 3/5a EN 3/5d EN 3/6a EN 3/6a EN 4.5/6b EN 4.5/6d EN 4.5/7b EN 4.5/7d		
▲ Pupils individually to evaluate across; progress; work produced; ways of working; individual contributions; plans for next session etc. Evaluation presented in the form of diary.	Pupils should have opportunities to: ● write in a range of forms, minding display; ● use writing to facilitate their own thinking and learning, recognising that not all written work will lead to a polished final product.	EN 3/3a EN 3/3d EN 3/4a EN 3/4b EN 4/tc. EN 3/5b	**WRITTEN** Ability to reflect on individual contributions in diary form.	

Table 12.1 'Count Alucard' project, National Curriculum planning chart

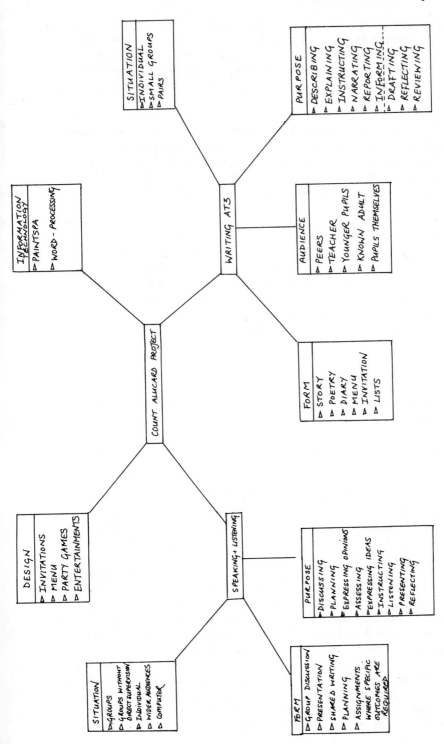

© JAT 1990

Figure 12.1 'Count Alucard' project, National Curriculum brainstorming web

to Paintspa. The pupils did not, unfortunately, have access to a colour printer. The computers were all prepared well in advance of the pupils' arrivals. Past encounters with technology had taught me some harsh lessons! It is also necessary to ensure that sufficient space has been allocated by the network manager to your specific user area. Paintspa can consume a great deal of memory.

The pupils were divided into groups of four, with two Daventry William Parker School pupils matched with two Grange Junior School pupils. The groups were provided with the 'Count Alucard' information sheet and asked to brainstorm ideas for the invitation, menu, party games and entertainments. The groups then sub-divided into pairs and began working on their allocated tasks, either by using the computer or by using card, paper, etc.

The formation of groups is an important aspect of curriculum continuity work. Some time had been spent discussing the constitution of the groups and pairings, in order to provide a balance of abilities and personalities. It does help to be aware, in advance, of pupils who find working in groups difficult, or pupils who tend to dominate situations. The SEAC 'A Guide To Teacher Assessment — Pack C: A Source Book Of Teacher Assessment' provides a checklist for the assessment of group work.[2] Chapter 4, section 4.12, 'Monitoring Performance' advises that:

> Group work requires teachers to determine carefully what tasks will be undertaken, who will compose the group, and how the outcomes will be assessed.... In the classroom, much learning takes place in a group, so the teacher needs to know how well each child has worked.

Teachers are advised to consider carefully how children share the tasks within the group, the level of involvement of individuals in the task, what kind of participation results in the task being taken forward, the kind of dialogue taking place and, most importantly, how the teacher will approach observation. En 1/4c specifically focuses on interaction between pupils and the three joint sessions provide many opportunities to observe and assess the pupils working in a new context — secondary and junior school pupils working together on a joint activity.

It is impossible to assess all the pupils on all of the Attainment Targets on the same occasion and the class teacher should not even seek to achieve this. It is better to assess specific Attainment Targets on a few children. The best adage is, 'little and often'. The class teacher needs to observe the groups very carefully and be flexible in the assessment arrangements. There are some variables which cannot be controlled; if a pupil is not performing well on a particular occasion, it is better not to assess. Team teaching, in such a context, helps to provide an organizational solution, but the nature of the task itself once set up and running also facilitates the assessment process.

'Real' and purposeful oral work is stimulated by pairs working at a computer station and creates a further invaluable opportunity for assessment of Attainment Target 1: Speaking and Listening. Pupils certainly were involved in giving, receiving and following accurately '. . . precise instructions when pursuing a task individually or as a member of a group' En 1/3d, as they jointly discovered how to use the computer program to achieve the desired results which they had discussed earlier. As time progressed, the pupils became more critical of the work they had produced on the computer screen and were anxious to re-shape their ideas. Some pupils certainly achieved, at least in part, En 1/5b 'contribute to and respond constructively in discussion, including the development of ideas; advocate and justify a point of view'.

The use of computers to help pupils recognize explicitly the different stages in the writing process proved to be most advantageous. Pupils were assembling ideas on a computer screen and demonstrating an ability at least at En 3/5d to 'produce a draft from them and then to revise and redraft as necessary'. On this occasion pupils certainly fulfilled En 4.5/6d, demonstrating most effectively '. . . some ability to use any available presentational devices that are appropriate to the task, so that finished work is presented clearly and attractively' and even reaching level En 4.5/7d. Pupils were certainly demonstrating En 4.5/6b and En 4.5/7b: 'check final drafts of writing for misspelling and other errors of presentation'. From a cross-curricular point of view, pupils also fulfilled aspects of the Information Technology Statements of Attainment (DES 1990b). Some pupils demonstrated an ability to use IT to retrieve, develop, organize and present work at least to level 4 (AT 5: Information technology capability, level 4a).[3]

The time provided for the joint sessions was limited, but it provided an opportunity for pupils to work under pressure to meet the deadline set. Some pupils opted not to use the computers to produce their work because of the practical difficulties. There were some obvious problems: time taken to print the work, pupils omitting to store work and the lack of a colour printer, but taken as a whole, the sessions in the computer room were very successful.

Some extracts from diary entries completed by Daventry William Parker School pupils, at the end of each session, will illustrate how the pupils responded. Anne wrote:

> We worked on the food for the party and instructions for the journey to the castle. We tried to make the food sound spooky and we have four courses, starters, main meal, dessert and drinks. I think our work was of a good standard and should be good on the computer next week . . .

Simon wrote:

> On Friday, we finished using the computer. Jim and I did the menu on the computer. We tried to think of some party games and in the end did things like Murder in the Dark, Musical bites etc. We looked at each others' work and commented upon it. His work was better

than I expected. We printed out the menu, but it was too small, so we enlarged it on the duplicating machine.

Maria wrote:

> Whilst doing the menu cover, we discovered we couldn't fit it on, though by working together we managed to change it. I was pleased with my work, yet I wished we had more time as the lesson went really quickly. My partner worked well and she was very inquisitive about the school. By the end of the lesson, we had prepared the poster and most of the menu. Sally seemed very keen to work and had prepared a lot of work at home. So far, we are a bit behind work-wise, but producing good work.

The pupils were quite clearly using their writing to record thoughts, capture immediate responses and collect and organize ideas so they were available for reflection, (AT 3 POS). The pupils will certainly have fulfilled, at least in part, the En 3/4b: '... produce other kinds of chronologically organised writing'. The quality of the polished pieces of work were superb. How could you resist an invitation like this from Fiona?

> Don't get scared and don't get a fright,
> The party will start around midnight.
> Don't get scared, I'll tell you again,
> The party will end at 7.00 a.m.

And with this sort of entertainment on offer, how could you refuse the invitation?

ENTERTAINMENTS

Starring The Transylvanian Philharmonic
Orchestra with:
Fatal Attraction,
Scream and Shout,
Bone Marrow,
Rock and Roll Your Intestines (John)

... and if you're wondering how to get there, follow the set of instructions shown in Figure 12.2. Also provided, as a 'taster', are a series of rather gruesome menus (Figures 12.3 and 12.4). As indicated in Table 12.1, the pupils were quite clearly demonstrating an ability to write in a range of forms, write for a range of purposes, organize and express their meaning appropriately for a specified audience and use appropriate methods of presentation. The examples of pupils' work also demonstrate so much more. The pupils were clearly accomplished language users, who were enjoying the opportunity to 'play' with language for humorous effects.

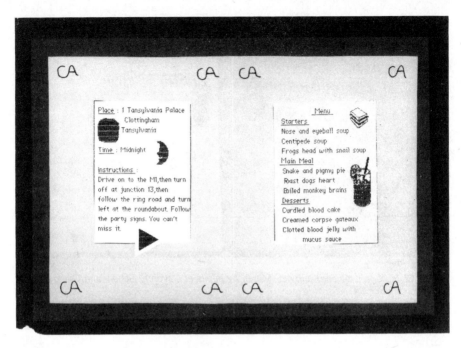

Figure 12.2 'Count Alucard' project, Instructions and Menu, by pupils at Daventry School and Grange Junior School

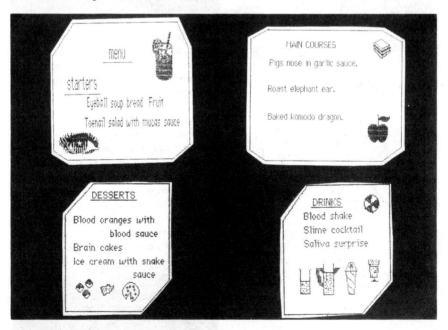

Figure 12.3 'Count Alucard' project, Menu, by pupils at Daventry School and Grange Junior School

Figure 12.4 *'Count Alucard' project, Menu, by pupils at Daventry School and Grange Junior School*

Figure 12.5 *'Escape', by a pupil at Daventry William Parker School.*

Horror Stories and Poems

The next stage of the project involved the pupils in an individual creative writing activity. Daventry William Parker School pupils wrote stories and poems for their primary school partners. The stimulus used for creative writing is outlined in the 'Creative Language' photocopiable English resource pack produced by Stanley Thornes (Publishers).[4] Each pupil was provided, on an arbitrary basis, with a creature, an object, a place and a horror words card. The pupils were then asked to incorporate all these elements in either a story or poem. The pupils had previously worked on the drafting process and some of the final polished pieces are shown below.

The fact that the pupils knew they were writing for a specific audience, other than the class teacher, provided an additional incentive and improved the overall quality of work produced. Whilst the English National Curriculum does not state that pupils must write in the poetic form to achieve a certain level, the Programme of Study for Attainment Target 3 does stipulate that pupils should: 'be able to write in a range of forms, including poems' and 'write in aesthetic and imaginative forms'. To a certain extent, the direct assessment of poetry in terms of the writing Attainment Targets could prove to be problematical; but Michael's poem 'The Forbidden Place' must surely fulfil in part En 3/5a: 'write in a variety of forms for a range of purposes and audiences, in ways which attempt to engage the interest of the reader.' The way in which Michael creates a humorous effect, by building up the suspense in the poem and then reaching an anti-climax, reveals a mature and perceptive sense of audience.

The Forbidden Place

There's a place which I know of, where vampires roam,
A place where it's not safe to be on your own,
And where dreadful, rotting skulls abide,
Which give you an ominous feeling inside,
It's not really safe to enter this room —
To disappear inside, would be to meet your doom!
It's a living cemetry inside of there —
If you manage to reappear, you'll have grey hair.
Now this room is spring-loaded, and booby-trapped,
To actually get through it, you really need a map.
To get to this room, you have to ascend some stairs,
A rickety, groaning, rotting affair.
The sight of this place, would make you swoon,
But the fact still remains
IT'S MY BEDROOM!!
(Michael aged 13)

The castle

In the distance
Is the darkness.

The Castle,
Derelict and deserted,
No sound,
No movement,

Just the flapping wings
of ferocious bats.
Inside damp and ancient,
Evil-smelling, ivy-clad,
In the corners skulls and
fungus,
Lurking in the chill of
night.

Skulls drawn and
battered,
Sunken eyes,
Bone-chilling smiles,
Enchanted cackles
Are all hidden away in
This antiquated castle.
(Karen aged 13)

There it was, hidden under the ivy-clad
stairway,
He reached out his evil-smelling hand. Staring
at the enchanted skull,
A bone-chilling laugh disturbing the silence, then
floating up the derelict staircase,
Stumbling upon an ancient sceptre, shaped like a bat
digging its' mysterious fangs into the metal,
Starving, he licked the skull, hoping to find blood,
Failing in his attempt,
He plunged his blood-thirsty fangs deep into his arms,
Sending a chill down his spine,
Travelling toward the antiquated graveyard, he fell,
His blood drained,
He lay there, dying slowly but surely,
The skull glowing with rising spirit,
The sceptre vanishing, as the life disappears from his body.
(Stuart aged 13)

Presentation Session

The last session of the project was held in the library and intended as a celebration of the work the pupils had jointly produced. Each group proudly displayed their work on tables and were invited to view the work produced by the other pupils. The Deputy Head was invited to join this last session, as he had kindly helped with the transport arrangements by driving the mini bus! He welcomed the Grange Junior School pupils and talked to all the pupils about their work and involvement in the project. Some pupils had also invented a rather disgusting drink, which was served to all who dared drink it. 'The Stomach Churner', comprising of Cherry 7-Up, Coca-Cola, lemonade, crushed biscuits and vanilla ice-cream, proved to be surprisingly popular.

The rest of this session involved a presentation of the poems and stories to the Grange Junior School pupils. A pupil, in the role of Count Alucard, welcomed everyone to the party in a most frightening fashion, and the pupils from the Grange Junior School sat enthralled as the pupils presented their work. Some pupils presented their stories with sound effects, some presented their poems dramatically in groups and some read aloud sections of their work. A real sense of audience was provided for the pupils from Daventry William Parker School and most fulfilled, more than adequately, the En 1/6c 'contribute to the planning and organisation of, and participate with fluency in, a group presentation or performance.' On reflection, it might have been even more productive for the mixed junior and secondary groups to have planned and performed a polished performance, but unfortunately only a limited amount of time was available for the joint sessions. The entire session was video taped and played back to the class during the next lesson.

The final piece of work involved pupils in the writing of an evaluative report on the entire project. The pupils were asked to include comments on the following areas:

1   An evaluation of the whole project;
2   An evaluation of their own contributions and work produced;
3   What they felt they had gained from the experience and what they felt the juniors had gained;
4   How the work or project could have been improved.

The reports proved to be interesting reading and provided a sound basis for a complete teacher review of the project. Elizabeth wrote a detailed report, of which only a portion is reproduced here:

In the Count Alucard project, I made a menu shaped like a ghost, with snake decorated inner and menu contents. I also made a small book, which is a story about a man returning from the dead in a coffin called Driving Dead. The menu has a striking cover and the food is very appropriate to the work, with some good word twisting. The story is a bit long though and in a way rather boring. Maybe if it were shorter and snappier, it would have been better.

Michael, commenting upon what he thought the Junior School pupils had gained from the project, wrote:

... The Junior School children will have had a taste of the Senior School, which might have helped them. They will also have learnt new skills in writing and what will be expected of them when they are older ...

Commenting upon the project as a whole, Elizabeth wrote:

... From this project, I have gained the ability to work with younger people. I enjoyed this project. I think it gave us a lot of freedom as to what we did and could do. Working with the juniors was good and I learnt to work better with other people and understand them. Overall, the project was fun and worth the effort ...

I would not seek to claim that the project was without its faults, or that it provides a panacea for the delivery of the English National Curriculum. The chapter has not addressed the problem of recording assessment, for example. Certainly, if the same project was used on another occasion, there are some aspects which would need to be changed and some aspects which need to be developed: more joint sessions to facilitate a mixed oral presentation would be one of the improvements which would greatly enhance the project from a curriculum continuity point of view. Yet the quality and variety of work produced successfully demonstrates the way in which much of the English Programmes of Study and Attainment Targets have been fulfilled in a cohesive, stimulating and exciting way. There was no loss of freedom and no sense of being restricted by the National Curriculum requirements. We, as teachers, need not fear the 'many headed' monster, but seek to use it as a vehicle for enriching our curriculum delivery. I agree with Elizabeth; the project was fun and worth the effort!

Follow-up Interviews

At the end of the project interviews were conducted with Jude Eddon and some of the pupils involved in the project, from both schools[5]. Jude Eddon felt that the project had been of great social value to her pupils, and even the shyest had benefited. She was pleased with the amount of oral work that the project had generated, and the increased motivation that resulted from the juniors working in groups with older pupils. She liked the cross-curricular nature of the work, especially the use of computers, and the way the juniors were the experts, because they'd used the Paintspa computer program before.

Jude Eddon was aware how the perceptions of the pupils altered during the project. The pupils from Daventry William Parker School were clearly amazed at how gifted some of the juniors were. The Grange juniors were impressed by the presentations given by the older pupils, and the quality of their booklets. The project made transition easier for the juniors, and helped them to become more familiar with the school.

The project had been planned as an 'extra' and didn't fit in with other curriculum planning for the term, but Jude Eddon found it easy to organize. The travel arrangements had gone more smoothly than the previous year, and she had enjoyed working with Jackie Turner on the project.

The junior school pupils were very enthusiastic about the project. They had enjoyed working with the older pupils, using the computers, and watching the final presentations. Most of them felt more confident about transition as a result. A few pupils admitted that they had felt anxious at the start of the project, though the majority had looked forward to it.

> Karen: I was nervous at first but we got a lot of work done and it was nice working with them.
>
> Dennis: Well, I thought it would be a good experience for us to go up to our new school and see what the work was like.

The pupils' enjoyment of working with the computers came through very clearly; the following extracts are typical.

> Dennis: I enjoyed the computers, because it was good to learn how to use computers, drawing on them ... The work was quite hard at first, but it got easier as you went on.
>
> William: I liked it when ... playing on computers, we had to tell the seniors what to do, instead of them telling us all the time.
>
> Karen: I think working on the computers was fun!
>
> Teacher: Did you know more about the Paintspa program than your senior school partner?
>
> Karen: Yes, because we'd done it at school before.
>
> Teacher: How did you find it, that you were the teacher in that situation?
>
> Karen: It was funny!

The juniors wrote most of their stories at the Grange Junior School, and discussed the first drafts with their classmates. Subsequently, they read the stories to their partners at Daventry William Parker School. Helga, Karen and Dennis gave this account of the story-writing process:

> Helga: We did this for the seniors ... we writ the stories in rough, and then we went round the class showing them, asking people what they thought about it ... and try to make it better for us.
>
> Teacher: Did anyone make suggestions to help you improve your story?
>
> Helga: Yes ... I didn't really need to put 'and' most of the time and I could put a few more interesting words.
>
> Teacher: What describing words?
>
> Helga: Some were describing words but others were to make it a bit more interesting.

Teacher:	Right. What did you do when you got all those sugges-tions?
Helga:	I writ them down and put them in ... We took it up to William Parker and showed it to our groups.
Karen:	When I took my story back to William Parker School my partner was very helpful in ... they showed me where I'd gone wrong over spelling and helped me with some phrases.
Teacher:	Did you have a chance to read their stories?
Karen:	Yes.
Teacher:	What did you say about that?
Karen:	I really liked their stories, I was impressed by them!
Dennis:	I didn't really have a chance to read Tim's story because ... um ... it was long and we didn't have much time to read.
Teacher:	What did you think of Tim's work?
Dennis:	Yeah, it was good. The drawing was good.
Teacher:	What was he like to work with?
Dennis:	He was helpful, and he explained what to do.

All the junior school pupils interviewed felt that they had benefited considerably from the project. The following extract is typical of their responses:

Dennis:	I think we got a lot out of the project because we were learning on the computers as well as writing.
Teacher:	Janet, what do you think you got out of it?
Janet:	Working with older children and ... people you were just getting to know, people who are going to be in the next school.
Karen:	I think that we learned that it wasn't so bad in the senior school, and that we could actually work with the seniors and they weren't as bad as we thought.
Heidi:	I think we learned a lot, and spellings and that.
Luke:	I think it gave us more experience for when we go up because ... they're not so bad and we got to know them.
William:	It helped with putting expression into your words ... and writing stories.

The children also felt more confident about transition as a result of the project, as this extract shows:

Dennis:	I feel it's helped us because we know where the computer room is, and if we need anything and we get lost. It helped us with bigger pupils so we know if we get lost or something ... we know where to find them.
Teacher:	Janet, how do you feel it helped you?

Janet:	By knowing what the people are like.
Teacher:	Did it make you feel more confident?
Janet:	I'm still a bit nervous, but I'm more confident because I know what it's like now, and I'll be able to get through.
William:	Some people were scared about the older school, but we've been there for a couple of days ... so we're less scared.
Luke:	Instead of being nervous you're just calmer and not worrying.

Some of the pupils at Daventry William Parker School who took part in the project were interviewed as well. Like the juniors, they had also felt apprehensive before meeting their partners. Much of the initial anxiety had centred round the difference in ages.

Verity:	I thought they were all going to be very small, not know a thing and be a bit thick.
Teacher:	Were you anxious about it?
Verity:	Yeah, I thought I wouldn't get on with them very well.
Daniel:	At first I thought they might be a bit thick because they were younger than us but then I thought that I wasn't *that* thick when I was in the fourth year.
Tim:	I felt nervous! Might make a fool of myself or something!
Teacher:	How would you have done that?
Tim:	Well, you never know how to react with that sort of age group, do you? Well, I don't, anyway!

However, good personal relationships quickly developed, and most of the pupils felt that they had worked well with their junior school partners.

Verity:	I had a very chatty person, she was always talking. She was very anxious about the school, and didn't seem to want to get on with the work.
Teacher:	So the main interest for her when she first met you was to find out all about the school?
Verity:	Yes, about what they could and couldn't do.
Tim:	My partner was an easy–come, easy–go person. I enjoyed working with him actually because he always got on with the work, and did some of his own ideas. He had a lot of his own ideas when he came, he didn't leave it all to me, so I thought that was good.
Teacher:	You mean, he brought ideas with him before you started working?
Tim:	Yeah, I thought it would just be my ideas and me over-powering him, but he had quite a few ideas of his own ... We worked on the computers mostly and it was

good fun. We talked quite a lot, but we got the work done sufficiently.

Daniel: I found my partner knew more about Paintspa than me, because he'd used it at school.

Teacher: So your partner was the expert, compared to you?

Daniel: Yes.

Teacher: How did you feel about that?

Daniel: Didn't bother me.

Verity: I was learning how to use the computer program as I went along. I had used one in the Art Block, but it was a different one, I think, and we decided to do it all by hand in the end.

Daniel: Well, I kept finding that I was producing the ideas and ... I didn't want it to be that I was doing all the work, so I kept getting him to make suggestions.

Tim: I did most of the work but Dennis didn't seem to mind so it was quite a good partnership, and he went along with the ideas ... He didn't really want to do his own ideas, but he did a couple, like he did this crossword thing and it was good, so I tried that, and he did quite lot of the presentation.

Kathy: The partner I had was quite lively, and we got on quite well.

Nigel: My partner was OK, he tended to agree with my answers though ... sometimes I let him come up with his suggestions.

Kathy: Well, I enjoyed the work, I liked the way that we all worked together and the way we co-operated ...

Peter: I liked doing all the work and drawing the covers in the computer lab for the menus.

The older pupils were also sensitive to the personal benefits which they gained from working with the younger children.

Tim: I learned how to work with another person, and not to be overpowering and bossy, and I thought it was a good experience working with a younger person.

Daniel: Well, I agree with what Tim said about working with someone younger than you.

Verity: You begin to understand them a bit more ... being a youngest child I don't get on with younger people.

Teacher: What do you think you got out of the project personally?

Nigel: Learning to work with someone younger than you from a different school.

Peter: Um ... same as Nick ... Well, like it gives more experience to work with other people when you get older.

Kathy: Well, learning to co-operate with younger people and respect them more.

Nigel: The worst part was during the presentation. Robert was reading his story, and I'd taped some screams on a tape. I went to press it for the screams and it wouldn't come, so I had to stop it.

Peter: I put different music on during our presentation, because I said I'd change the music, but I didn't tell the person who was acting out what it was.

Teacher: What effect did that have?

Peter: Well, laughing.

Kathy: Was he trying to play the keyboard?

Peter: Yeah, well the organ ... it came up like different music!

The transcripts clearly reveal the range of benefits that both groups of pupils felt they had gained from working with each other. Greater self-confidence and mutual respect, increasing competence in the use of computers, and improvements in oral and writing skills had resulted from the project. A bridge had also been created for the juniors, who were about to transfer to Daventry William Parker School in September.

Notes

1 I am sincerely grateful to Jude Eddon, who had the original idea for the project and with whom the project was planned and delivered. I would also like to thank the pupils of Daventry William Parker School and Grange Junior School for their boundless enthusiasm and sense of commitment to the project. My thanks also to Daniel Tabor and Bob Armstrong for their encouragement and practical support.

2 'A Guide To Teacher Assessment' (1990) Packs A, B, and C is published by Heinemann Educational on behalf of SEAC. It was produced under contract with the STAIR Consortium by SEAC. Copies should have been sent to all Key Stage 1 and 2 teachers. Whilst in places an unwieldy document, pack C does provide some useful tips and advice.

Additional copies are available from:

Information Section
SEAC
Newcombe House
45 Notting Hill Gate
London W11 3JB

3 The pupils were also fulfilling the following element in the Programme of Study for KS 3: '... integrate more than one form of information, *for example words and pictures; symbols; pictures and sound*, into a single presentation or report for a particular audience;' (DES 1990b, p. 55). I am grateful to HMSO for permission to quote this statement.

4 'Creative Language', Editor David Orme (1990), is a photocopiable resource published three times a year by Stanley Thornes. Some very practical lesson ideas, along with poems from the Schools Poetry Association are included.
5 This section was written by Daniel Tabor, based on the interviews which he conducted at the end of the 'Count Alucard' project.

Evaluation of the Projects

Independent evaluation of five of the projects was carried out by John Follett, Head of Daventry PDC; his report conveys the flavour of the joint sessions.

> *Language Continuity Project — William Parker and*
> *Contributory Primary Schools*

I have provided a few notes on each of the projects I have visited. I must say how much I have enjoyed the experience and how impressed I have been with the level of cooperation, enjoyment and commitment to the work I have witnessed during these times. I was only sorry I could not be available to come in on more occasions. I will make a few observations on each of the sessions I saw.

Wednesday 14th February: Periods 1 and 2 (Library): Mrs. S. Herlihy's Year 8 group and Barby School's top juniors
There was a high level of mutual support involved in the group work. The level of communication between individuals was good and the standard of work high. I thought the short input from Mrs. Herlihy in preparation for the poetry writing was very well pitched to meet the needs of the group and laid the groundwork well for the poetry work about to be undertaken.

Friday 2nd March: Periods 5 and 6 (Computer Room): Jackie Turner's Year 8 group and Grange Junior School top juniors
Again, there was a high level of mutual support in the group work. The children very much enjoyed the IT element using Newspaper and the tasks set. There was a minimum of 'listening to the teacher' as a class and both teachers' time, as well as mine, was used giving help to individual groups. I found that members of one group were only too happy to show another group how to carry out certain functions in the programme. Again, the level of communication was both supportive and of a high order.

Monday 5th March: Periods 1 and 2: Mrs. W. Collins' Year 7 group and Grange Junior School top juniors
I was accompanied by Margaret Riley (INSET Inspector) on this occasion and both she and I were impressed by the degree of mutual support and cooperation amongst the children. The degree of difficulty of the poetry

work was such that it stretched the more able, while at the same time gave the weaker pupils a sense of achievement.

Wednesday 14th March: Periods 1 and 2 (Library): Mrs. Herlihy
This was the follow up to the groups I saw working on the 14th February. The same general comments apply and in fact as the session developed all the adults felt that they were in danger of cutting the flow of communication by making inputs into the groups because they were working so well together.

Friday 23rd March: Periods 3 and 4 (Library): Mr. D. Tabor's Year 8 group,
Grange Junior and Staverton Primary School
Mixed small groups of primary and secondary school pupils had worked together previously to plan a 'TV news spot'. This session involved filming the work. There was a high level of involvement and commitment on behalf of pupils and teachers. Those watching were very good, both in terms of their behaviour/noise level and in their support/advice to groups performing.

The work involved planning, co-operation/collaboration on the project by all concerned as well as performance before the camera, which is working very much towards the aim of 'creating a sense of audience' among pupils in the way language work and the media studies are moving.

Monday 26th March: Periods 1 and 2 (Library): Mrs. L. Unwin's Year 9 group and
Braunston top juniors
This group work followed the same style but with a different agenda. The mixed groups were working on advertising by whatever means their imaginary sports/leisure centre/ shopping centre. Again there was a high degree of involvement of all concerned, a high degree of decision-making and creativeness was evident and some novel and interesting advertising ploys were coming out. Watch out Saatchi and Saatchi!

Conclusion

This book has charted the development of a curriculum continuity programme in English over a period of four years. Though the book has been written largely from the viewpoint of a secondary school teacher, the written and spoken words of pupils and teachers in both phases have been used as much as possible. We have tried to show how the approach developed here has enabled primary and secondary pupils to work together successfully on a series of joint projects, thereby contributing to curriculum continuity in English. These projects have provided a variety of child-centred learning experiences for all the pupils involved. The children were not only working *with* each other, but also *for* each other, the sense of audience being an important part of most projects.

Much good oral work resulted from the interactions of pupils, and writing for a 'real' audience undoubtedly stimulated many pupils' creativity, and increased their motivation. The projects have covered a wide range of topics, including IT, Media Studies, and workshops with practising writers. We have also demonstrated how the projects hit a wide band of levels in the Attainment Targets for English, and covered many elements in the Programmes of Study.

The projects were owned by the teachers in both phases who planned them. Liaison with our contributory primary schools was improved as a result, and colleagues gained greater understanding of each other's approaches to language work. Good relationships developed between the pupils who worked together, and follow-up interviews and surveys showed that this helped pupils in Year 6 to make the transition to the secondary school more easily. Over 1100 primary and secondary pupils have participated so far.

Derricott has suggested that curriculum continuity implies an agreed curriculum plan between primary or middle contributory schools, and the secondary school to which pupils are transferred (Derricott 1985, p. 16). We have not attempted to draw up a 'grand plan' with our primary schools. Rather, we have approached curriculum continuity from a different perspective. Through working together, we have provided primary school pupils with continuity in their curricular experience of English. Many of the primary pupils who took part felt that they gained some idea of what English at the secondary school would be like.

We have shown that these projects provided many opportunities for the assessment of Attainment Targets, though this was not a determining factor in planning the projects. Clearly, the National Curriculum should not be regarded as a strait-jacket, though it does force us to think more precisely about what we are expecting children to do, and which elements we want to assess at any one time. Jackie Turner has demonstrated in detail (in Chapter 12) how the activities in a project can be aligned with the Attainment Targets, Programmes of Study, and opportunities for assessment.

We are trying to start a National Curriculum Language Planning Group in Daventry in 1990, involving all the primary schools, and both secondary schools, to address issues of common concern. The experience of working together on joint projects, and the relationships between teachers that have developed as a result, should contribute much to the success of such a group. More generally, the approach described here could be broadened in scope, and used in the planning of cross-curricular projects across the primary-secondary divide.

Curriculum continuity is a complex issue, particularly at a time when education is undergoing radical change. It is hoped that the present study will contribute to the development of a 5–16 perspective among practising teachers of English.

Appendix 1

A Month in the Country: An Account of a Month's Flexi-Secondment (6 June–8 July 1988)

This report has been reproduced with a few minor alterations. It gives a picture of our contributory schools, and the language work which was observed during the flexi-secondment. Much of it remains valid in spite of the introduction of the National Curriculum. It also shows how we were trying to 'build bridges' with our primary school colleagues at this stage of our curriculum continuity work.

Part 1

Introduction

This flexi-secondment grew out of two years' work in curriculum continuity with three of our contributory schools. One of the aims of the flexi-secondment was to observe in detail the different opportunities for language development at the Grange Junior School and Welton Primary School, spending a week in each school. In the second half of the secondment I visited all our other contributory schools, spending a day at each one observing classes. I was able to take three of my colleagues from the English Department with me, and each of them visited two schools. The other aims of the secondment were to improve liaison between the contributory schools and the English Department at Daventry School, and to lay the groundwork for joint projects in 1988/89. We hope that these projects will involve all of our contributory schools. The secondment was divided into two blocks of a fortnight each, with a week's interval, and it ran from 6 June–8 July 1988.

My role in the contributory schools was as an observer, not an evaluator, and inevitably I can only present a series of personal impressions. I have focused on the junior classes in Years 5 and 6, since many of these pupils were about to make the transition to Daventry School. Where possible, I have included examples of pupils' work, and other materials from the schools. I have written this report as an English teacher, but with an interest in language across the curriculum. It is intended primarily for my colleagues at Daventry School, though I hope my perceptions will also be of interest to our colleagues in the contributory schools.

I have presented the range of language activities which I observed, or which were described to me, in tabular form. In Part 2 I have described my visits to each of the schools in more detail. I was made very welcome by the Headteachers and staff of our contributory schools, and given every assistance. My first draft of this account of the secondment was circulated to colleagues at our contributory schools, and I have incorporated their suggestions and corrections in this version.

Outcomes of the Flexi-Secondment

1 I made a video of the range of language activities at the Grange Junior School and Welton Primary School, and I showed extracts of it to my colleagues in the English Department at Daventry School.
2 The visits by three of my colleagues to some of the contributory schools enabled them to make the initial contacts from which we shall develop joint projects in 1988/89. A programme of visits by primary school staff to Daventry School, planned for 1988/89 through INSET will take place in the context of our curriculum continuity work.
3 I hope this report, and our work in curriculum continuity, will give colleagues in the English Department at Daventry School (and in other departments) a clearer picture of the range of language activities and approaches to teaching used in the contributory schools. This should help us to plan our first year teaching with greater understanding.

Recommendations

1 I was impressed by the colourful display work and the child-centred environment in most classrooms. In part this was a result of each class being taught everything by one teacher. Hence it was necessary to have most teaching resources at hand. Surely we could adapt or recreate something of this child-centred environment in our own specialist teaching rooms? To take two small examples, we could have a selection of dictionaries and reference books in each classroom, and more resources for display work. What I am principally concerned about is the approach of our colleagues in the contributory schools. I am sure we can learn much from talking to them, and visiting their classrooms.
2 It seemed to me that the most creative language work grew out of projects, whilst language skills were often developed through rather formal language exercises. Perhaps we could widen the scope of our English teaching, and adopt a multi-disciplinary approach for certain

topics e.g. the Vikings, or the First World War, through collaboration with colleagues in (say) the Humanities Department.

3   We should reconsider the place of skills work in the curriculum of the English Department. Most of us would not to wish to set children formal exercises from course books, but would prefer to use the children's own writing as the starting point for teaching grammar, punctuation etc. Considering the change in the nature of our intake which will result from reorganization, surely this is a good opportunity for reconsidering the place of skills work in the syllabus.

4   The Maths Department sends a check list to the contributory schools, so that teachers can tick the Maths skills which each child has acquired. Could we not devise a 'can do' check list of skills for English? However this will only be useful if we have a departmental policy about the range of skills which we are trying to impart to first year pupils at Daventry School.

5   There is quite an overlap between the fiction which the brighter pupils at primary school read in Year 6, and the fiction they encounter at Daventry School. We need to be informed of this. Our contributory schools vary greatly in size, in the nature of their intakes, and in the teaching styles of their staff. We need to be aware of these differences when meeting our new pupils in Year 7 at the beginning of the academic year.

Acknowledgments

I am most grateful to the Headteachers, staff and pupils of our contributory schools for their generous help and cooperation, and to Mr. Doherty for his support. I am grateful to the LEA, and to Mrs. Rashida Spencer, for enabling me to have the flexi-secondment. Thanks are also due to Mrs. F. Start, Head of Daventry Teachers' Centre (1987–88), for her help and encouragement.

Part 2

The Grange Junior School (6–10 June 1988)

Introduction

The Grange Junior School is one of the largest in the county, with 395 pupils. They were divided into thirteen classes, each with over thirty pupils. Year 5 was the largest, with four classes; the other years were divided into three classes. Each class encompassed the full ability range. The children were taught everything by one teacher during the year, and moved on to a different teacher in the following year. In addition to the thirteen class teachers there was the Special Needs Coordinator, who organized the reading schemes throughout the school, and the Acting Head Teacher. There were a number of ancillary teachers who came for short periods during the week to

CHART OF LANGUAGE ACTIVITIES		ORAL WORK							LISTENING TO....							READING....								WRITING									
		Discussion in pairs, small groups	Discussion with T.: one-to-one	T-directed, with whole class	Giving instructions	Giving a talk or presentation	Role play, acting	a pupil reading	T. reading	instructions from T.	instructions from peers	a presentation by pupil	a broadcast	a talk by a visitor	music	a coursebook	a reference book	own choice book	instructions	aloud to the class	to the T.	first draft of own work	first draft of partner's work	Handwriting exercises	Note taking	Copying	Drafting, editing, correcting	Making a neat copy	Creative writing	Project work: T. directed	Project work: own choice	Skills work: formal exercises	Group work on story or booklet
THE GRANGE JUNIOR SCHOOL (6-10 June)	Year 3		✓	✓				✓	✓				✓	✓	✓	✓		✓							✓								
	Year 4	✓	✓	✓		✓			✓	✓			✓	✓			✓							✓					✓	✓		✓	
	Year 5			✓				✓	✓				✓	✓		✓		✓											✓		✓		✓
	Year 6	✓		✓		✓		✓	✓	✓			✓	✓		✓	✓			✓		✓	✓	✓		✓	✓		✓	✓	✓	✓	
WELTON PRIMARY SCHOOL (13-17 June)	Top Class	✓	✓	✓	✓		✓	✓	✓	✓			✓	✓	✓	✓	✓	✓	✓		✓	✓	✓	✓	✓	✓	✓	✓	✓	✓	✓	✓	✓
	Middle Class	✓	✓	✓	✓			✓	✓					✓	✓	✓		✓	✓	✓							✓	✓	✓	✓	✓		✓ ✓
	Infants and Reception Class	✓	✓	✓	✓			✓	✓				✓	✓	✓	✓	✓	✓		✓	✓				✓		✓			✓	✓		✓
CRICK PRIMARY SCHOOL (27 June)	Years 5 & 6	✓	✓		✓												✓							✓	✓	✓				✓	✓		
	Years 3 & 4	✓	✓														✓			✓	✓				✓	✓					✓		✓
	Year 2		✓		✓																												
	Year 1							✓																									
STAVERTON PRIMARY SCHOOL (28 June)	Juniors (Years 3-6)	✓	✓													✓																	✓
BRAUNSTON PRIMARY SCHOOL (30 June)	Year 6			✓					✓																						✓		
	Year 5		✓	✓									✓	✓															✓	✓	✓		
	Year 4	✓	✓																											✓			
	Year 3			✓																							✓		✓			✓
	Infants (Year 2)	✓	✓																														✓
	Infants (Year 1)			✓																													
	Infants (Reception)	✓					✓																										
KILSBY PRIMARY SCHOOL (1 July)	Years 5 & 6	✓	✓						✓		✓		✓	✓						✓	✓					✓							
	Years 3 & 4 & Infants				✓				✓		✓			✓					✓														
BARBY PRIMARY SCHOOL (4 July)	Years 5 & 6	✓	✓		✓				✓								✓				✓	✓			✓	✓	✓	✓	✓	✓	✓ ✓		
THE ABBEY PRIMARY SCHOOL (8 July)	Years 5 & 6	✓	✓					✓	✓	✓						✓										✓	✓	✓	✓	✓	✓		

Table Appendix 1.1   Chart of language activities

help pupils with hearing problems, or pupils from the ethnic minorities with specific language problems. The school was going through a period of transition, with a new Head Teacher taking up her post in September. The reorganization of education in Daventry, and the impending closure of the Grange Secondary School, resulted in the fourth year pupils that I saw going to Daventry School or Southbrook School in September 1988.

Language Policy

The school's policy on language had been shaped by the teacher with special responsibility for this area of the curriculum. The school's language policy document emphasized the importance of the pupils' own experiences, and their interaction with parents and teachers in the development of language. Dramatic play, movement and dance, mime and the senses, were identified as some of the areas which could provide stimuli for language development, starting with oracy, and leading into writing and reading.

A complementary view was to be found in 'The Development of Work in English', which identified specific skills that pupils should master in four stages while at the Grange Junior School. Each stage was subdivided into comprehension, sentences, paragraphs and composition, vocabulary and spelling, and grammar and punctuation. The individual skills were more complex at each succeeding stage. Other documents, for example, to help staff with the teaching of spelling or handwriting, had been produced within the school.

Reading

The reading policy within the school was very well organized. The teacher concerned had developed a reading scheme built round the Oxford Junior Readers, Reading 360 and a selection of other books, arranged in seven sections of increasing difficulty (see Table 1.2). Each pupil was tested with the Schonell word recognition test at the beginning of the first year, and put on the appropriate reader. The whole school was tested for reading in November and May; the Spar Tests A and B were given to Years 3 and 4, and the 'Daniels and Diack Test 12' was given to Years 5 and 6.

Reading was very important, and each class teacher heard every pupil read at least once a week, and noted the pupil's progress on a special form (see Table 1.3). This usually occurred at the beginning of the morning. Those pupils who had reading difficulties went to the teacher with reponsibility for Special Needs every day, in year groups of ten to twelve thirty-five to forty minutes, and usually when they were not missing one of their 'core' subjects. The teacher saw sixty-two such pupils every day, and felt that the number of children needing special help had increased over the years, largely due, it seems, to an increase in social pressures. Pupils entered the school in Year 3, from the adjacent infant school. In 1987–88 Year 3 contained twenty-two pupils out of ninety who needed help with reading. The teacher identified the underlying problems as those of language acquisition, and basic vocabulary, which many children lacked.

Within the Special Needs room I observed children reading to the

REVISED READING SCHEME

SECTION 1 READABILITY – 7 years
Reading 360 Level 6 Books 1–7
Oxford Junior Readers Book 1 (4 Titles)
Roundabouts D Books 1–4
Reading 360 Level 7 Books 1–7

SECTION 2 READABILITY – 7½/8 years
Oxford Junior Readers Book 2 (4 Titles)
Reading 360 Level 8 Books 1–7
Flightpath A (Yellow) Books 1–8
Storyline Geography 1
Wide Range – Stories from World Religions
          1 Science Stories 1

SECTION 3 READABILITY 8/8½ years
Oxford Junior Readers Book 3 (4 Titles)
Flightpath B (Blue) Books 1–8
Dolphin D (12 Titles)
Reading 360 Level 9 Books 1–5
Storyline Geography 2
Wide Range – Stories from World Religions 2
          Science Stories 2
Flightpath C (REd) Books 1–8

SECTION 4 READABILITY 9/9½ years
Oxford Junior Readers Book 4 (4 Titles)
Roundabouts G Books 1–4
Roundabouts H Books 1–4
Flightpath D (Green) Books 1–8
Dolphin E Books 1–6

SECTION 5 READABILITY 9½/10 years
Oxford Junior Readers 5 (4 Titles)
Dolphin F Books 1–6
Roundabouts I Books 1–4
Buccaneers Books 1–8
New Buccaneers Books 1–8
Storyline Geography 3
Wide Range – Stories from World Religions 3
          Science Stories 3

SECTION 6 READABILITY 10/11 years
Oxford Junior Readers 6 (4 Titles)
Dolphin G Books 1–7
Dolphin H Books 1–6
The Gay Dolphin
Storyline Geography 4
Wide Range – Stories from World Religions 4
          Science Stories 4

SECTION 7 READABILITY 11+ years
Windmill Series

Appropriate reading books supplementary to
each section can be found on the bottom
shelves.

Table Appendix 1.2 Revised reading scheme

SUPPLEMENTARY READING BOOKS

SECTION 1
Language Patterns Stage 1. Yellow
Wide Range 1 Blue
    "   " 1 Green
    "   " Interest 1
    "   " More Interest 1

SECTION 2
Language Patterns Stage 2 Blue
Wide Range 2 Blue
    "   " Interest 2
    "   " More Interest 2
Carry On Reading 1

SECTION 3
Wide Range 3 Blue
    "   " 3 Green
    "   " Interest 3
    "   " More Interest 3
Dolphin C

SECTION 3/4
Carry on Reading 2 (8½/9½ years)

SECTION 4
Wide Range 4 Blue
    "   " 4 Green
    "   " Interest 4
Carry on Reading 3

SECTION 5
Wide Range 5 Blue
    "   " 5 Green
    "   " 5 Green (New Edition)
Carry on Reading 4

SECTION 6
Wide Range 6 Blue
    "   " 6 Green
    "   " 6 Red
    "   " Myths and Legends
Carry on Reading 5

11 + SECTION
Carry on Reading 6
Wide Range Red Book 8 (12+ Reading Age)
Reading On Book 1 Yellow
Reading On Book 1 Red
Reading On Book 2 Yellow
Reading On Book 2 Red

READING RECORD		STEVEN ROBINSON		
DATE	C.A.	R.A		
MAY '86	9.4	10.8 SPAR	Nov 87. 10.11. 12.6.	
NOV 86		11.6		
MAY '87	10.4	11.2 Daniels & Diack 12		
BOOK	DATE	PAGE	COMMENT	
COR Red 3	11/9	p61	The Ghost of T.Kang.	
OJR5 Orange		p123(19/9)	114-116 7/1 GONS/1	
OJR5 History	3/10	107(3/10)		
~5 Myths & Legends	14/10	42 (9/10)	WR4 Holey. comp 20/1.	
			OJR6 comp 26/1.	
G1 The Ashworth Growler	22/10	60 (29/10)	W R Science ③ 29/1.	
G2 Nobody's Pony	3/11		COR No6. comp.11/2.	
G4 The Great Expedition	11/11	8(11/11) 76 (19/11)	W.R. Readers. 6g. " 29/2.	
G5 Adventure in the Sky	20/11		The Insect Man comp 15/2	
G6 Moon Adventure	27/11			
G7 ?			Wideling 9 Rely J 3 comp	
CCR 4 ?			12/4.	
OJR6 Myths & Legends	22/1		CORb comp 18/4	
OJR6 Orange Series	18/2		W R Red 8. comp. 16/5.	
OJR6 New Series	6/3			
OJR6 History	20/3			
...	-/1.			
H3	31/1			
H ?	14/5.			
H 4	2/6			
H5 Singapore Story	13/7	comp 9/9.		
H6. comp.		p28 ... 8/10.		
Roundabout 14		50-52. comp. 13/10.		
"		comp n/c		
...		comp 21/10.		
.3		comp 22.o.		
Wide Range 4.		comp. s/11.		
Carry On Reading	5	comp 14/11.		
The Grey Dolphin				
The Day the Rilly fell		comp 2/12.		

Table Appendix 1.3 Oral reading record

teacher on a one-to-one basis, working quietly in small groups, and discussing and interpreting pictures.

In addition to an Oxford Junior Reader (or similar type of book), most pupils at the school had an individual class reader, chosen from a selection of books kept in their classroom, as well as being able to choose a book from the school library (see Table 1.4).

Classes in Year 3
I observed each of the three classes in Year 3 and in the first I saw the following activities: handwriting exercises, where pupils were learning to join up letters, and individual work on multiplication (using 'Mathematics for Schools' by Fletcher *et al.*). There was a lot of oral work, between the teacher and the pupils, and among the pupils themselves, particularly when the class discussed a poem about a cottage garden. This lead to the pupils writing their own poems about cottage gardens, using alliteration, which most pupils finished before the end of the lesson.

In another class in Year 3 a taped music lesson from the radio was used. The pupils discussed the words of the song, the technical terms connected with the length of the beats and rests, and listened carefully to the instruc-

Book Title	Author	Publisher	ISBN
The Enormous Crocodile	Roald Dahl	Puffin.	
The Magic Finger	Roald Dahl	Puffin.	
Fantastic Mr Fox	Roald Dahl	Puffin.	
The Witch of Monopoly Manor	Margaret Stuart Barry	Lions	
Danny Fox	David Thomson.	Puffin.	
The Pocket Mouse	Barbara Willard.	Julia MacRae	
The Lost Merbaby	Puffin	Puffin.	
The Wishing Nut Tree	M ~ M Baker.	—	
Lotta.	Astrid Lindgren	Magnet	
The Worst Witch	Jill Murphy	Puffin	
The Worst Witch Strikes Again	—		
A Bad Spell for the Worst Witch	Jill Murphy	Kestrel	
The Wild Swans	H.C. Anderson.	Macmillan.	
A Book of Giants			
Ghosts ~ Goblins	Ruth Manning Sanders	Magnet	
Wizards			
Witches			
Gods, Men ~ Monsters from the Greek Myths	Michael Gibson.	Peter Lowe.	
Wolves of Willoughby Chase	Joan Aiken	Puffin.	
The Children of Green Knowe	Lucy M Boston	Puffin.	
James ~ the Giant Peach	Roald Dahl	Puffin	
Elidor	Alan Garner.	Lions	
The Iron Man	Ted Hughes	Faber.	
Charmed Life	Diana Wynne-Jones	Puffin.	
Stig of the Dump	Clive King	Puffin.	
Tom's Midnight Garden	Philippa Pearce	Puffin.	
The Cricket in Times Square	George Selden	Puffin.	
(2) Charlotte's Web	E. B White.	Puffin.	
Finn Family Moomintroll	Tove Jansson.	Puffin	
The Eighteenth Emergency	Betsy Byars	Puffin	
Danny Champion of the World	Roald Dahl	Puffin.	
The Railway Children	E. Nesbit	Puffin	

Table Appendix 1.4   *Some recent acquisitions for the school library*

tions for clapping, which were difficult and required concentration. They clearly enjoyed singing the songs. The same class then spent twenty-five minutes performing country dancing in the hall to a tape, and again they had to listen carefully to follow instructions, which most pupils did successfully.

In the third class in Year 3 some of the pupils were planting runner beans with the teacher's help, as part of their project on 'Plants and Trees'; others were drawing pictures for the project. The class also asked me questions about Daventry School. These impressions indicate the range of activities which pupils in Year 3 were involved in. I was struck by the friendly atmosphere in all classes, and the responsive nature of the children.

Oral skills were developed through drama or role play:

... I put them in a situation they know of, such as going shopping, having breakfast, going on holiday, that sort of thing. Or they act out plays that they write or choose for themselves ... At the beginning of the year they're very reticent, very giggly and don't know how to work together. Now there's been a lot of improvement. We do quite a lot of discussion ... in all kinds of work, not just English.

In general, oral work was important with all years, and was developed across the curriculum. More formal comprehension skills and grammar were developed by the use of course books e.g. by Haydn Richards, and the more recent series 'Developing Comprehension', while spelling was improved through the use of Spelling Workshop cards.

Classes in Year 4

One class, engaged on a project about the Vikings, measured out a Viking longboat in the playground, and simulated rowing. This involved virtually the whole class in discussion and working together. In a Maths lesson the pupils were working at their own rate through 'Mathematics for School', Books 2 and 3, discussing their work quietly with a neighbour or the teacher.

Where writing was concerned, the teacher felt that her aim was to improve the pupils' fluency. To this end she used précis skills, cloze procedures (where pupils fill in missing words in a passage) and close reading of passages. The need for formal skills was also emphasized; 'Junior English' (Gregory 1980) was used for grammar and comprehension work.[1] Some pupils showed me their project folders on the Vikings, which had involved them in note-taking, creative writing and illustration. They were all excited about their forthcoming visit to York.

In another class, the pupils had watched a TV programme about rocks, and were discussing the specialized words (e.g. 'igneous', 'sedimentary') with the teacher. The pupils examined a selection of rocks in detail using magnifying glasses, talking about them with the teacher and members of their group. The pupils enjoyed doing this. The teacher discussed with the class the sort of vocabulary they would use to describe the rock, and by the end of the lesson all the pupils had started to write a short piece entitled 'My Rock'.

The teachers of the Year 4 pupils felt that the children were not yet ready to draft and rewrite their work, though ideas might first be put down in a rough book. Pupils in Years 3 and 4 watched the TV programme 'Look and Read' for two terms, which helped them with phonics, punctuation etc.

Classes in Year 5

A great deal of creative work took place in Year 5. I was only able to visit two Year 5 classes briefly, when the pupils were doing language work. In one class the pupils were doing the Blackwells Spelling Workshop in groups of three or four. The same teacher used 'Sound Sense' (Tansley 1970) and 'Junior English' for comprehension and grammar work, and was keen to instill in her pupils correct spelling, neat writing and accurate recording of information. Stories and poems were written straight into exercise books, without preliminary drafting. This class had started to write in ink in the summer term.

In the other Year 5 class I observed, the pupils read a short extract from an Alison Uttley story in 'Complete English', Book 2, by E.G. Thorpe (1962). The pupils discussed the comprehension questions with the teacher, and then spent the rest of the lesson writing the answers in their exercise books. The teacher felt that her class found creative work difficult, possibly due to the pupils' poor vocabulary. There was a large box of new books for the library in the classroom, and some of the pupils volunteered to help the teacher with the school library at break.

Given the short time I spent with these classes, the activities which I saw were not representative of the range of work which the children were involved in.

One morning all the pupils in Years 5 and 6 went into the hall to hear a half-hour religious broadcast, which included a dramatized extract from 'Pilgrim's Progress'. In the third class which I observed, pupils discussed the use of the inverted comma with the teacher, and spent the lesson doing exercises on this from 'Mainline English'. Pupils who finished early continued with on their project on Ironbridge, by copying an introductory paragraph from the board.

Classes in Year 6
I felt that all the work of Years 3–5 bore fruit with the pupils in Year 6. In one class the pupils were working in groups of threes or fours, mapping an imaginary desert island, and then planning a joint adventure story about it. Most pupils were discussing their ideas animatedly, and were able to give me a clear account of what they were doing. Their ideas were worked out on rough paper, and then each pupil made a neat copy of the final version of the story. The pair and group discussions were intended to help the pupils improve the quality of their written work.

This class had one poetry anthology lesson a week, when they read a wide selection of anthologies, and copied out the poems they liked into their poetry books, and illustrated them. Towards the end of the lesson the pupils read out the poems they had chosen, and discussed what they liked about them with the teacher and the other pupils. The teacher was keen to improve performance, and corrected poor intonation and expression when the poems were being read.

The class spent a part of most days at some stage of drafting a story or poem, or a piece of writing connected with a project. The pupils had produced some beautiful books on their canals project. The teacher emphasized that she did not neglect formal skills, e.g. comprehension, and used the 'Developing Comprehension' series by Lynskey and Stillie, which also gave scope for creative work. This series was used by one of the other Year 6 teachers.

When watching TV programmes or videos connected with projects, the teacher showed the programme twice, so that the pupils would learn to take notes the second time. Sometimes pupils had read a short passage from a course book, and then wrote out the gist of the passage from memory, as a way of learning précis skills.

In another class I was used as a resource. I went in, looked at the class, and walked out. The class discussed my appearance, and possible profession, with great enthusiasm. I revisited the class the next day, and the pupils read out their descriptions, and discussed their initial theories about my occupation. The suggestions were highly imaginative; I was described as children's clothes designer, a professor, an inventor, a child psychologist, a manager of a basketball team looking for tall children etc. The discussion was animated, and a consensus emerged that I might be an inventor looking for children of a certain size to operate a new machine. All the children started to design the sort of machine they thought I had invented.

By the next day, most of the children had discovered who I really was, but they continued to design their machines (mainly for space travel). The teacher had prepared an information leaflet which the children filled in with the specifications of their machines.

In the third class I visited pupils were working on their projects on the Victorians. The pupils were involved and interested in what they were doing; some were finishing off their poems about transport, others were using reference books to research topics that interested them, and copying out extracts. The pupils had produced some attractive pictures of Victorian costumes. All the pupils in Year 6 that I talked to were looking forward to going to the senior school. Those who had written letters to, and visited my class in Year 7 at Daventry School felt they already had friends there.

Planning, Resources and Records
All teachers had to plan their work using a half termly forecast, according to the subject area. The forecast usually combined creative and formal activities (see Figure 1.1). A record was kept of which activities or topics were actually covered. The teachers in each year met regularly to discuss project topics, and developed a list of topics to cover several curriculum areas. For example, the projects in Year 6 included a historical project on canals, a geography project on the seaside, a science project on the flora and fauna of the coastline. Language work pervaded all these areas, and the project could be used as an opportunity for creative work, comprehension skills, oral work etc.

Classes were timetabled for certain activities or rooms, e.g. Maths, TV programmes, the hall (for dancing or PE). Apart from that teachers devised their own timetables, though most started with English and Maths in the morning, when the pupils were freshest. They heard their pupils read from the course readers at least once a week, and most classes did spelling work-shops, comprehension and/or grammar exercises, and a piece of creative writing once a week. As already indicated, there were several sets of course books for comprehension, grammar and punctuation work, which were widely used.

Pupils' work was corrected for spelling and punctuation, and com-mented upon. Good work was sometimes indicated with a star, but it wasn't given a mark or a grade. Parents received a yearly report, and at the end of the year the County's green forms, covering all areas of the curriculum, were completed by the teacher for each pupil.

There was a well-stocked resource area, with information packs, videos, films, etc. which had been carefully planned. The school library contained new fiction, bought with money raised by staff as part of a fun run. There was some overlap between these books, and the fiction we use with classes in Year 7 at Daventry School. Several visitors came to talk to the children;

HALF-TERMLY FORECAST   DATE:- Jan '85.

CLASS TEACHER:- M. Linden   YEAR:- 4th.

SUBJECT:- English.

Following theme of topic - Underground. In poetry - prose and comprehension + Drama.

Literature - Our Exploits at West Poley. Th. Hardy.

Spelling - Words from project. - minerals + metals. terms. etc. Spelling workshop.

Handwriting - emphasising the need for good presentation with emphasis on certain letter formation with individual children.

Special Emphasis on Theme of Exploration as theme for exhibition.

Grammar. The place of adjectives and adverbs.

T.V. Prog. Middle Eng. a weekly series to stimulate interest in language both oral and written, and in literature, poetry + drama.

HEAD TEACHER'S COMMENT AND SIGNATURE

I like the topicality of the controversial topic. *

K.B. Dawson

WEEKLY RECORD OF WORK

DATE W.B.	
11-1-84.	Exploration Discussion and beginning rough draft of story of a safari for yeti type creature - in a group of 3 or 4.
	Grammar.
14-91-85	(1) Exploring the dictionary - finding our favourite adjective. - Aim - to extend vocabulary and introduce children to adverbs in dictionary - (n) (v) (adj)(adv)
16-1-85.	(2) Working on presentation of work on adjectives + illustrations.
18-1-85	Introduce idea of a poem and asking children to think about it and collect words + ideas for next week.
	Middle Eng. Fieldsports + Bloodsports. follow up by group discussion on whether or not we agreed with hunting. - lead on to class discussion on the controversy aroused in town about the forthcoming visit of circus - asked children to look in local papers for articles and letters on the debate.
25-1-85	Follow up to circus debate read articles discussed our views children wrote about their views on animals performing in circus.
26-1-85	Poems on cave exploration (2 days).
1-2-84	Hom. Continue with Exploration theme log book of expedition. Working for creative.
1-2-84	Completed rough stage of log books
8-2-84	Complete final log book. 3 lessons.
15-2-84	Cont theme of animals in circus, writing a first draft of poem on caged animals.
	Cont with theme previous 2 days.

HEAD TEACHER'S COMMENT AND SIGNATURE :

Figure Appendix 1.1   Half-termly forecast

while I was there the visitors included a 'magician' who talked to the children about road safety, and a lady from the Schools' Library Service who read extracts from stories and poems. It will be apparent that though I have concentrated on English, language work extended across the curriculum, and encompassed a rich variety of activities.

Examples of Pupils' Work with Teachers' Evaluations:
The Grange Junior School

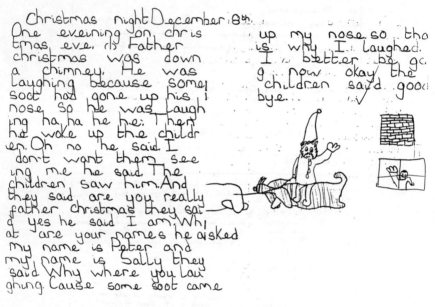

Christmas night December 8th.
One eveining on chris
tmas eve. as father
christmas was down
a chimney. He was
Laughing because some
soot had gone up his
nose. so he was laugh
ing ha ha he he; Then
he woke up the childr
en. Oh no he said I
don't want them see
ing me he said. The
children saw him. And
they said are you really
father christmas they sai
d yes he said I am, Wh
at are your names he asked
My name is Peter and
my name is Sally they
said Why where you Lau
ghing. Cause some soot came

up my nose so tha
is why I laughed.
I better be go
g now okay the
children sayd good
bye. ✓

Figure Appendix 1.2   Year 3, 'good' (teacher's evaluation)

Farmyard   Animals
One big dog barking at a cat
two fat pigs rolling in the mud.
Three large duck's swimming
in the pond, four large hens
pecking at the grain. Five big
sheep saying baa baa baa,
six small geese running all
about. Seven little chicks
hatching from their eggs. And
this was happening all day
long. ✓

April 27th Ice-cream
An ice-cream is soft and
smooth in your mouth and
the cornet is crispy. And
My favourite ice-cream is
chocolate and when it
down your hand it feel
cold. ✓

Figure Appendix 1.3   Year 3, 'below average' (teacher's evaluation)

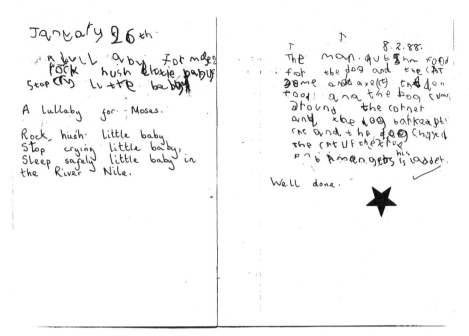

January 26th.

...lull aby For moses
rock   hush likkle baby
stop (ry) little baby

A lullaby for Moses.

Rock, hush little baby
Stop crying little baby,
Sleep safely little baby in
the River Nile.

T   ↑   8.2.88
The man gve thm food
for the dog and the CAT
some and axe (it) the don
food   a na the dog cvm
around the corner
and the dog barkeapt
the and the dog chsed
the cat up the xtop
          his
r n b a man gets is ladder.

Well done. ★

Figure Appendix 1.4   Year 3, 'average' (teacher's evaluation)

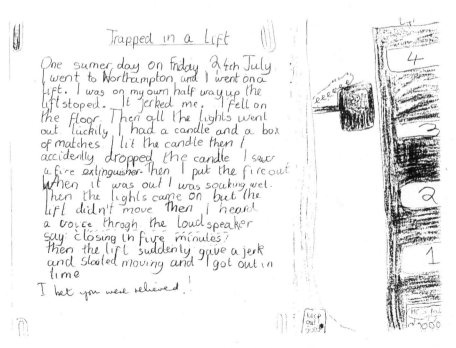

Trapped in a Lift

One sumer day on Friday 24th July
I went to Northampton and I went on a
lift. I was on my own half way up the
lift stoped.   It jerked me.   I fell on
the floor. Then all the lights went
out. luckily I had a candle and a box
of matches. I lit the candle then I
accidently dropped the candle I saw
a fire extinguisher. Then I put the fire out
When it was out I was soaking wet.
Then the lights came on but the
lift didn't move then I heard
a voice throgh the loud speaker
say: closing in five minutes?
then the lift suddenly gave a jerk
and started moving and I got out in
time
I bet you were relieved !

Figure Appendix 1.5   Year 4, 'above average' (teacher's evaluation)

Volcano

a volcano scwut and suv
down the side and noch how
trees sprck and Red hot lruuf
rolle and blos up hosis bay
the top of the volcano has
espeldid sprck flams fliy at
of the top and pipll run fur
ther livs smock cumes up and
bolvs hit pipll prfs esspiudil
and chage in to runing lruur
pipll diy pipll criy but now one
can Hulp.

A volcano squints and slithers
down the side and knocks down
rolls and knocks down houses bury the top
of the volcano has vlooded spares rus us
fly out of the top and pepils run for their
lives· smoke comes up and boulders hit
people· paths explode and change into running
river of lava people die people cry but no
one can help

Figure Appendix 1.6   Year 4, 'weak' (teacher's evaluation); first draft, with neat copy incorporating teacher's corrections

Spring Thoughts

Spring is here come and sing,
Hear the birds in their song.
Flowers sprouting everywhere,
Sunny days here and there.
Spring brings flowers,
And some showers.
Clear blue sky's,
And longer days.
The squirrel out of hibernation.
Buds on trees,
New green leaves,
Fisherman in their trawlers,
Spiders crawl in dusty corners.
After the Spring clean,
All the houses gleam.

by
Ian
Kemp

Figure Appendix 1.7   'Spring Thoughts', Year 5

Introduction

Welton Primary School had seventy-six children, divided into three classes, from reception (4 years old) up to the top juniors (11 years old). The week I was there, the whole school was engaged on its 'Africa' project, culminating in an open evening for parents, when pupils displayed their work and performed African dancing. The school was a hive of activity, and I was struck by the range of activities that pupils were involved in.

Étienne Zombra, the French assistant at Daventry School, spent a morning with the pupils, talking to them about his country (Burkina Faso), and teaching them various dances. There was also a visit at one assembly from two representatives of 'World Vision', a charity concerned to raise money for the Third World. These are examples of how links with the outside world, particularly Africa, were brought into school. The open evening was enjoyed by parents, pupils and teachers.

The Headteacher had been at the school for two years, during which time there had been a reassessment of the school's language policy. The aims of this policy were to give the children as many opportunities for writing as possible, and to make sure that by age 11 they were able to communicate fluently in writing and verbally, for a variety of different audiences. Written work grew out of the pupils' own experiences: '. . . we are in the business of giving them many opportunities for experience . . .' The emphasis was on trying to improve the quality of the children's work. Word processing was also used as often as possible, from 6 to 7 years onwards. For example, the top class built up a data base about Weedon, using old census returns, interviews with residents etc.

Project work was chosen to give good all round development, which would provide opportunities for work in most areas of the curriculum. There was flexibility, in that a class teacher could choose a topic for a mini-project (three weeks), or there might be a major project involving the whole school, and lasting half a term.

Infants and Juniors

This class included pupils from reception to top infants (5–7 years). Every day the pupils had to write an exercise, do a page of maths, and read to an adult. Pupils also had their own private readers. Handwriting was worked at continually, as an on-going activity. Spelling grew out of phonic work, e.g. pupils copied or traced new words, and then wrote their own sentences. Pupils had to write short sentences about themselves in their 'News Books'. The teacher read poems and nursery rhymes to the children which they often learned, but they didn't write stories at this stage. The pupils had one period of RE a week with another teacher, and four periods of PE. Once a week they watched the TV programme 'Words and Pictures'. The class always had a project in hand, and craft and painting were usually related to it. A recent project on farming had involved a visit by the pupils to a farm to see sheep being sheared. As a result they had learned a lot of new vocabulary, and this had lead to writing and art-work. The pupils had also written about Welton, as part of the school project on the village.

Language skills were developed initially through oral work. A great deal of discussion and talking occurred, in groups and with the teacher. Pupils continuously asked for guidance and reassurance.

Listening skills were developed through listening to the teacher's instructions — most of the time! The pupils listened to instructions and music for dancing, and to a weekly TV programme. In groups they listened to taped stories, using headphones.

Each pupil did some reading every day, if possible to the teacher, or to the part-time teacher who came three days a week. Pupils also read stories by themselves, as well as reading the instructions in their maths books. I saw these pupils consulting reference books on African animals. The 'One, Two, Three and Away' reading series was used regularly, as well as the 'Beacon' and 'Wide Range Readers' books. The pupils' progress on these schemes was recorded by the teacher.

I saw some writing taking place, for example, pupils copied two sentences about Africa from the board and produced their own illustration to go with it, for display purposes. Some pupils copied words and wrote simple sentences; most had written something in their 'Newsbooks' about their activities during the week.

Middle Class

The class contained eighteen pupils in Year 3 and seven top infants. The core of their language work was the 'Primary Language Programme' (Masson *et al.* 1983), which involved mainly cloze tests, comprehension activities and a range of creative work. The SRA Reading Laboratory was used to develop reading, the 'Sound Sense' (Tansley 1970) series for vocabulary, while spelling was developed through the use of 'Superspell' or 'Word Perfect' (Ridout 1977). Creative writing was stimulated through the use of pictures, opening lines, 'Picture Starters' (a series of pictures designed to stimulate writing), discussion, etc.

A great deal of discussion took place in class. For example, the teacher discussed with the class the different layers of the rain forest, and showed them pictures of orchids, as preparation for the pupils' own paintings of the jungle. The teacher talked to the class about the sorts of things that are found in a jungle, putting key words on the board, and subsequently discussed the rough drafts of these stories with each pupil, correcting the mistakes. She also talked to the class, and with individual pupils, about their crêpe paper designs for animals and jungle flowers. Pupils cut up cloth into strips to make jungle pictures, and discussed this in small groups, and with the teacher.

The teacher liked to hear the pupils read to her from a class reader once a week if possible. While I was in the classroom, the pupils read a short extract describing a jungle from the 'Primary Language Programme', as a stimulus for writing. I heard pupils read the rough drafts of their stories to the teacher, and they also read the instructions in their maths books. If they had finished tidying up in the afternoon before the end of school, they were allowed to go to the library area, and choose a book to read. This usually occupied the last twenty minutes of the day.

Much of the oral work outlined above was preparation for writing. For example, the discussion before the pupils wrote their stories, 'In the jungle'. The first drafts were written in rough books, and the corrected versions were copied out for display. The class had produced an impressive project about Welton School, using a questionnaire to interview their grandparents or other old people to find out what the school was like in the past. The answers were presented by each pupil as a continuous piece of writing, and all the work was put into a book, and illustrated with old photos.

Top Class
This class consisted of twenty-seven children: five in Year 4, thirteen in Year 5, and nine in Year 6. The pupils were taught by the Headteacher, who did a lot of work on poetry. The children usually wrote one poem a week, as well as other types of writing. The teacher was critical and demanding, trying to improve the quality of each child's writing. Grammar points, paragraphing, punctuation etc. grew out of the pupils' own work.

The core of the Language Programme was the 'Primary Language Programme', which developed a full range of language skills, and was linked to extracts from modern children's fiction. The books from which the extracts were taken were kept in class, and pupils were encouraged to read them. They kept a card on which to record their reading. Pupils covered different units, depending on their level (assessed by a cloze test). Some weeks they might use the programme four or five times; other weeks (when they were doing a project) not at all, but it provided the continuity in all areas of language work. A record sheet was used to record pupils' activities in the Programme. Small poetry sets were also used, particularly for stretching the brighter pupils. Not much drama work was done with this group.

The pupils had considerable opportunity for talking about their work with each other, in pairs or in small groups; or individually with the teacher or as a class. This applied across the curriculum, for example, as part of the Africa project, pupils planned and wrote acrostics in small groups, and discussed the display work they were doing. Some pupils discussed their stories with a neighbour. The teacher talked to small groups of pupils about the problems they were having in Maths; the Scottish Primary Maths Programme was used.

The pupils' listening skills were developed mainly through listening to instructions from the teacher, or listening to a partner in a group. Other activities included watching a video about African grasslands, listening to African music, listening to several visitors in Assembly, including Étienne Zombra, who told a story in his own language (Bisa), and taught the pupils African dancing.

The range of reading activities included reading first drafts of stories to the teacher, reading reference books, following instructions in their maths books and private reading from a story book. There was no reading round the class; most pupils read very well, and very few needed individual help.

I observed many opportunities for writing, for example pupils wrote an African story with a moral in two drafts, the first draft being corrected by the teacher. The pupils were encouraged to 'review' and improve their first drafts. They each compiled a fact sheet on an African country which they researched in reference books, and had to write up in their own words. In small groups they wrote an acrostic on the word 'Africa'. Pupils regularly made display copies of their work.

My overall impression was of a lively, dynamic school, with responsive pupils working in a child-centred environment.

Crick Primary School (27 June 1988)

This school had ninety-two pupils divided into two junior classes, and two infant classes. I spent most time with the top junior class of twenty-seven children; eleven were in Year 5, and sixteen were in Year 6. Four of these children were going to Daventry School in September 1988. The classroom was large and light, with attractive display work on the walls, and it looked onto the school garden and pond. The class teacher was there for a year only, so the work I observed may not have been representative of what occurred in other years.

The pupils were engaged on their Natural History project. They had watched TV programmes on insects and had caught insects in the local churchyard. They studied one insect a week, using reference books. The information was written out in rough in their own words, corrected by the teacher, and then turned into an illustrated leaflet.

The pupils had two exercise books for non-project work. One was for creative work, and the other for formal language work. This consisted mainly of comprehension exercises etc. In the autumn term, SRA comprehension exercises were used; GINN comprehension exercises were used in the spring term. By the summer term exercises from course books were combined with exercises which the teacher devised from the mistakes in the pupils' work.

The timetable was flexible, but Monday mornings were usually used for Maths and formal English; Tuesday mornings for creative work; Wednesday mornings were allocated for SRA or GIN work; and on Thursdays RE was taught. Monday and Tuesday afternoons were set aside for project work, though the activity might vary e.g. art work, writing etc. Other activities were fitted in where possible.

Pupils had a wide selection of fiction to choose from, including the 'Carry On' and 'Reading 360' series. Each pupil had a reading notebook, in which the teacher recorded the pupil's progress. She heard the poorer readers up to four times a week; two parent helpers came once a week to help. The teacher read to the class at the end of the day for a quarter of an hour; recent

My Granny Mrs Rm pimlett went to
Welton church of England.
She Stared in 1926
There were two Classes.
There were 45-50 children.
She was five when She Started school and
was there Until She was fourteen.
She did lots of lessens Such as
prayers, Scripture) Arithmetic) English)
Geogrophy) History) Needle work) knitting) Reading)
poetry) gardening, Singing, Games) Spelling)
physical) Training) painting) Raffi work) Baskets
and Bags.
There were two playgrounds One of the
playgrounds for the girls on the (Southside)
and one for the boys (north Side).
They played roundrès
hopscoth) Skiping) inand Out the windows) farmers
in his den) gathering nuts in may)
Houses. The Toys that She had doll and pram)
Puppets) puppet the theatre) Builing bricks
Jig puzlese

These are the Sports that my granny did
Netboll and roundes

Figure Appendix 1.8 Middle class: Year 3, 'above average' (teacher's evaluation)
Welton Primary School

books included Nina Bawden's *The White Horse Gang* and Roald Dahl's
Danny, The Champion of the World.

I observed the same group in the afternoon, and they were working on
individual projects such as electricity, British birds, dogs etc. They were
making rough notes from reference books, showing them to the teacher for
corrections, and then making a neat copy. This involved discussion in pairs,
in small groups, and with the teacher.

I also visited the class of juniors in Years 3 and 4 where the pupils were

My Nan Mrs. Muir went to School at Nelson primary and Junior school. She Started in 1925. There were 10 classes and 300 children in the School. There were no helpers. She Started School when She was 5 and left School at 16. Her lessons were English, geography, History, welsh, French, Latin, chemisry, physics, biology, Maths, cookery, Religiaus Education, Physicl Education, needle work. The playground had a Hockey pitch, Tennis courts. She played Tennis, net ball, cricket, hop Scotch, She played with dolls, prams, Books, Jigsaws, whip and tops. She wore dresses and School uniform a gymslip. my hairStyle was a short bob. She had Sand witches in the cookery room. She had a flip top desk and ordinary chair. She read Enid Blyton Charles Dickens. Her pen was a nib pen. She had a pencil case. She Started School at 9oclock and finished School at 4pm. She had assembly. She had prayers and Sang hymns She did p.e. and had aparatus She wore pants and a blouse. She got to School by bus.   Richard
                                        RamSden

Figure Appendix 1.9 Middle class: Year 3, 'quite good' (teacher's evaluation) Welton Primary School

working in groups on a project about roadside verges. In groups of four they were making large illustrated booklets about the plants and animals found there. The pupils used reference books and their own observations, discussing their work with each other and the teacher. Some of their work formed a display around the classroom.

The class of top and middle infants (5½–7½ year olds) were having a discussion session with the teacher. A few pupils gave a short, informal talk to the class about something of interest, with prompting and help from the teacher. For example, some pupils had brought shells, two books received as a

Rachel Bichener

My Father attended Braunston b of E school from 1954 to 1960 under Mr Gallie, Mrs Bole, Miss Jones Miss Hivens and another teacher he can't remember. There were 75 to 100 children and no helpers. He started when he was 5 and left when he was 11. He learnt maths, English, history, geography, games and gardening. The playground was a good tarmac area surrounded by trees with a climbing frame at one end. Games were football, netball and rounders. Bricks and sand were the toys and sports were football, running and jumping. For school he wore a dark blue blazer, grey shirt and short grey trousers. He had a short back and sides hairstyle. School meals were provided and eaten in the hall and tables and chairs were double desks with ink wells and benches attached to them. First year infants used slates and chalk and the rest used exercise books. Ink pens with removable nibs that he thought made good darts were used. School started at 9 o'clock and carried on until 10 to 4. There were no pencilcases. In assembly he sang hymns and said prayers. He did not do P.E. He walked to school and the houses were modern with no central heating

Figure Appendix 1.10   Middle class: Year 3, 'best in class' (teacher's evaluation)
Welton Primary School

birthday present, and holiday photos, which they discussed with the class. The other pupils were interested and responsive; this activity occurred every day for about twenty to thirty minutes, to develop oral skills.

These pupils developed their reading through the core scheme 'One, Two, Three and Away', which was supplemented by readers with a matching colour code, though pupils did not have to stick to the same level in their private reading. The teacher listened to each child read at least once a week, and read to them regularly; recent books included E.B. White's *Charlotte's Web* and Roald Dahls' *The BFG*.

The pupils had to do some reading, one piece of writing, and some number work every day; then they could choose what they wanted to do. Each pupil had a word book in which to try out and then record the correct spelling of new words. Pupils also had access to a word processor which they shared on alternate weeks with reception. I was impressed by the imaginative display work and project work in the classroom.[2]

Staverton Primary School (28 June 1988)

I was made welcome by the Headteacher, and the Headteacher Designate, who was very keen to be involved in our curriculum continuity projects. This is a small school, and the class which I observed consisted of sixteen pupils, and included top infants and juniors from years 3–6. Two or three of the juniors in Year 6 were intending to come to Daventry School in September 1988. The other class in the year contained infants and the reception year. In 1988/89 the top class will consist of twenty-two pupils, who will range from reception to Year 6 juniors.

I observed the pupils in the top class working individually on language cards, made by the teacher, which tested their comprehension skills. A few pupils worked on their Maths. Comprehension or language work was done two or three times a week, and creative work of some sort once a week.

The 'Reading 360' scheme, with accompanying language work, was used once or twice a week, and the pupils had access to class library books. Pupils were encouraged to read, and there was a Book Club where they could save up on a weekly basis to buy a book. The teacher read to the class most days; a recent book was *The Day of the Spaniards* (a historical novel).

Literature was usually used in relation to a particular project. For example, pupils were engaged on a project called 'Villages, Towns and Cities', and were making a model of a medieval castle for the Primary Celebration exhibition. As part of their work, pupils had recently read poems or stories about town life. Their written work did not involve much drafting or rewriting, though there was an emphasis on good presentation and display work.

Braunston Primary School (30 June 1988)

Braunston Primary School had 175 pupils divided into four junior classes (years 3–6), three classes of infants and one reception class. Though I was able to see nearly all the classes in the school, I spent most time with the juniors. Junior 4 (the top class) was a class of eighteen pupils in Year 6, who were making presentation books about their recent visit to Quincy-Voisins in France. The pupils were binding their books, following precise instructions from the teacher. The pupils were responsive, polite and articulate in answering my questions about their trip. The classroom contained interesting display work, including an impressive collection of bottles.

Junior 3 (Year 5) had a talk from the local policeman about the dangers of strangers, bicycles and canals, and the need for vigilance and safety. The pupils were very attentive, demonstrating good listening skills, and asking intelligent questions. Later on in the morning the pupils listened to part of a radio broadcast about a new boy at school, and started to write a story on a theme linked to the play. The pupils wrote a rough version in the back of their exercise books, discussed the story individually with the teacher, who corrected it, and started the neat copy on display paper.

In the afternoon I visited the younger pupils, albeit briefly. In Junior 2 (Year 4: 8–9 year olds) the pupils were writing Viking stories using 'Junior Projects Sheets' which had the beginnings of three different stories. The pupils had to write a sequel, and the teacher went round discussing each child's work individually. There was a lot of oral work, pupils discussing their stories in pairs and with the teacher.

The pupils in Junior 1 (Year 3: 7–8 year olds) were working on a project on aircraft, and had recently visited Shuttleworth Museum. The pupils were answering questions on the museum, copying a passage from the board, using reference books, and writing a story. A group of pupils talked to me about their visit, and were very lively and responsive.

In the Infants 3 class (Year 2: 6–7 year olds) pupils had just finished doing crosswords, which they showed to me. Some pupils were working on a cloze test, and the teacher checked each pupil's work on a one-to-one basis. A number of the pupils found writing and reading very difficult. The teacher made extensive use of remedial-type materials to develop pupils' basic language skills.

In Infants 2 (Year 1: 5–6 year olds) the pupils discussed with the teacher what they thought my job was, and then the teacher lead a discussion about their recent visit to Lings Wood, where they had been pond-dipping. In Infants 1 (Reception: 4–5 year olds) the pupils had set up market stalls and were playing shops. This summary indicates the range of activities in which pupils were involved, and some of the different ways language skills were developed.

Kilsby Primary School (1 July 1988)

I had visited the school several times, because the top class had done a project with my fourth year group. I was able to take Richard Kemp, and we attended the assembly, in which a class of juniors in Year 3 and some infants read poems, acrostics and stories on the theme of 'Home', and showed pictures that they'd painted. The children appeared self-confident, and performed well. The whole school listened to a steel band from another school during the second part of the assembly. I covered Richard Kemp's lessons at Daventry School for the rest of the morning, and returned to Kilsby in the afternoon.

In the afternoon the pupils in Year 6 had a bicycling proficiency test, while a group of pupils in Year 5 read through a play based on Frank L. Baum's *The Wizard of Oz*, which two of the boys had written. Usually pupils in Years 5 and 6 were taught together by the Headteacher. He tended to set Monday aside for a variety of activities, the children often working in small groups. Tuesdays were used for topic work, and a debate or discussion activities leading to writing. On Wednesdays the pupils did fairly formal comprehension and grammar work, the pupils in Year 6 using the comprehension exercises by Haydn Richards. On Thursdays they wrote a composition or story, and in the afternoons did RE sometimes drawing a picture to illustrate a Bible story, or some written work. Fridays were set aside for follow-up work to TV programmes, and project work.

Written work was usually done in one draft only, unless it was going to be used for display purposes, in which case it was corrected and copied out. The teacher marked according to what he was trying to teach, e.g. targetting formal points, spelling etc. He rarely put a mark or grade, and there was no school policy about assessment. Pupils' writing skills were also developed through project work, which involved note-taking, creative work, etc. as well as some copying out.

Reading was developed through the 'Wide Range Readers' scheme, though by Year 5 pupils read library books of their own choice, and there was a good selection of fiction in the school. Pupils could also choose from the library van every half-term.

Towards the end of the afternoon, the group of pupils who had read through their versions of *The Wizard of Oz* earlier on acted it out in front of the class. Afterwards the teacher read some of the poems about school from our anthology 'Poetry in the Making', and discussed them with the pupils.

Barby Primary School (4 July 1988)

I took Alison Gadsden with me, since she planned to work with the top class in 1988/89. We were given a warm welcome by the Headteacher, and by the teacher in charge of the top class of pupils in Years 5 and 6. The language work of the class was basically a mixture of project work and basic skills work, supplemented by language work across the curriculum.

The whole school had been involved in a project on the Caribbean for the Primary Celebration exhibition, and there was beautiful display work around the school; pupils were obviously encouraged to take a pride in their work.

Year 6 pupils were working on their individual projects, which were the culmination of all the skills they had learned such as reference skills, note-taking, creative writing, etc. Pupils in Year 5 had worked on a bottle project, and the class was starting work on an Armada Project.

Basic skills work was organized on a 'wheel' basis, using 'Better English' (Ridont 1961) for language work, spelling tests, comprehension exercises and a book for the development of reference skills. Each child worked at his or her own pace, and there was a checklist in the file which was ticked when each task was completed. Pupils worked in various areas, depending on their particular weaknesses.

Supplementary materials were used to develop language across the curriculum, such as poetry, letter writing etc. These were slotted in where possible. The teacher felt that pupils needed to learn to work more in groups, to develop their skills at note taking, and to work more through drafting and rewriting. All the pupils, except one, were competent readers, and there was no need for a reading scheme. Pupils chose their own reading books, and the teacher also read to them twice a week, which they thoroughly enjoyed.

Falconer's Hill Junior School (5 July 1988)

I paid a half-day visit to the school, and reviewed the progress of our joint projects over the last two years with the colleagues involved. We agreed that they had been successful and of benefit to the pupils, and that we all wanted to continue this work next year. We discussed ways in which the projects could be improved, and the need to devise activities that were not so 'teacher-intensive', particularly where less able pupils were concerned. We also agreed that the projects should be more closely related to the project work that the junior school pupils were already engaged in, rather than being something extra.

The Grange Junior School (7 July 1988)

I spent half a day at the school, and took Richard Kemp and Jackie Turner with me, so that they could visit two of the classes in Year 5 and their teachers. Both enjoyed the visit and expressed the wish to return for a longer period. I visited the top classes (in Year 6), and talked to colleagues about our plans for next year.

The Abbey School (8 July 1988)

My first impression on entering the school was the amount of colourful display work. The classes were arranged in vertical groups, so that in 1987/88 there were four top classes of pupils in Years 5 and 6 together, a total of about sixty pupils from each year. For example, one top class continued thirteen pupils in Year 5, and fourteen pupils in Year 6. They were working on their Japan project, and were completing decorated folders. The contents were mainly factual, and taken from reference books. The pupils explained to me that they took rough notes first, and then put the information into their own words. I talked to most of the pupils about their projects, what they'd enjoyed, and about their visit to the Victoria and Albert Museum. I interrogated one student about the Japanese language, and he coped very well.

The pupils followed the 'Reading 360' scheme; they followed it up to reading age 12 with the accompanying written work. A few could manage the readers at level 13, though not the written tasks. The teacher usually planned to have one structured lesson a week with the scheme. The pupils could also choose a book from two shelves of class library books, which were mainly non-fiction, and there was a selection of fiction available on the trolley outside the classroom.

I visited another class of pupils in Years 5 and 6, all very well behaved. When I came in they were starting a piece of continuous writing which they had to do without any help from the teacher. She suggested that they write on an Egyptian theme, since this was the subject of their current project. In the afternoon the class worked on their project folders. The pupils were interested and involved in what they were doing, and able to talk with ease about what they had learned. The folders were beautifully decorated, and there was much fine display work, including models around the walls.

In the other top class which I visited, pupils were working on a number of different tasks, though the majority were finishing off their projects on the human body. For example, two boys were writing up an experiment about touch for their folders. Other pupils were making puppets from rolls of paper. This classroom was also bright and cheerful, in spite of a skeleton resting in the corner. Next year the top classes will be doing projects on the four elements.

Notes

1 Where possible, details of books and other materials cited in this report will be found in the Bibliography. However, I have not been able to trace all the materials referred to.
2 No pupils from Crick Primary School have come to Daventry William Parker School since September 1989.

Appendix 2

Attainment Targets for English

Attainment Target 1: Speaking and Listening[1]

The development of pupils' understanding of the spoken word and the capacity to express themselves effectively in a variety of speaking and listening activities, matching style and response to audience and purpose. From level 7, pupils should be using Standard English, wherever appropriate, to meet the statements of attainment.

Level	*Statements of Attainment*	*Example*
	Pupils should be able to:	
1	a) participate as speakers and listeners in group activities, including imaginative play.	*Suggest what to do next in a practical activity; tell stories; play the role of shopkeeper or customer in the class shop.*
	b) listen attentively, and respond, to stories and poems.	*Ask questions about a story or poem; retell a story; enact a poem; draw a picture to illustrate a story or poems.*
	c) respond appropriately to simple instructions given by a teacher.	*Follow two consecutive instructions such as 'Choose some shells from the box and draw pictures of them'.*

---

[1] The statements of attainment at levels 1 to 3 are as specified by Order and published in the statutory Document entitled *English in the National Curriculum* (ISBN 0 11 270682 7) on 31 May 1989.
Reprinted from *English in the National Curriculum* (No. 2) (DES 1990a), pp. 3–19, by permission of HMSO.

2   a) participate as speakers and listeners in a group engaged in a given task.

Compose a story together; design and make a model; assume a role in play activity.

　　b) describe an event, real or imagined, to the teacher or another pupil.

Tell the listener about something which happened at home, on the television or in a book.

　　c) listen attentively to stories and poems, and talk about them.

Talk about the characters; say what they like or dislike about a story or poem

　　d) talk with the teacher, listen, and ask and answer questions.

Talk about events or activities in or out of school — such as a school trip, a family outing or a television programme.

　　e) respond appropriately to a range of more complex instructions given by a teacher, and give simple instructions.

Follow three consecutive actions such as 'Write down the place in the classroom where you think your plant will grow best, find out what the others on your table think and try to agree on which is likely to be the best place'.

3   a) relate real or imaginary events in a connected narrative which conveys meaning to a group of pupils, the teacher or another known adult.

Tell a story with a beginning, middle and end; recount a series of related incidents that happened at home or in a science activity.

　　b) convey accurately a simple message.

Relay a simple telephone message in role-play or real life; take an oral message to another teacher.

　　c) listen with an increased span of concentration to other children and adults, asking and responding to questions and commenting on what has been said.

Listen to the teacher or to a radio programme on a new topic, then discuss what has been said.

　　d) give, and receive and follow accurately, precise instructions when pursuing a task individually or as a member of a group.

Plan a wall display or arrange an outing together.

4   a) give a detailed oral account of an event, or something that has been learned in the classroom, or explain with reasons why a particular

Report on a scientific investigation, or the progress of a planned group activity, to another group or the class.

course of action has been taken.

b) ask and respond to questions in a range of situations with increased confidence.

Guide other pupils in designing something; conduct an interview on a radio programme devised with other pupils.

c) take part as speakers and listeners in a group discussion or activity, expressing a personal view and commenting constructively on what is being discussed or experienced.

Draft a piece of writing, with others, on a word processor; contribute to the planning and implementation of a group activity.

d) participate in a presentation.

Describe the outcome of a group activity; improvise a scene from a story or poem or of the pupils' own devising.

5 a) give a well organised and sustained account of an event, a personal experience or an activity.

Describe a model which has been made, indicating the reasons for the design and the choice of materials.

b) contribute to and respond constructively in discussion, including the development of ideas; advocate and justify a point of view.

Explain the actions taken by a character in a novel; work in a group to develop a detailed plan of action; provide arguments in favour of an approach to a problem.

c) use language to convey information and ideas effectively in a straightforward situation.

Provide an eye witness account of an event or incident; explain how a personal possession was lost, describing the item in question.

d) contribute to the planning of, and participate in, a group presentation.

Compile a news report or a news programme for younger children; perform a story or poem by means of improvization, making use of video, or audio recorders where appropriate.

e) recognize variations in vocabulary between different regional or social groups, and relate this knowledge where appropriate to personal experience.

Talk about dialect vocabulary and specialist terms; discuss the vocabulary used by characters in books or on television.

6 a) contribute, to group discussions, considered

Present or develop a line of reasoning in discussion of an issue opinions or clear statements of personal feeling which are clearly responsive to the contributions of others.

raised by a story and comment on other viewpoints.

b) use language to convey information and ideas effectively in a variety of situations where the subject is familiar to the pupils and the audience or other participants.

Explain a technical aspect of a hobby to someone with a general interests; present a news report on a local issue.

c) contribute to the planning and organization of, and participate with fluency in, a group presentation or performance.

Participate in a group presentation of a scripted or improvized episode from a story or novel; present to the class the results of a group investigation.

d) show in discussion an awareness of grammatical differences between spoken Standard English and a non-standard variety.

Take note of different ways in which tense and person are marked in the verb 'to be' after listening to recordings or participating in classroom improvizations.

7   a) express a point of view clearly and cogently to a range of audiences and interpret accurately a range of statements by others.

Present a personal opinion or a belief to younger pupils, another teacher, or another adult.

b) use and understand language which conveys information and ideas effectively on occasions where the situation or topic is less readily familiar to the pupils and/or their audience.

Explain to a younger pupil how to construct a model, or make a book; describe the reasons why a character in a book, or in improvised or text-based drama, behaved in a particular way.

c) take an active part in group discussions, contributing constructively to the development of the argument.

Introduce a new, relevant idea to a group discussion about the planning of a visit, or the making of a database; show respect for the contributions of others.

d) show in discussion an awareness of the appropriate use of spoken language, according to purpose, topic and audience.

Analyse and reflect upon the language appropriate for a job interview, or an argument with a parent or another pupil following a presentation.

8   a) express points of view on complex matters clearly and cogently and interpret points of view with accuracy and discrimination.

Debate a contentious issue and summarize the main arguments.

  b) convey information and ideas in a variety of complex situations involving a range of audiences and in language which is matched to context and purpose.

Explain causes and effects; speculate upon outcomes of a policy or a given course of action; take part in interviews for, or on behalf of, a school mini company.

  c) take an active part in group discussions, contributing constructively to the sustained development of the argument.

Take part in a real or simulated committee discussion which requires an agreement; express views and cite evidence in group discussions of books or poems.

  d) show in discussion and in writing an awareness of the contribution that facial expressions, gestures and tone of voice can make to a speaker's meaning.

Comment on the varied use of these features noted in a stage presentation, a television drama, or film. Comment on what may be conveyed (intentionally or inadvertently) in advertisements, speeches, interviews or in observed behaviour around the school.

9   a) give a presentation expressing a personal point of view on a complex subject persuasively, cogently and clearly, integrating talk with writing and other media where appropriate, and respond to the presentations of others.

Introduce a researched environmental topic for discussion, using slides, OHP transparencies, notes or diagrams in the presentation.

  b) take an active part in group discussion, displaying sensitivity, listening critically and being self-critical.

Discuss a film or television programme, recognizing and helping to develop the views of others, accepting and offering alternatives in positive ways.

  c) show in discussion and in writing an awareness of the ways in which language varies between different types of spoken communication.

Describe how different kinds of language use, such as jokes, anecdote, conversation, commentary, lecture, etc. could be explained to a foreign visitor.

10 a) express a point of view on complex subjects persuasively, cogently and

Devise and mount an advertising campaign concerned with a matter of principle.

            clearly, applying and
interpreting a range of
methods of presentation and
assessing their own
effectiveness accurately.

b)	take a variety of leading roles in group discusssion, including taking the chair, listening with concentration and understanding and noting down salient points.	*Summarize an argument and help to formulate a conclusion.*
c)	show in discussion and in writing an awareness of some of the factors that influence people's attitudes to the way other people speak.	*Using the results of a survey, make a report on the attitudes to spoken language held by the class and the community.*

Note: Pupils unable to communicate by speech may use other means including the use of technology, signing, symbols or lip-reading as alternatives to speaking and listening.

Attainment Target 2: Reading[2]

The development of the ability to read, understand and respond to all types of writing, as well as the development of information-retrieval strategies for the purposes of study.

Level	*Statements of Attainment*	*Example*
	Pupils should be able to:	
1	a) recognize that print is used to carry meaning, in books and in other forms in the everyday world.	*Point to and recognize own name; tell the teacher that a label on a container says what is inside or that the words in a book tell a story.*
	b) begin to recognize individual words or letters in familiar contexts.	*In role-play, read simple signs such as shop names or brand names; recognize 'bus-stop', 'exit', 'danger'.*
	c) show signs of a developing interest in reading.	*Pick up books and look at the pictures; choose books to hear or read.*

[2] The statements of attainment at levels 1 to 3 are as specified by Order and published in the statutory Document entitled *English in the National Curriculum* (ISBN 0 11 270682 7) on 31 May 1989.

	d) talk in simple terms about the content of stories, or information in non-fiction books.	*Talk about characters and pictures, including likes and dislikes.*
2	a) read accurately and understand straightforward signs, labels and notices.	*Read labels on drawers in the classroom; read simple menus.*
	b) demonstrate knowledge of the alphabet in using word books and simple dictionaries.	*Turn towards the end to find words beginning with 's', rather than always starting from the beginning.*
	c) use picture and context cues, words recognized on sight and phonic cues in reading.	*Use a picture to help make sense of a text; recognize that 'Once' is often followed by 'upon a time'; use initial letters to help with recognising words.*
	d) describe what has happened in a story and predict what may happen next.	*Talk about how and why Jack climbs the beanstalk and suggest what may be at the top.*
	e) listen and respond to stories, poems and other material read aloud, expressing opinions informed by what has been read.	*Talk about characters, their actions and appearance; discuss the behaviour of different animals described in a radio programme.*
	f) read a range of material with some independence, fluency, accuracy and understanding.	*Read something unprompted; talk with some confidence about what has been read; produce craftwork related to reading work.*
3	a) read aloud from familiar stories and poems fluently and with appropriate expression.	*Raise or lower voice to indicate different characters.*
	b) read silently and with sustained concentration.	
	c) listen attentively to stories, talk about setting, story-line and characters and recall significant details.	*Talk about a story, saying what happened to change the fortunes of the leading characters.*
	d) demonstrate, in talking about stories and poems, that they are beginning to use inference, deduction and previous reading experience to find and appreciate meanings beyond the literal.	*Discuss what might happen to characters in a story, based on the outcome of adventures in other stories.*

e) bring to their writing and discussion about stories some understanding of the way stories are structured.

Refer to different parts of the story such as 'at the beginning' or 'the story ends with'; notice that some stories build up in a predictable way, e.g. 'The Three Little Pigs', 'Goldilocks and the Three Bears'.

f) devise a clear set of questions that will enable them to select and use appropriate information sources and reference books from the class and school library.

Decide that the wildlife project needs information about the size and colour of birds, their food and habitat, and look it up.

4 a) read aloud expressively, fluently and with increased confidence from a range of familiar literature.

Vary the pace and tone of the voice to express feelings, or to represent character or mood.

b) demonstrate, in talking about a range of stories and poems which they have read, an ability to explore preferences.

Describe those qualities of the poem or story which appeal and give an indication of personal response.

c) demonstrate, in talking about stories, poems, non-fiction and other texts, that they are developing their abilities to use inference, deduction and previous reading experience.

Recognise and use those clues in a text which help the reader predict events.

d) find books or magazines in the class or school library by using the classification system, catalogue or database and use appropriate methods of finding information, when pursuing a line of inquiry.

Use search reading to contribute to an inquiry into health and safety at school or in the home.

5 a) demonstrate, in talking and writing about a range of stories and poems which they have read, an ability to explain preferences.

Make simple comparisons between stories or poems; offer justification for personal preference.

b) demonstrate, in talking or writing about fiction, poetry, non-fiction and other texts that they are

Discuss character, action, fact and opinion, relating them to personal experience.

developing their own views
and can support them by
reference to some details in
the text.

c) show in discussion that they
can recognize whether
subject matter in non–literary
and media texts is presented
as fact or opinion.

*Look for indications which suggest
the difference: whether evidence is
offered or whether persuasion is used
in the absence of facts.*

d) select reference books and
other information materials
and use organizational
devices to find answers to
their own questions and
those of others.

*Decide what information is required
for a project on a topic of their own
choice and locate it by reference to
chapter titles, subheadings,
typefaces, symbol keys, etc.*

e) show through discussion an
awareness of a writer's
choice of particular words
and phrases and the effect on
the reader.

*Recognise puns, word play,
unconventional spellings and the
placing together of pictures and text.*

6 a) read a range of fiction and
poetry, explaining their
preferences through talking
and writing, with reference
to details.

*Show involvement and independent
choice over a range of genres.*

b) demonstrate, in talking and
writing about literature,
non–fiction and other texts
that they are developing
their own insights and can
sustain them by reference to
the text.

*Make judgements about characters
and their actions, developing those
characters and events in their own
writing or drama.*

c) show in discussion or in
writing that they can
recognize whether subject
matter in non–literary and
media texts is presented as
fact or opinion, identifying
some of the ways in which
the distinction can be made.

*Look for indications which will help
determine the difference: unsupported
assertion, the use of statistics, attacks
upon character which distract from
an opponent's reasoning or evidence.*

d) select from a range of
reference materials, using
appropriate methods to
identify key points.

*Research a public figure using
posters, interviews, publicity
material, databases etc.*

e) show in discussion of their
reading an awareness that

*Understand that technological
developments, euphemism, contact*

words can change in use and meaning over time and demonstrate some of the reasons why.

with other languages or fashion all contribute to language change.

7 a) read a range of fiction, poetry, literary non–fiction and drama, including pre-20th century literature, explaining their preferences through talking and writing, with reference to detail.

Read letters, diaries and autobiographies; works from a range of cultures, and in translation.

b) talk and write about literature and other texts giving evidence of personal response and showing an understanding of the author's approach.

Write further episodes of a book under discussion; write journals or letters in character; compose imaginary letters to characters in books or to their authors; assess the development of a relationship in a play or novel.

c) show in discussion that they can recognize features of presentation which are used to inform, to regulate, to reassure or to persuade, in non–literary and media texts.

Note the effect of the enhancement or suppression of colour, page layout, illustration, style and size of print, verbal emphasis through repetition, exclamation or vocabulary.

d) select, retrieve and combine information independently from a wide range of reference materials.

Write a background briefing for a group presentation, drawing upon an encyclopaedia or database.

e) show in discussion or in writing an awareness of writers' use of sound patterns and some other literary devices and the effect on the reader.

In a group discussion on poems, advertisements or other materials, refer to rhyme, alliteration and figures of speech such as similes, metaphors and personification.

8 a) read a range of fiction, poetry, literary non–fiction and drama, including pre-20th century literature.

Read texts whose content, length, organization or language make demands on the reader.

b) talk and write about literature and other texts, giving evidence of personal response and showing an understanding of the devices and structures used by the

Write essays commenting upon points of style, character or plot in comparison with other texts; show how or why a dramatist or novelist used questions and/or repetition to build up emotion in an episode

writers, with appropriate reference to details.

involving two characters.

c) show in discussion and writing an ability to form a considered opinion about features of presentation which are used to inform, regulate, reassure or persuade, in non-literary and media texts.

Compare two reports of the same event, or devise two texts which serve contrasting purposes or audiences.

d) select, retrieve, evaluate and combine information independently and with discrimination, from a comprehensive range of reference materials.

Write a short study drawing upon ideas from different parts of a text or different texts.

e) discuss and write about changes in the grammar of English over time, encountered in the course of their reading.

Comment on examples such as pronouns (from 'thou' and 'thee' to 'you'), verb forms and negatives.

9   a) read a range of fiction, poetry, literary non-fiction and drama, including pre-20th century literature.

b) talk and write clearly about literature and other texts giving sustained evidence of personal response and showing an understanding of the devices and structures used by the writer, making comparisons within texts and between different texts.

Analyse the differences and similarities between two novels, showing a sustained personal response to both texts.

c) show in discussion and in writing an ability to recognize techniques and conventions of presentation in non-literary and media texts, and judge the effectiveness of their use.

Recognize the structure of news stories or the ways in which television programmes and newspapers match style and content to specific audiences; produce text in a number of media, drawing on these techniques.

d) select, retrieve, evaluate and combine information

Prepare a well-argued report drawing on information from a

independently and with discrimination, from a comprehensive range of reference materials, making effective use of the information.

e) demonstrate some understanding of the use of lexical and grammatical effects in the language of literature.

variety of sources.

Consider the repetition of words or structures, dialect forms, archaisms, etc.

10

a) read a range of fiction, poetry, literary non-fiction and drama, including pre-20th century literature.

b) talk and write cogently and knowledgeably about literature and other texts giving sustained evidence of personal response and showing an understanding of the devices and structures used by the writer, making detailed comparisons within texts and between different texts.

Compare the treatment by different authors of similar themes, providing detailed evidence and a clear grasp of relevant background.

c) show in discussion and in writing an ability to evaluate techniques and conventions of presentation in non-literary and media texts, and judge the effectiveness of their use.

Compare the presentation of news or commentary in similar broadcasts on two television channels or between radio and television; compare the treatment of the same event in two newspapers.

d) select, retrieve, evaluate and combine information independently and with discrimination, from a comprehensive range of reference materials, making effective and sustained use of the information.

Make appropriate use of a variety of techniques, and, in devising a presentation, make use of a range of media consistently and appropriately for the audience.

e) demonstrate in discussion and in writing some understanding of attitudes in society towards language change and of ideas about

Comment on the arguments, attitudes and styles displayed in a running correspondence, on an issue of language usage or perfomance, in a newspaper or weekly periodical.

appropriateness and
correctness in language use.

Note: Pupils who need to use non-sighted methods of reading, such as braille, may use alternatives which do not demand a visual approach. Pupils unable to read aloud may use other means such as signing.

Attainment Target 3: Writing[3]

A growing ability to construct and convey meaning in written language matching style to audience and purpose.

Level	Statements of Attainment	Example
	Pupils should be able to:	
1	a) use pictures, symbols or isolated letters, words or phrases to communicate meaning.	*Show work to others, saying what writing and drawings mean.*
2	a) produce, independently, pieces of writing using complete sentences, some of them demarcated with capital letters and full stops or question marks.	
	b) structure sequences of real or imagined events coherently in chronological accounts.	*An account of a family occasion, a practical task in mathematics or an adventure story.*
	c) write stories showing an understanding of the rudiments of story structure by establishing an opening, characters, and one or more events.	*A story with an opening which suggests when or where the action takes place and which involves more than one character.*
	d) produce simple, coherent non-chronological writing.	*Lists, captions, invitations, greetings cards, notices, posters etc.*
3	a) produce, independently, pieces of writing using	

---

[3] The statements of attainment at levels 1 to 3 are as specified by Order and published in the statutory Document entitled *English in the National Curriculum* (ISBN 0 11 270682 7) on 31 May 1989.

complete sentences, mainly
demarcated with capital
letters and full stops or
question marks.

b) shape chronological writing, *but when after so because*
beginning to use a wider
range of sentence
connectives than 'and' and
'then'.

c) write more complex *Stories which include a description of*
stories with detail beyond *setting and the feelings of characters.*
simple events and with a
defined ending.

d) produce a range of types of *Plans and diagrams, descriptions of a*
non-chronological writing. *person or place, or notes for an*
activity in science or design.

e) begin to revise and redraft in
discussion with the teacher,
other adults, or other
children in the class, paying
attention to meaning and
clarity as well as checking
for matters such as correct
and consistent use of tenses
and pronouns.

4   a) produce, independently, *Make use of titles, paragraphs or*
pieces of writing showing *verses, capital letters, full stops,*
evidence of a developing *question marks and exclamation*
ability to structure what is *marks; set out and punctuate direct*
written in ways that make *speech.*
the meaning clear to the
reader; demonstrate in their
writing generally accurate
use of sentence punctuation.

b) write stories which have an *Write, in addition to stories,*
opening, a setting, *instructions, accounts or*
characters, a series of events *explanations, perhaps of a scientific*
and a resolution and which *investigation.*
engage the interest of the
reader; produce other kinds
of chronologically organized
writing.

c) organize non-chronological *Record in writing an aspect of*
writing for different *learning; present information and*
purposes in orderly ways. *express feelings in forms such as*
letters, poems, invitations, posters,

etc.

d) begin to use the structures of written Standard English and begin to use some sentence structures different from those of speech.

Begin to use subordinate clauses and expanded noun phrases.

e) discuss the organization of their own writing; revise and redraft the writing as appropriate, independently, in the light of that discussion.

Talk about content and those features which ensure clarity for the reader.

5 a) write in a variety of forms for a range of purposes and audiences, in ways which attempt to engage the interest of the reader.

Write notes, letters, instructions, stories and poems in order to plan, inform, explain, entertain and express attitudes or emotions.

b) produce, independently, pieces of writing in which the meaning is made clear to the reader and in which organizational devices and sentence punctuation, including commas and the setting out of direct speech, are generally accurately used.

Make use of layout, headings, paragraphs and verse structure; make use of the comma.

c) demonstrate increased effectiveness in the use of Standard English (except in contexts where non–standard forms are needed for literary purposes) and show an increased differentiation between speech and writing.

Understand that non-standard forms for literary purposes might be required in dialogue, in a story or playscript; use constructions which reduce repetition.

d) assemble ideas on paper or on a VDU, individually or in discussion with others, and show evidence of an ability to produce a draft from them and then to revise and redraft as necessary.

Draft a story, a script, a poem, a description or a report.

e) show in discussion the ability to recognize variations in vocabulary according to purpose, topic and audience and whether language is spoken or

Discuss the use of slang in dialogue and narrative in a published text and in their own writing and comment on its appropriateness.

written, and use them
appropriately in their
writing.

6   a)   write in a variety of forms
for a range of purposes,
presenting subject matter
differently to suit the needs
of specified known
audiences and
demonstrating the ability
to sustain the interest of
the reader.

Write an illustrated story which is suitable for a younger reader.

b)   produce, independently,
pieces of writing in which
the subject matter is
organized and set out
clearly and appropriately
and in which sentences
and any direct speech are
helpfully punctuated.

Employ a wider range of uses of the comma and make use of brackets or pairs of dashes, where necessary.

c)   demonstrate the ability to
use literary stylistic
features and those which
characterise an impersonal
style, when appropriate,
using Standard English
(except in contexts where
non-standard forms are
needed for literary
purposes).

Alter word order for emphasis or deliberately repeat words or sentence patterns.

d)   recognize when redrafting
and revising are appropriate
and act accordingly, either
on paper or on a computer
screen.

Write a second draft of an account of a group activity following the group's discussion of the first draft.

e)   demonstrate, through
discussion and in their
writing, grammatical
differences between spoken
and written English.

In a group, identify some of the differences between the language used in a tape recording of someone talking and a piece of writing by the same person.

7   a)   write in a wider variety of
forms, with commitment
and a clear sense of purpose
and awareness of audience,
demonstrating an ability to

Write notes, personal letters, formal letters, instructions, essays, newspaper articles, reviews, biographies, stories, poems, playscripts, radio and TV scripts.

anticipate the reader's response.

Plan, formulate hypotheses, inform, explain, compare and contrast, persuade, entertain, express attitudes or emotions, describe experience imaginatively.

b) produce well-structured pieces of writing, some of which handle demanding subject matter; punctuate their writing so that meaning and structure are clear to the reader.

Devise a news broadcasts of topical interest for a particular channel or develop a playscript from an improvisation. Go beyond first hand experience.

c) make a more assured and selective use of a wider range of grammatical and lexical features, characteristic of different styles, that are appropriate for topic, purpose and audience; use Standard English (except in contexts where non-standard forms are needed for literary purposes).

In transactional writing, choose neutral vocabulary; in imaginative writing, choose vocabulary which conveys attitudes, responses and emotions.

d) demonstrate an increased awareness that a first draft may be changed, amended and reordered in a variety of ways.

Change the form from a story to a film script; restructure text on a VDU or alter sentence structure or choice of vocabulary.

e) show in discussion and in writing an awareness of what is appropriate and inappropriate language use in written texts.

Appreciate the need to take account of topic, purpose and audience.

8   a) write in a wide variety of forms, with a clear sense of purpose and audience, demonstrating an ability to judge the appropriate length and form for a given task and to sustain the interest of the reader.

Produce editorial columns for a broadsheet newspaper and for a tabloid.

b) produce, independently, well-structured pieces of writing, providing evidence that the function

Separate distinct ideas and events and unify related ones in their writing.

of paragraphing has been
grasped; punctuate writing
so that meaning and
structure are clear to the
reader.

c) make an assured and selective
use of a wide range of
grammatical constructions,
which are appropriate for
topic, purpose and audience;
use Standard English (except
in contexts where non-
standard forms are needed for
literary purposes).

*Forms of writing might include:
alteration of word order, lexical or
structural repetition, passive
constructions, adverbial connectives
and varied and appropriate
vocabulary such as colloquial,
formal, technical, poetic or
figurative.*

d) demonstrate knowledge of
organizational differences
between spoken and written
English.

*Talk and write about the fact that
speech is interactive, spontaneous
and informal while writing is more
tightly planned.*

9   a) write in a wide variety of
forms, with an assured sense
of purpose, organizing and
presenting subject matter
appropriately for specified
audiences, both known and
unknown, showing
awareness of the need to
sustain the interest of the
reader; present subject
matter from a point of
view other than their own,
showing evidence of
commitment to the topic;
produce a sustained piece of
writing when the task
demands it.

*Write an essay justifying the actions
of a character in a novel or play of
whom they disapprove.*

b) organize and present
complex subject matter in
coherently linked sentences
within paragraphs; punctuate
writing so that meaning and
structure are clear to the
reader.

*Present an investigative report about
a contentious issue, drawing on a
number of conflicting points of view;
weave more than one strand into a
story.*

c) make an assured and
selective use of a wide range
of grammatical constructions
which are appropriate for

*Vary sentence beginnings; alter word
order; use lexical or structural
repetition, passive constructions,
adverbial connectives, elliptical*

topic, purpose and audience, demonstrating awareness of the means whereby a writer may choose to achieve a desired emphasis; show an ability to sustain the chosen style; use Standard English (except in contexts where non–standard forms are needed for literary purposes).

constructions, non-finite subordinate clauses and choose varied and appropriate vocabulary such as colloquial, formal, technical, poetic or figurative.

d) demonstrate in discussion and in writing knowledge of ways in which language varies between different types of texts.

Identify what is distinctive about the language used in personal letters, formal letters, printed instructions, reports in different newspapers, playscripts or films.

10 a) write, selecting an appropriate length, in a wide variety of chosen forms, demonstrating an assured sense of purpose and audience and a commitment to the topic.

Write a report of their chosen investigation into language use, which is well-judged in length and form for the audience and uses a range of techniques of presentation, including accounts of interviews, descriptions of people, analyses of tabulated data and summary conclusions.

b) organize complex, demanding or extended subject matter clearly and effectively; produce well–structured pieces of writing in which the relationship between successive paragraphs is clear; punctuate their writing so that meaning and structure are clear to the reader.

Present the similarities and differences between conflicting points of view or handle elements of a story which involve characters in very different contexts.

c) sustain a personal style, making an assured, selective and appropriate use of a wide range of grammatical constructions and an extensive vocabulary, choosing to use Standard English (except in contexts where non–standard forms are needed for literary

Use a variety of sentence lengths, structure and openings and achieve striking effects through an apt choice of words.

purposes) and maintaining
the interest and attention of
the reader.

d) demonstrate, in discussion
and in writing, knowledge
of criteria by which different
types of written language
can be judged.

*Make use of criteria such as clarity,
coherence, accuracy, appropriateness,
effectiveness, vigour and awareness
of purpose and audience.*

Note: At each level of attainment the use of technological aids by pupils who depend on them physically to produce their written work is acceptable.

Attainment Target 4: Spelling[4]

Level	Statements of Attainment	Example

Pupils should be able to:

1   a) begin to show an
understanding of the
difference between drawing
and writing, and between
numbers and letters.

b) write some letter shapes in
response to speech sounds
and letter names.

Initial letter of own name.

c) use at least single letters or
groups of letters to
represent whole words
or parts of words.

2   a) produce recognizable
(though not necessarily
always correct) spelling of a
range of of common words.

b) spell correctly, in the course
of their own writing, simple
monosyllabic words they use
regularly which observe
common patterns.

see car man sun hot cold thank

c) recognize that spelling has
patterns, and begin to apply
their knowledge of those

[4] The statements of attainment at levels 1 to 3 are as specified by Order and published in the statutory Document entitled *English in the National Curriculum* (ISBN 0 11 270682 7) on 31 May 1989.

patterns in their attempts to
spell a wider range of words.

d) show knowledge of the
names and order of the
letters of the alphabet.

*Name the letters when spelling out
loud from a simple dictionary or
word book.*

3 a) spell correctly, in the course
of their own writing, simple
polysyllabic words they use
regularly which observe
common patterns.

*because after open teacher animal
together*

b) recognize and use correctly
regular patterns for vowel
sounds and common letter
strings.

-ing -ion -ous

c) show a growing awareness
of word families and their
relationships.

grow growth growing grown grew

d) in revising and redrafting
their writing, begin to check
the accuracy of their
spelling.

*Use a simple dictionary, word book,
spell checker, or other classroom
resources; make spelling books or
picture books.*

4 a) spell correctly, in the course
of their own writing, words
which display other main
patterns in English spelling.

*Words using the main prefixes and
suffixes.*

Note: Pupils may be exempted from this target if they need to use a non-sighted
form of writing such as braille or if they have such a degree of physical disability that
the attainment target is unattainable.

Attainment Target 5: Handwriting[5]

Level	*Statements of Attainment*	*Example*

Pupils should be able to:

1 a) begin to form letters with
some control over the size,
shape and orientation of
letters or lines of writing.

---

[5] The statements of attainment at levels 1 to 3 are as specified by Order and
published in the statutory Document entitled *English in the National Curriculum* (ISBN
0 11 270682 7) on 31 May 1989.

2   a) produce legible upper and   *Produce capital letters and lower case*
        lower case letters in one style   *letters which are easily*
        and use them consistently   *distinguishable.*
        (i.e. not randomly mixed
        within words).

    b) produce letters that are   *b and d,*
        recognizably formed and
        properly oriented and that   *p and b*
        have clear ascenders and
        descenders where necessary.

3   a) begin to produce clear and
        legible joined-up writing.

4   a) produce more fluent
        joined-up writing in
        independent work.

Attainment Target 4/5: Presentation

Level	Statements of Attainment	Example
	Pupils should be able to:	
5	a) spell correctly, in the course of their own writing, words of greater complexity.	*Words with inflectional suffixes, such as **-ed** and **-ing,**, where consonant doubling ('running') or **-e** deletion ('coming') are required.*
	b) check final drafts of writing for misspelling and other errors of presentation.	*Use a dictionary or computer spelling checker when appropriate.*
	c) produce clear and legible handwriting in printed and cursive styles.	
6	a) recognize that words with related meanings may have related spellings, even though they sound different; recognize that the spelling of unstressed syllables can often be deduced from the spelling of a stressed syllable in a related word.	*Sign, signature; medical, medicine; muscle, muscular; history, historical; grammar, grammatical; manager, managerial.*
	b) check final drafts of writing for misspelling and other errors of presentation.	*Use a dictionary or computer spelling checker when appropriate.*

c) write fluently and legibly.

d) show some ability to use any available presentational devices that are appropriate to the task, so that finished work is presented clearly and attractively.

Handwriting, typewriting, computer printout, artwork, computer graphics, desk-top publishing.

7

a) spell (and understand the meaning of) common roots that have been borrowed from other languages and that play an important role in word-building; recognize that where words have been borrowed in the last 400 years, there are some characteristic sound-symbol relationships that reflect the word's origin.

micro-, psych-, tele-, therm-; ch- in French words like 'champagne', 'chauffeur', 'charade', and ch- in Greek words like 'chaos', 'chiropody', 'chorus'; compared with the ch- in long-established English words like 'chaff', 'cheese', 'chin'.

b) check final drafts of writing for misspelling and other errors of presentation.

Use a dictionary or computer spelling checker when appropriate.

c) write fluently and legibly.

d) show an increased ability to present finished work appropriately, clearly and attractively.

Note: At each level of attainment the use of technological aids by pupils who depend on them physically to produce their written work is acceptable. Pupils may be exempted from the statements of attainment which require handwriting if they need to use a non-sighted form of writing such as braille or if they have such a degree of physical disability that those statements of attainment are unattainable.

Appendix 3

Two Play Scripts

These are two of the other scripts produced by groups of children who took part in the drama project 'Fear and Suspense', described in Chapter 10.

The Tigers
by Stella, Simon, Laura, Andrea and Philip.

Cast:

Simon:	Animal Rights Man (ARM)
Laura:	Brave Girl (Janine)
Andrea:	Scared Girl (Kerry)
Linda:	Narrator
Philip:	Zookeeper.

Narrator:	At 1.30 in the morning a tall dark stranger makes his way to the tiger cages. He opens the cage and two tigers run out the man says:
ARM:	Another two of God's animals set free. (Later that morning.)
Narrator:	At 7.30 a.m., an alarm went off in a small cottage in a wood.
Janine:	Ah! What a lovely morning.
Kerry:	Why don't you shut up, I'm tired.
Janine:	Kerry get up and go get the milk.
Kerry:	OK, I will, Janine.
Narrator:	She went down stairs opened the door and ...
Kerry:	Aaaaahh!
Narrator:	She fainted. Her friend Janine went down to find two tigers standing in the door way. Janine quickly shut the door and tried to wake Kerry up. She eventually got her awake.
Kerry:	Tigers, tigers, where are they?
Janine:	Shut up, I've shut the door.
Kerry:	If we throw some meat out of the window they might go away.
Narrator:	They threw meat out and then they looked out of the window

and the two tigers are still there. Then Kerry and Janine went back to bed. The next day Kerry phoned the zookeeper.

Kerry:	Hello I think two of your tigers are here.
Zookeeper:	Right I'll be over about 5.20 p.m.
Kerry:	Thank you very much. Bye.
Janine:	Is he coming over?
Kerry:	Yes about 5.20 p.m.
Janine:	That's a bit late.
Kerry:	But that's the only time he's got free.
Narrator:	Later the zookeeper came at 5.15 p.m.
Janine:	Look, he is going round to the back where the tigers are.
Kerry:	Quick open the door but don't let the tigers in.
Narrator:	One of the tigers tried to attack the zookeeper but he ran into the house.
Zookeeper:	Quick shut the door, shut the door!
Janine:	OK I'm shutting it.
Kerry:	Do you want some tea?
Zookeeper:	Yes please.
Janine:	We'll go and sit down in the living room.
Narrator:	They went in to the living room, Kerry brought the tea in.
Janine:	Shall we watch the end of *Blue Peter*?
Kerry:	Yes, OK.
Narrator:	The tigers were sitting outside. Then all of a sudden one of the tigers jumped through the window.
Janine:	Quick run upstairs.
Narrator:	The zookeeper and Janine ran upstairs but Kerry stood frozen and screamed.
Kerry:	Aaaahh! Help!
Narrator:	All of a sudden *Neighbours* started, and everyone sat down to watch it. When it had finished everybody went back to their places. The zookeeper went and got his dart-gun to put the tigers asleep. The zookeeper put the tigers asleep then the zookeeper took them back and everything went back to normal.
Janine:	I fancy having a pussy cat.
Kerry:	Not a big pussy cat?
Narrator:	Then she fainted again.

The End

Lost in the Ghost House
by Diane, Helen, Mark, Andrew and John.

Scene 1

At the fair one night eating candy floss and drinking Pepsi, when Nyree decides to go in the Ghost House and take a ride on the ghost train ...

Helen:	Come on you lot, let's go in the Ghost House.
Diane:	Yeah come on let's go.
Mark and John:	No I don't want to go in there you might get scared.
Diane and Helen:	More like you'll get scared.
John:	No we won't come on then let's go.

Scene 2

In the Ghost House when suddenly the lights go out.

Helen:	Where have they gone?
Diane:	Helen I'm scared.
Helen:	So am I.

Scene 3

Helen and Diane are trying to find the boys when they hear scary noises.

| Diane: | I wish the boys were here because I'm scared. |
| Helen: | Yeah, I'm really scared. |

Scene 4

John and Mark find the girls.

John:	We were making the noise because we were trying to muck about.
Diane:	Don't do it again, you really scared us.
Helen:	Yeah, stupid.
Mark:	Sorry we didn't mean to.
John:	We promise we won't do it again.
Mark:	Ahhh
John:	Mark, where are you? This is no time for jokes.
Diane and Helen:	Mark!!

Scene 5

Diane, Helen and John carry on shouting down the tracks in the Ghost House.

Helen:	I'm scared I want to go home.
Diane:	It's your fault, you wanted to come in here.
Helen:	So did you.
John:	Stop arguing you two and let's get out of here.
Diane:	We got to find Mark first.

Scene 6

They are all looking for Mark when . . .

Diane:	Ahhh
John:	What is it?
Diane:	It feels like a dead body.

262

Helen:	It could be Mark.
Diane:	I hope not.
Helen:	Why?
Diane:	Because it feels dead.
John:	Well, if it is Mark, he's not dead.
Mark:	Groan ... groan.
John:	Mark, is that you?
Mark:	John (says it slowly)
Diane:	Mark, what's happened?
Mark:	Groan ... groan.

Scene 7

	They get Mark up and are asking questions he can talk a bit better ...
Diane:	Mark what happened?
Mark:	I can't remember, honest.
Helen:	At least we're all back together again ...
Diane:	And safe.
Helen:	Yeah, that too.
John:	I hate to tell you this but we should split up ...
Helen:	No way!
John:	Just hear me out. Mark and I will try to find the train and Diane and you can find it too.
Diane:	We'll go this way and you go that way.
John:	Right, see ya.
Helen:	John seems scared I mean.

Scene 8

	Helen gets pulled suddenly although she can't scream because she's in so much shock. Diane carried on walking, thinking Helen is still there, until ...
Diane:	Helen do you still want to come to my house? Helen? Helen?
Andrew:	Here I am.
Diane:	Don't do that again, or ...
Helen:	... Diane, who are you talking to?
Diane:	You, silly.
Helen:	You can't be because I'm here.
Diane:	Then who am I ...?
Andrew:	Me, the ghost of the Ghost House.
Diane:	Ahhh!
Helen:	Come on Diane, run, I'm over here.

Scene 9

	The girls reach the train and the boys are there.
Helen:	Thank God for that.
Diane:	I wouldn't, he could come back.

Helen: He won't any way. Look for a button under your seat.
Everyone: Ahhh!

Scene 10

The train starts to come out of the Ghost House ...

Gerald: Did you enjoy your ride? Oh sorry about the lights ... ha ...
             ha ... ha!

Diane: It was all planned, I feel a fool.

Helen ⎤
Mark ⎬   So do I.
John ⎦

Scene 11

They all walk off.

The End

Bibliography

ALLEN, D. (1987) *English, Whose English?*, Sheffield, NATE.

BEYNON, L. (1981) 'Curriculum Continuity', *Education 3–13*, **9**, 2, pp. 36–41.

BROWN, J.B. and ARMSTRONG, M.P. (1986) 'Transfer from junior to secondary: The child's perspective', in YOUNGMAN, M.B. (Ed.) *Mid-Schooling Transfer*, Windsor, NFER, Chapter 2.

BULLOCK REPORT DES (1975) *A Language For Life*, London, HMSO.

CASTLE, J. and LAWRENCE, I. (Eds) (1987) *Continuity Models In The Curriculum: A Handbook for Teachers*, London, West London Press.

COLLIN, D. (1984) 'Language: Curricular Continuity at Transfer', in DODDS, P. and LAWRENCE, I. (Eds) *Curriculum Continuity: Fact or Fiction?*, London, Education Department of the West London Institute of Higher Education, Chapter 4.

COX REPORT, DES (1989) *English for Ages 5 to 16*, London, HMSO.

CREASEY, M., FINDLAY, F. and WALSH, B. (1983) *Language Across the Transition: Primary/Secondary Continuity and Liaison in English*, York, Longman for the Schools Council.

CRINSON, J. (1987) 'Transfer and Liaison: A Survey of Current Work', in FINDLAY, F.D. (Ed.) *Moving On: Continuity and Liaison in Action*, Sheffield, NATE, pp. 84–92.

CROLL, P. (1984) 'Moving from the Primary Classroom', in DODDS, P. and LAWRENCE, I. (Eds) *Curriculum Continuity: Fact or Fiction?*, London, Education Department of the West London Institute of Higher Education, Chapter 6.

CUTLER, V. (1984) 'Liaison between primary and secondary school', *Secondary Education Journal*, **14**, 1, pp. 7–8.

DERRICOTT, R. (Ed.) (1985) *Curriculum Continuity: Primary to Secondary*, Windsor, NFER–Nelson.

DES (1984) *English from 5 to 16: Curriculum Matters 1 — An HMI Series*, London, HMSO.

DES (1985a) *Better Schools*, London, HMSO.

DES (1985b) *Science 5–16*, London, HMSO.

DES (1990a) *English in the National Curriculum (No. 2)*, London, HMSO.

DES (1990b) *Technology in the National Curriculum*, London, HMSO.

DIXON, R.T. (1985) 'Linking Primary and Secondary Schools through a Language and Learning Group,' *Education 3–13*, **13**, 1, pp. 29–31.

DODDS, P. (1984) 'Research into Curriculum Continuity', in DODDS, P. and LAWRENCE, I. (Eds) *Curriculum Continuity: Fact or Fiction?*, London, Education Department of the West London Institute of Higher Education, Chapter 2.

DODDS, P. and LAWRENCE, I. (Eds) (1984) *Curriculum Continuity: Fact or Fiction?*, London, Education Department of the West London Institute of Higher Education.

DOHERTY, P. (1984) 'Moving On', *Junior Education*, **8**, 6, p. 13.

FINDLAY, F.D. (1983) 'Continuity and Liaison in Language', *Education 3–13*, **11**, 1, pp. 21–24.

FINDLAY, F.D. (Ed.) (1987a) *Moving On: Continuity and Liasion in Action*, Sheffield, NATE.

FINDLAY, F.D. (1987b) 'A Primary/Secondary Joint Project', in FINDLAY, F.D. (Ed.) *Moving On: Continuity and Liaison in Action*, Sheffield, NATE, pp. 41–43.

GALTON, M. and WILCOCKS, J. (1983) *Moving from the Primary Classroom*, London, Routledge and Kegan Paul.

GALTON, M. (1983) 'Changing Teachers and Changing Schools', in GALTON, M. and WILCOCKS, J., *Moving from the Primary Classroom*, London, Routledge and Kegan Paul, Chapter 1.

GARDINER, H. (1988) 'Perspectives for Kingman', in JONES, M. and WEST, A. (Eds) *Learning Me Your Language*, London, Mary Glasgow Publications, pp. 15–20.

GINNEVER, S. (1986) 'Liaison and Curriculum Continuity', in YOUNGMAN, M.B. (Ed.) *Mid-Schooling Transfer*, Windsor, NFER, Chapter 10.

GORWOOD, B.T. (Ed.) (1984) *Intermediate School*, Aspects of Education No. 32, University of Hull.

GORWOOD, B.T. (1986) *School Transfer and Curriculum Continuity*, London, Croom Helm.

GREGORY, O. (1980) *Oxford Junior English*, Oxford, Oxford University Press.

HADOW REPORT, BOARD OF EDUCATION (1926) *Report of the Consultative Committee on the Education of the Adolescent*, London, HMSO.

HORNER, S. (1987) 'Writing at the Transition — National Writing Project (Sheffield)', in FINDLAY, F.D. (Ed.) *Moving On: Continuity and Liaison in Action*, Sheffield, NATE.

HOWE, A. (1988) *Expanding Horizons: Teaching and Learning Through Whole Class Discussions*, Sheffield, NATE:

HUGHES, T. (1967) *Poetry in the Making*, London, Faber and Faber.

ILEA (1985) *The Island*, The English Centre.

JENNINGS, K. and HARGREAVES, D.J. (1981) 'Children's Attitudes to Secondary School Transfer', *Educational Studies*, **7**, 1, pp. 35–39.

JONES, A.W. (1985) 'Perceptions Across the Infant-Junior Transfer', *Education 3–13*, **13**, 1, pp. 44–48.

JONES, M. and WEST, A. (Eds) (1988) *Learning Me Your Language*, London, Mary Glasgow Publications.

KINGMAN REPORT, DES (1988) *Report of the Kingman Committee of Enquiry into the Teaching of English Language*, London, HMSO.

LAYCOCK, A. (1987) 'New Forms of Record Keeping', in FINDLAY, F.D. (Ed.) *Moving On: Continuity and Liaison in Action*, Sheffield, NATE, pp. 54–57.

MARLAND, M. (1977) *Language Across the Curriculum*, London, Heinemann.

MASSON, M.G. MONAGHAN, F. and THOMSON, L. (1983) *Primary Language Programme*, London, Heinemann.

MASTERMAN, L. (1985) *Teaching the Media*, London, Comedia Publishing Group.

McGREGOR, L., TATE, M. and ROBINSON, K. (1977) *Learning Through Drama*, London, Heinemann Educational Books for the Schools Council.

MEASOR, L. and WOOD, P. (1984) *Changing Schools: Pupil Perspectives on Transfer to a Comprehensive*, Oxford, Oxford University Press.

MURDOCH, A. (1986) 'Forty-two children and the transfer to secondary education', in YOUNGMAN, M.B. (Ed.) *Mid-Schooling Transfer*, Windsor, NFER–Nelson, Chapter 3.

NATIONAL CURRICULUM COUNCIL CONSULTATIVE REPORT (1989) *English in the National Curriculum*, York, National Curriculum Council.

NEAL, P.D. (1975) *Project 5 — Continuity in Education*, Birmingham, City of Birmingham Education Department.

NEELANDS, J. (1984) *Making Sense of Drama*, Oxford, Heinemann Educational Books.

NISBET, J.D. and ENTWISTLE, N.J. (1969) *The Transition to Secondary Education*, London, University of London Press.

NORFOLK ASSOCIATION OF MIDDLE SCHOOL HEAD TEACHERS (1983) *Discussion Document: Patterns of Liaison — Middle to Secondary*.

ORME, D. (Ed.) (1990) *Creative Language*, Cheltenham, Stanley Thornes.

PADGETT, C. (1987) 'Writing for Infants', in FINDLAY, F.D. (Ed.) *Moving On: Continuity and Liaison in Action*, Sheffield, NATE, pp. 46–47.

PERERA, K. (1987) *Understanding Language*, Sheffield, NATE.

PLOWDEN REPORT, DES (1967) *Children and Their Primary Schools*, London, HMSO.

POTTER, J. (1987) 'A Primary/Secondary Joint Project', in FINDLAY, F.D. (Ed.) *Moving On: Continuity and Liaison in Action*, Sheffield, NATE, pp. 44–45.

RIDOUT, R. (1961) *Better English*, Aylesbury, Ginn and Co. Ltd.

RIDOUT, R. (1977) *Word Perfect* (17th impression), Aylesbury, Ginn and Co., Ltd.

SCDC (1986) *Curriculum Issues No. 2*, London, SCDC.

SCDC (1988) *Information Packs on Curriculum Continuity, Units 1 and 2*, London, SCDC.

SEAC (1990) *A Guide to Teacher Assessment: Packs A, B and C*, Oxford, Heinemann Educational Books.

SPENCER, R. (1988) 'Continuity, Liaison and Progression: The Northampton-shire Approach', in *Curriculum Continuity Information Pack, Unit 1*, London, SCDC, pp. 36–44.

STEED, E. and SUDWORTH, P. (1985) 'The Humpback Bridge', in DERRICOTT, R. (Ed.) *Curriculum Continuity: Primary to Secondary*, Windsor, NFER–Nelson, Chapter 3.

STILLMAN, A. (1984) 'Some reflections on planning the transition in transfer', in GORWOOD, B. (Ed.) *Intermediate School*, Aspects of Education No. 32, University of Hull.

STILLMAN, A. and MAYCHELL, K. (1984) *School to School*, Windsor, NFER–Nelson.

SUMMERFIELD, G. (1968) *Voices (The First Book)*, Middlesex, Penguin.

SUMNER, R. and BRADLEY, K. (1977) *Assessment for Transition: A Study of New Procedures*, Windsor, NFER–Nelson.

TABOR, D.C. and RICHARDS, N. (1987) 'Building Bridges', *Junior Education*, **11**, 12, pp. 30–31.

TABOR, D.C. (1988) 'Building More Bridges', *Curriculum Continuity Information Pack, Unit 1*, London, SCDC, p. 34.

TABOR, D.C. (1988) 'Children's Writing and the Sense of an Audience', *Education 3–13*, **16**, 2, pp. 26–31.

TABOR, D.C. and RAYNHAM, P. (1989) 'Poetry in the Making', *Junior Education*, **13**, 3, pp. 36–37.

TABOR, D.C. (1990) 'Poetry Across the Divide', *Education 3–13*, **18**, 1, pp. 33–40.

TALBOT, C. (1990) 'When the Talking Stops: an Exercise in Liaison', *Education 3–13*, **18**, 1, pp. 28–32.

TANSLEY, A.E. (1970) *Sound Sense*, Leeds, E.J. Arnold.

TARLETON, R. (1988) *Learning and Talking*, London, Routledge.

THORPE, E.G. (1962) *Complete English*, Book 2, London, Heinemann.

VAN GENNEP, A. (1909) *Les Rites de Passage*, Translated by VIZEDOM, M. and CAFFE, G. (1960) London, Routledge and Kegan Paul.

WALLEN, M. (1987) 'The National Writing Project in Dorset', in FINDLAY, F.D. (Ed.) *Moving On: Continuity and Liaison in Action*, Sheffield, NATE, pp. 33–34.

WHALEN, F.E. and FRIED, M.A. (1973) 'Geographic mobility and its effect on student achievement', *Journal of Educational Research*, **67**.

YOUNGMAN, M.B. (Ed.) (1986) *Mid-Schooling Transfer: Problems and Proposals*, Windsor, NFER–Nelson.

YOUNGMAN, M.B. and LUNZER, E.A. (1977) *Adjustment to Secondary Schooling*, Nottingham, Nottinghamshire County Council and Nottingham University School of Education.

Index